Pragmatic Internet of Everything (IOE) for Smart Cities: 360-Degree Perspective

Edited by

Satya Prakash Yadav

Department of Computer Science and Engineering
GL Bajaj Institute of Technology and Management
India

Graduate Program in Telecommunications Engineering
(PPGET)
Federal Institute of Education, Science and Technology of
Ceará (IFCE)
Brazil

Sansar Singh Chauhan

Department of Computer Science & Engineering
Noida Institute of Engineering & Technology
India

Sanjeev Kumar Pippal

NSBT MGM University, Cidco, Aurangabad
Maharashtra 431003
India

&

Victor Hugo C. de Albuquerque

Department of Teleinformatics Engineering (DETI) Federal
University of Ceará
Brazil

Pragmatic Internet of Everything (IOE) for Smart Cities: 360-Degree Perspective

Editors: Satya Prakash Yadav, Sansar Singh Chauhan, Sanjeev Kumar Pippal & Victor Hugo C. de Albuquerque

ISBN (Online): 978-981-5136-17-3

ISBN (Print): 978-981-5136-18-0

ISBN (Paperback): 978-981-5136-19-7

need for a court order if at any point you breach any terms of this License Agreement. In no event will any delay or failure by Bentham Science Publishers in enforcing your compliance with this License Agreement constitute a waiver of any of its rights.

3. You acknowledge that you have read this License Agreement, and agree to be bound by its terms and conditions. To the extent that any other terms and conditions presented on any website of Bentham Science Publishers conflict with, or are inconsistent with, the terms and conditions set out in this License Agreement, you acknowledge that the terms and conditions set out in this License Agreement shall prevail.

Bentham Science Publishers Pte. Ltd.
80 Robinson Road #02-00
Singapore 068898
Singapore
Email: subscriptions@benthamscience.net

CONTENTS

CHAPTER 4 UNDERSTANDING THE FUTURE OF SMART CITIES FROM TECHNOLOGICAL AND COMMERCIAL POINT OF VIEW 61

Arushi Kapoor, Vartika Agarwal, Muskan Jindal and *Shashank Awasthi*

CHAPTER 5 DYNAMIC INVOLVEMENT OF DEEP LEARNING AND BIG DATA IN SMART CITIES 87

Nidhi Shah, Arushi Kapoor, Namith Gupta, Vartika Agarwal and *Muskan Jindal*

PREFACE

Pragmatic Internet of Everything (IOE) for Smart Cities: 360-degree perspective has emerged as a powerful paradigm for representing and solving complex problems. Pragmatic Internet of Everything (IOE) for Smart Cities: 360-degree perspective is the branch of Internet of Everything (IOE) concerned with coordinating behaviour among a collection of semi-autonomous problem-solving agents: how they can coordinate their knowledge, goals and plans to act together, to solve joint problems, or to make individually or globally rational decisions in the face of uncertainty and multiple, conflicting perspectives.

The inspiration and need for this book specifically on smart cities arose due to the sheer absence of any literature which amalgamates different perspectives, thereby giving a 360 degree perspective to the reader, even though there is plenty of literature available on the topic. An insight from subject matter experts from various vivid fields will not only substantiate the knowledge on the subject but, also give some inputs towards the implementation of practical ventures of the same. This process not only included excessive research and review of available literature and practical ventures but also included extensive surveys to get the gist of the topic from citizens of smart cities, along with the analysis of the same from a financial or business perspective and using policymakers' mind to optimize the same.

This book presents a collection of articles surveying several major recent developments in the Pragmatic Internet of Everything (IOE) for Smart Cities: 360-degree perspective. The book focuses on issues and challenges that arise in building practical Internet of Everything (IOE) for Smart Cities systems in real-world settings, and covers some solutions to the issues faced. It provides a synthesis of recent thinking, both theoretical and applied, on major problems of the Internet of Everything (IOE).

Satya Prakash Yadav
Department of Computer Science and Engineering
GL Bajaj Institute of Technology and Management
India
Graduate Program in Telecommunications Engineering (PPGET)
Federal Institute of Education, Science and Technology of Ceará (IFCE)
Brazil

Sansar Singh Chauhan
Department of Computer Science & Engineering
Noida Institute of Engineering & Technology
India

Sanjeev Kumar Pippal
NSBT MGM University, Cidco, Aurangabad
Maharashtra 431003
India

&

Victor Hugo C. de Albuquerque
Department of Teleinformatics Engineering (DETI) Federal University of Ceará
Brazil

List of Contributors

Arushi Kapoor	Robert R Mcormick School of Engineering and Applied Science, Northwestern University, Illinois, United States
Arushi Kapoor	Department of Biotechnology, Amity Institute of Biotechnology, Amity University, Noida, India
A. Kumaraswamy	Sri Venkateswara College of Engineering, Sriperumbudur, Tamilnadu, India
Chandra Sekhar Kolli	Department of Computer Science, Gandhi Institute of Technology and Management, Visakhapatnam, Andhra Pradesh, India
C. Muruganandam	Department of Computer Science, AVVM Sri Pushpam College, Affiliated to Bharathidasan University, Poondi, Thanjavur, Tamil Nadu - 613503, India
Dimitrios A. Karras	National and Kapodistrian University of Athens (NKUA), Hellas, Greece
Debajit Mishra	Department of Ocean Studies & Marine Biology, Pondicherry University, Port Blair Campus, India
G. Harish	Department of Computer Science & Engineering, Dr. Ambedkar Institute of Technology, Mallathahalli, Bangalore, Karnataka - 560056, India
J. Viswanatha Rao	VNR Vignana Jyothi Institute of Engineering and Technology, Hyderabad, India
K. N. Asha	Department of Computer Science & Engineering, Dr. Ambedkar Institute of Technology, Mallathahalli, Bangalore, Karnataka - 560056, India
K. P. Asha Rani	Department of Computer Science & Engineering, Dr. Ambedkar Institute of Technology, Mallathahalli, Bangalore, Karnataka - 560056, India
K. R. Swetha	Department of CSE, BGS Institute of Technology, Adichunchanagiri University, Mandya, Karnataka, India
Muskan Jindal	Department of Computer Science, Amity School of Engineering and Technology, Amity University, Noida, Uttar Pradesh, India
Mahaveer Singh Naruka	G.L. Bajaj Institute of Technology and Management, Greater Noida, U.P, India
Muskan Jindal	Amity School of Engineering and Technology, Noida, Uttar Pradesh, India
M. G. Skanda	Department of Industrial & Production Engineering, JSS S&T University, (SJCE) Mysore, India
M. Lakshminarayana	Department of Medical Electronics Engineering, M S Ramaiah Institute Of Technology, Bengaluru, Karnataka, India
N. Chitra Kiran	Department of Electronics and Communication Engineering, Alliance University, Bengaluru, Karnataka, India
Namith Gupta	Amity School of Engineering and Technology, Amity University, Noida, India
Nidhi Shah	Department of Life Sciences, University of Mumbai, Mumbai, India
N. Mohan	Department of EEE, JSS Science and Technology University Mysuru, Karnataka-570006, India
P. Vasantha Kumar	School of Excellence in Law, The Tamil Nadu Dr. Ambedkar Law University, Chennai, India

Rishabh Jain	Ajay Kumar Garg Engineering College (AKTU), Ghaziabad, Uttar Pradesh, India
Rajesh Kumar Patnaik	Department of Electrical and Electronics Engineering, GMR Institute of Technology, Rajam, Andhra Pradesh-532127, India
Ranjan Walia	Department of Electrical Engineering, Model Institute of Engineering and Technology, Jammu, Jammu & Kashmir - 181122, India
Shashank Awasthi	Department of Computer Science and Engineering, G.L. Bajaj Institute of Technology and Management, Greater Noida, U.P., India
Srishti Jain	Indira Gandhi Delhi Technical University for Women, India
Sumedha Jain	Chandigarh College of Engineering and Technology, Chandigarh, India
Satya Prakash Yadav	Department of Computer Science and Engineering, G.L. Bajaj Institute of Technology and Management, Greater Noida, U.P, India
Sagaya Aurelia	Department of Computer Science, CHRIST University, Bengaluru, Karnataka, India
S. Kirubakaran	Department of ECE, KPR Institute of Engineering and Technology, Coimbatore, Tamil Nadu-641407, India
Smitha Shekar	Department of Computer Science & Engineering, Dr. Ambedkar Institute of Technology, Mallathahalli, Bangalore, Karnataka - 560056, India
S. B. Prathibha	Department of Computer Science and Engineering, Sri Siddartha Institute of Technology, Tumakuru, Karnataka, India
Udayabalan Balasingam	Department of Information Science and Engineering, East Point College of Engineering and Technology, Bengaluru, Karnataka, India
Urmila R. Pol	Department of Computer Science, Shivaji University, Kolhapur, Maharashtra-416003, India
Vartika Agarwal	Department of Biotechnology, Savitribai Phule Pune University, Pune, Maharashtra, India
Vartika Agarwal	Amity School of Engineering and Technology, Noida, Uttar Pradesh, India

CHAPTER 1

Investigating the Features of Physical Layer Structure for Employment of Smart City Models

Rishabh Jain[1,*], Srishti Jain[2], Muskan Jindal[3] and Mahaveer Singh Naruka[4]

[1] *Ajay Kumar Garg Engineering College (AKTU), Ghaziabad, Uttar Pradesh, India*

[2] *Indira Gandhi Delhi Technical University for Women, India*

[3] *Amity School of Engineering and Technology, Noida, Uttar Pradesh, India*

[4] *G.L. Bajaj Institute of Technology and Management, Greater Noida, U.P, India*

Abstract: In today's world, when everything around us is getting smart, be it the "phone" or "television", there is an utter need and high time for the cities to get smart to solve the major problems of mankind. It is a futuristic approach to alleviate obstacles caused due to day by day increasing population of India. It will help the government as well as the common people to fight daily life problems such as water scarcity, waste management, and lack of interconnectivity in a city that can cause serious problems like delayed responses to emergency situations. This paper mainly focuses on the salient features of the smart city "Dholera" in Gujarat, India. The city uses futuristic technologies like Artificial Intelligence (AI) and the Internet of Things(IoT) to automate city resources. It has AI-based smart grids, transportation, water and waste management. This paper explains why Cholera is a smart, intelligent and fast-responsive city and how it is a boon for the masses.

Keywords: Case Study, Employment Framework, IOT, Smart City.

1. INTRODUCTION

India today has a population of around 136 crores out of which 34% is the urban population. Today, urbanisation is increasing rapidly in India [1, 2]. Urbanisation increases the economy of the country and also contributes majorly to the growth of the country. But, is it sufficient for a city to be just urban to solve all the problems? The answer to this question is NO [3, 60, 61, 64].

As the population is increasing, and people are shifting more to urban cities, and the waste and water management problems are increasing day by day [4, 37, 48, 52, 53]. So, there is an utter need to convert cities into smart cities. This project is

* **Corresponding author Rishabh Jain:** Ajay Kumar Garg Engineering College(AKTU), Ghaziabad, Uttar Pradesh, India; E-mail: 7as1827000423@gmail.com

Satya Prakash Yadav, Sansar Singh Chauhan, Sanjeev Kumar Pippal and Victor Hugo C. de Albuquerque (Eds.)

also called the Brownfield smart city project or the conversion of a barren land into a smart city is also called as Greenfield smart city project. We need some intelligent and smart solutions for problems that occur even in urban areas [5 - 7].

Let us consider the case of Mumbai, which is a metropolitan city in India. It faced heavy downpours in July 19, 2021, causing water logging in several low-lying areas in Kalyan-Dombivli, Ulhasnagar, Bhiwandi and Ambernath in Thane District [8 - 10]. Some people lost their lives as they got trapped in a massive mudslide. Also, according to news agencies, a 9-year-old boy fell and died in the open drain on Mira road. Had it been a smart city, the problem of water logging would have never occurred because of the excellent drainage system and such drastic incidents would have never occurred [11 - 13]. Let us consider another incident of Bengaluru's poor wastewater management system. Due to rapid urbanisation and development in Bengaluru, its groundwater is getting severely contaminated [71-73] as shown in Fig. (**1**).

Fig. (1). Water Logging [74].

Untreated waste from industries directly gets discharged into water bodies, polluting the water severely. This contaminated water when enters the ground, and later consumed, can directly cause fatal health diseases and if used for agricultural purposes, it can enter the food chain easily [14 - 16]. Many lakes in Bengaluru, such as Kaikondrahalli, Kasavanahalli and Kalkere lakes, have earlier also foamed, but the level of foam in Varthur and Bellandur lakes is alarmingly high. The foam sometimes overflows onto the roads, hindering the views of cars and other motor drivers leading to accidents. Some residents have reported skin irritation and many other life-threatening diseases. These issues can be addressed by using smarter solutions by encouraging the concept of smart cities in India. Smart cities make use of Information and Communication Technology(ICT) to overcome these problems and thereby enhance the standard of living [18 - 20].

Fig. (2). Froth in Bangalore City Causing Hindrance in Visibility [76].

Fig. (3). Smart City Infrastructure.

By making use of IoT along with Artificial Intelligence, we can collect data using sensors. Smart cities also have great infrastructure as shown in Fig. (**3**), to avoid problems like water logging, traffic management problems as shown in Fig. (**2**), waste-water and solid waste management problems. Smart cities also have separate residential and commercial areas for proper functioning and easier lives [21 - 24].

The Government of India has launched the smart city mission with the aim of developing 100 smart cities and many Greenfield cities across the country, making them citizen-friendly and sustainable. One of the cities in the mission is Dholera, which is India's first Industrial Greenfield city [25 - 28, 57, 68, 75].

Dholera consists of a smart water management system that solves waterlogging and wastewater problems [29 - 32]. It also has 4 ICT service centres, which will act as a central hub for all sensors. Supervisory control and data acquisition (SCADA), a computer system for collecting and analysing real-time data makes the city water supply robust. Smart city infrastructure elements include adequate water supply with smart management and maintenance, assured electricity, proper waste management, efficient urban mobility, and urban transport. Dholera smart city project is divided into 3 phases be investing in the Dholera project [33 - 36].

Each phase is of 10 years and the deadline for this project is 2042. It is the heaven on Earth project built with highly futuristic technologies like Artificial Intelligence and IoT [51, 54].

2. FUTURE OF DHOLERA SIR SMART CITY

The Dholera Smart City Project has a bright future because it is not just providing enormous benefits but at an affordable price also. People can buy houses at an affordable cost. Many large and renowned companies like Adani Group, M&M, HCC, Halcrow [39 - 41], torrent, *etc* will be investing in the Dholera project. Also, the French aerospace and defence firm Airbus group and Baba Kalyani group will also be investing in the project.

The Dholera Project will surely be attracting people from all over the world to come and settle in this world-class city. Dholera has IOT (Internet of Things) that will ensure that all the parts of the city be wirelessly interconnected with the internet. Adding to it, the combination of ICT- Internet, Communication and Technology will make it technologically stronger [40, 42, 43, 69].

Dholera Smart City will be twice the size of Delhi and will incorporate features like affordable housing and expansion of businesses [43, 45, 70]. Now the investors won't have to spend time in long queues for the documentation work and common attributes shown in Fig. (**4**). There will be a single window clearance and e-land allocation system [34, 46, 56]. The EWS (Economically Weaker Sections) will be allotted 10% of the residential areas of Dholera city. The city will also have a six-lane expressway and a metro line to reduce travel time. The city will also have its own international airport called the Dholera Airport having two parallel runways of 2910 metres and 4000 metres [56, 65, 67].

3. DEVELOPMENT OF DHOLERA SIR

Dholera SIR is a 'New Gujarat within Gujarat' built with all the future technologies like IOT(Internet of Technology) and Artificial Intelligence. It will prove to be the perfect abode for a person to stay with his/her family and a perfect place for investors to invest their money into. The city provides marvelous connectivity within the city so that we can reach our destination as fast as possible. The city will have its own airport, metro and a seaport covered with water on three sides [41, 43, 47]. So, with the excellent connectivity and extremely affordable rates of property, Dholera will attract many MNCs and manufacturing industries. Several reputed companies like Tata will open India's first electric vehicle's battery manufacturing plant in the city. Such developments will create many direct and indirect jobs in Dholera. Thus, the employment rate in the country will increase if more such smart cities are created [34, 62, 63].

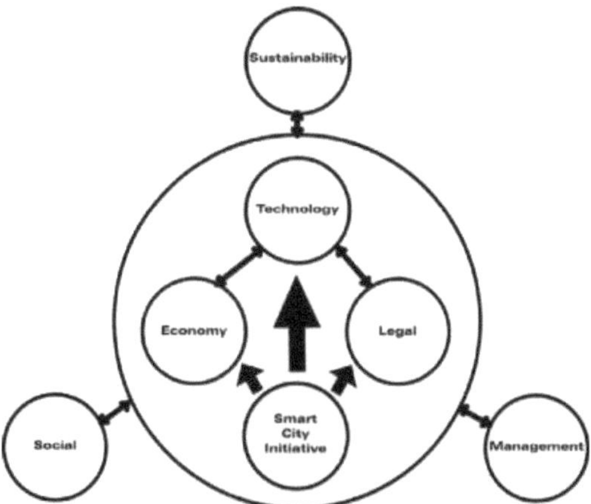

Fig. (4). Creative Commons Attribution-Non-Commercial-No Derivatives 4.0 International [77].

4. EMPLOYMENT FRAMEWORK IN DHOLERA

Dholera Smart City is envisaged to create 8 lakh employment opportunities and house 20 lakh people by 2042. Prime Minister Narendra Modi has visioned the smart city to be double the size of Delhi. ITI Aayog CEO Amitabh Kant opines that the key challenge for India is to grow at rates of 8-9 percent or more annually for three decades to uplift the vast segment of the population presently below the poverty line and to grow at rates of 15-16 percent annually for the next three decades. "Gujarat has taken this opportunity to meet the challenges by developing DSIR," he says [49].

You will get world-class facilities, amenities and Infrastructure in Dholera. Dholera is going to be very good for businesses and investors. This is because the rate of land is low right now which makes businesses very easy. It is also going to be a very accessible city. It is going to have multiple modes of transport which include 8-lane express highways, a new international airport, and even the metro. Dholera SIR is going to be a city connected by the metro which makes traveling in and around Dholera very easy. Dholera will have a port too. This makes transportation of goods in and out of Dholera very easy and hence a big bonus for companies and businesses to boom. Dholera Smart City is the best time to invest due to its metro smart city projects.

The Draft Development Plan of Dholera SIR aims at the creation of an economically and socially balanced, new age City with world-class infrastructure and high-quality of life as shown in Fig. (**5**).

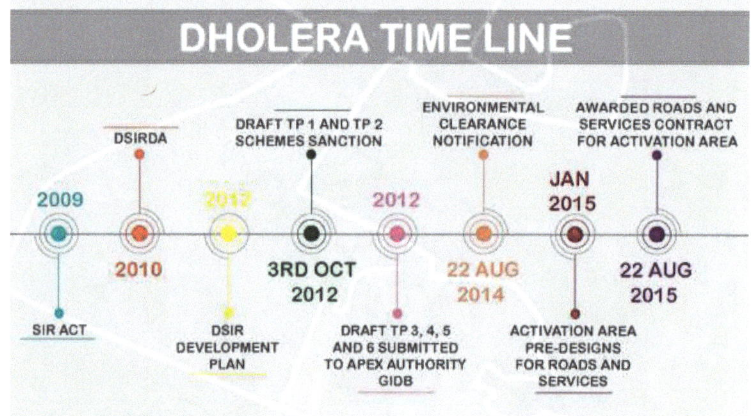

Fig. (5). Dholera TimeLine [77].

5. FUTURISTIC OPTIONS

In the actual urban development context, the smart city concept is frequently used. This concept does not have a unique definition, but is always defined as having a positive impact. At the base of this concept, there is a challenge to reduce the environmental impact and carbon footprint [45, 55, 58].

Smart cities focus more on renewable sources of energy rather than conventional resources depicted in Fig. (**6**). Thus, tapping the wind energy becomes necessary. So, vertical windmills are used in areas with low wind speeds [43, 44, 50].

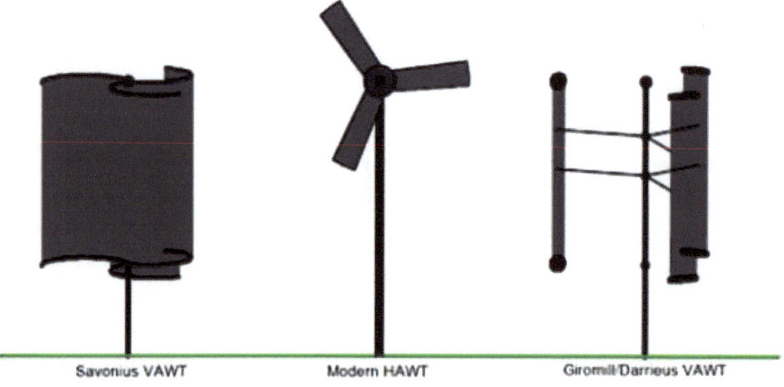

Fig. (6). Working of Renewable Sources of Energy.

The graph shows the vorticity magnitude for each TSR value and the power coefficient variation around each of the two wind turbines: the outer turbine is denoted Turine 1 in Fig. (7), and the inner turbine is Turbine 2 [17, 38, 59, 67].

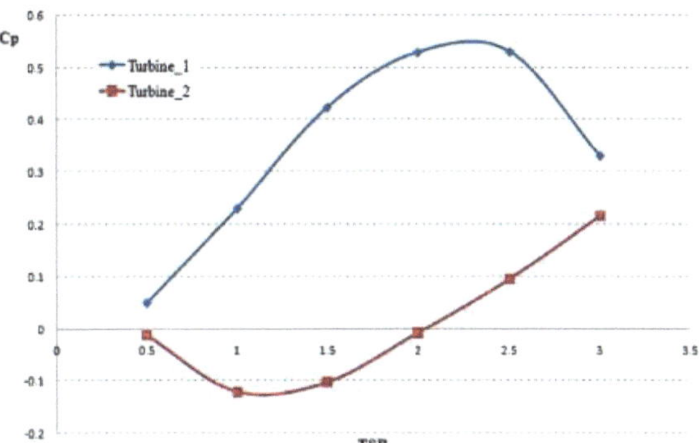

Fig. (7). Cp variations for both wind turbines. indicate an optimal TSR can be found with respect to the TSR value. Thus, the outer turbine power coefficient is maximum at about TSR = 2.5.

6. PROGRAM CODE

According to a report by the Texas Transportation Institute, drivers in the United States, spend around 42 h a year in traffic and waste more than 3 billion gallons of fuel per year. The following code is the implementation of the preferable traffic light in smart cities [26].

```
void A_CHANGE() {
  //Interrupt function to read the x2 timelapse of the encoder.

  if ( digitalRead(ENC_INB) == 0 )
  {
    if ( digitalRead(ENC_INA) == 0 )
    {
      // A fell, B is low
      timelapse++; // Moving forward
    } else
    {
      // A rose, B is high
      timelapse--; // Moving reverse
    }
  }
  else if(digitalRead(ENC_INB) == 1) {
    if ( digitalRead(ENC_INA) == 0 ) {
      timelapse--;
      //Serial.println(timelapse);// Moving reverse
    }
  }
}
```

Source: Github Profile -https://github.com/srishtijain123?tab=repositories

CONCLUSION

The concept of a smart city is the need of today because only urbanization cannot solve the problems we face in day-to-day life like water-logging, traffic management, *etc.* We need to make advancement today, and use the latest technologies like artificial intelligence and IOT to support the needs of India's growing population. Many countries in the world like Brazil, USA, and Singapore have adopted the concept of a Smart City. Singapore, Helsinki and Zurich are top-ranking in the global smart city index. Though many cities today are switching to smart cities, but most of them are Brownfield cities. And when we count Greenfield cities, unfortunately the count is extremely low. We need more greenfield cities because they are developed from scratch, and many barren lands come into use because of this concept. But when we build a brownfield city, we are not building from scratch, we are making changes in the already built infrastructure that has been standing for ages. I It becomes difficult to add features and new technology efficiently. In this research paper, we have thrown light on features of India's first Greenfield project, Dholera that makes use of the latest techniques like IOT(Internet of Things) to solve all the major problems. It is also affordable for both the residents as well as the investors who want to buy property in Dholera. Dholera has the capacity to accommodate the population of around 50,00,000. So we need 50 more such cities like Dholera to accommodate a population of 25,00,00,000.

REFERENCES

[1]   "HAWT or VAWT?", *Innovation in Wind Turbine Design,* pp. 277-290, 2018.
        [http://dx.doi.org/10.1002/9781119137924.ch13]

[2]   R. Wiser, and M. Bolinger, "2010 wind technologies market report", 2011.
        [http://dx.doi.org/10.2172/1219205]

[3]   K. Kim, "Implementation of climate smart city planning: Global climate smart city platform solution",
        Low-Carbon Smart Cities, pp. 285-323, 2017.
        [http://dx.doi.org/10.1007/978-3-319-59618-1_7]

[4]   F. Al-Turjman, and C. Altrjman, "Energy consumption monitoring in IoT-based smart cities",
        Intelligence in IoT-enabled Smart Cities, pp. 7-26, 2018.
        [http://dx.doi.org/10.1201/9780429022456-2]

[5]   I. Malael, G.B. Gherman, and I. Porumbel, "Increase the smart cities development by using an
        innovative design for vertical axis wind turbine", *Proceedings of the 27th International DAAAM
        Symposium,* 2016pp. 0506-0513.
        [http://dx.doi.org/10.2507/27th.daaam.proceedings.076]

[6]   J. Palsa, L. Vokorokos, E. Chovancova, and M. Chovanec, "Smart cities and the importance of smart
        traffic lights", *17th International Conference on Emerging eLearning Technologies and Applications
        (ICETA),* 2019 pp. 587-592 Starý Smokovec, Slovakia.
        [http://dx.doi.org/10.1109/ICETA48886.2019.9040086]

[7]   R. Bang, M. Patel, V. Garg, V. Kasa, J. Malhotra, and S. Sarode, "Redefining smartness in township
        with internet of things & artificial intelligence: Dholera city", *E3S Web of Conferences,* vol. 170, p.
        06001, 2020.

[http://dx.doi.org/10.1051/e3sconf/202017006001]

[8]   T. Jazeel, "Utopian urbanism and representational city-ness", *Dialogues Hum. Geogr.,* vol. 5, no. 1, pp. 27-30, 2015.
[http://dx.doi.org/10.1177/2043820614565866]

[9]   D. Monroe, *Challenges of gate-dielectric scaling, including the vertical replacement-gate MOSFET.* vol. 550. AIP Conference Proceedings, 2001, pp. 97-104.
[http://dx.doi.org/10.1063/1.1354379]

[10]   S. Joshi, S. Saxena, T. Godbole, and Shreya, "Developing smart cities: An integrated framework", *Procedia Comput. Sci.,* vol. 93, pp. 902-909, 2016.
[http://dx.doi.org/10.1016/j.procs.2016.07.258]

[11]   E. Alterman, "The uses and abuses of clausewitz", *Parameters,* vol. 17, no. 1, 1987.
[http://dx.doi.org/10.55540/0031-1723.1439]

[12]   G.I. Navaroj, and E. Julie, "Smart parking in smart cities using secure IoT", In: *Deployment of IoT Projects in Smart Cities* Handbook of Research on Implementation, 2019, pp. 165-188.
[http://dx.doi.org/10.4018/978-1-5225-9199-3.ch011]

[13]   R. Krishnamurthi, A. Nayyar, and A. Solanki, "Innovation opportunities through internet of things (iot) for smart cities", *Green and Smart Technologies for Smart Cities,* pp. 261-292, 2019.

[14]   D. Gavalas, P. Nicopolitidis, A. Kameas, C. Goumopoulos, P. Bellavista, L. Lambrinos, and B. Guo, "Smart cities: Recent trends, methodologies, and applications", *Wire Commun Mobi Comput,* pp. 1-2, 2017.
[http://dx.doi.org/10.1155/2017/7090963Ismagilova] E. Hughes, L. Dwivedi, K. Lambrinos, and K. R. Raman, "Smart cities: Advances in research—An information systems perspective", *Int. J. Info. Manag.,* vol. 47, pp. 88-100, 2017.
[http://dx.doi.org/10.1016/j.ijinfomgt.2019.01.004]

[15]   P.M. Santos, C. Queiros, S. Sargento, A. Aguiar, J. Barros, J.G.P. Rodrigues, S.B. Cruz, T. Lourenco, P.M. d'Orey, Y. Luis, C. Rocha, S. Sousa, and S. Crisostomo, "PortoLivingLab: An IoT-based sensing platform for smart cities", *IEEE Internet Things J.,* vol. 5, no. 2, pp. 523-532, 2018.
[http://dx.doi.org/10.1109/JIOT.2018.2791522]

[16]   A.C. Mangra, I. Porumbel, and F.G. Florean, "Experimental measurements of camelina sativa oil combustion", *Energy Sustain. Dev.,* vol. 44, pp. 109-116, 2018.
[http://dx.doi.org/10.1016/j.esd.2018.03.008]

[17]   K.H. Suffer, R. Usubamatov, G. Abdul Quadir, and K.A. Ismail, "Numerical simulation of a vertical Axis wind turbine having cavity vanes", *Int. J. Simulation. Systems. Sci. Techno,* 2020.
[http://dx.doi.org/10.5013/IJSSST.a.15.03.13]

[18]   P. Tchakoua, R. Wamkeue, M. Ouhrouche, T. Tameghe, and G. Ekemb, "A new approach for modeling darrieus-type vertical Axis wind turbine rotors using electrical equivalent circuit analogy: Basis of theoretical formulations and model development", *Energies,* vol. 8, no. 10, pp. 10684-10717, 2015.
[http://dx.doi.org/10.3390/en81010684]

[19]   D. T. Griffith, M. F. Barone, J. Paquette, B. C. Owens, D. L. Bull, C. Simao-Ferriera, A. Goupee, and M. Fowler, "Design studies for deep-water floating offshore vertical Axis wind turbines", *Engineering,* 2018.
[http://dx.doi.org/10.2172/1459118]

[20]   M. Raciti Castelli, and E. Benini, "Effect of blade inclination angle on a Darrieus wind turbine", *Industrial and Cogeneration; Microturbines and Small Turbomachinery; Oil and Gas Applications; Wind Turbine Technology.,* vol. 5, pp. 857-869, 2010 .Glasgow, UK.
[http://dx.doi.org/10.1115/GT2010-23332]

[21]   a. A. Kumar, and R. Saini, "Performance analysis of a single stage modified savonius hydrokinetic turbine having twisted blades", *Renewable Energy,* vol. 113, pp. 461-478, 2017.
[http://dx.doi.org/10.1016/j.renene.2017.06.020]

b. R. Y. Redlinger, P. D. Andersen, and P. E. Morthorst, "Wind energy in the twenty-first century", 2002.
[http://dx.doi.org/10.1057/9780230524279]

[22]   L.A. Mitulet, G. Oprina, R.A. Chihaia, S. Nicolaie, A. Nedelcu, and M. Popescu, "Wind tunnel testing for a new experimental model of counter-rotating wind turbine", *Procedia Eng.,* vol. 100, pp. 1141-1149, 2015.
[http://dx.doi.org/10.1016/j.proeng.2015.01.477]

[23]   B.K. Debnath, A. Biswas, and R. Gupta, "Computational fluid dynamics analysis of a combined three-bucket Savonius and three-bladed Darrieus rotor at various overlap conditions", *J. Renew. Sustain. Energy,* vol. 1, no. 3, p. 033110, 2009.
[http://dx.doi.org/10.1063/1.3152431]

[24]   A. Kumar, and R.P. Saini, "Performance analysis of a single stage modified Savonius hydrokinetic turbine having twisted blades", *Renew. Energy,* vol. 113, pp. 461-478, 2017.
[http://dx.doi.org/10.1016/j.renene.2017.06.020]

[25]   "What should we teach?", *World Class,* pp. 26-37, 2017.
[http://dx.doi.org/10.4324/9781315650678-4]

[26]   L. Cseke, *Smart urbanism: Utopian vision or false dawn?,* S. Marvin, A. Luque-Ayala, C. McFarlane, Eds., vol. 65. Hungarian Geographical Bulletin, 2017, no. 4, pp. 444-446.
[http://dx.doi.org/10.15201/hungeobull.65.4.13]

[27]   A. Vanolo, "Smartmentality: The smart city as disciplinary strategy", *Urban Stud.,* vol. 51, no. 5, pp. 883-898, 2014.
[http://dx.doi.org/10.1177/0042098013494427]

[28]   M. Finka, V. Ondrejička, and Ľ. Jamečný, "Urban safety as spatial quality in smart cities", *Smart City 360°,* pp. 821-829, 2016.
[http://dx.doi.org/10.1007/978-3-319-33681-7_73]

[29]   L. Cseke, *Smart urbanism: Utopian vision or false dawn?,* S. Marvin, A. Luque-Ayala, C. McFarlane, Eds., vol. 65. Hungarian Geographical Bulletin, 2017, no. 4, pp. 444-446.
[http://dx.doi.org/10.15201/hungeobull.65.4.13]

[30]   A.T. Barker, "Electromagnetic therapies real or imaginary?", *Phys. World,* vol. 5, no. 1, pp. 14-16, 1992.
[http://dx.doi.org/10.1088/2058-7058/5/1/15]

[31]   "Smart sustainable cities", *Encyclopedia of the UN Sustainable Development Goals,* pp. 605-605, 2020.
[http://dx.doi.org/10.1007/978-3-319-95717-3_300126]

[32]   F. Chang, and D. Das, "Smart nation Singapore: Developing policies for a citizen-oriented smart city initiative", *Developing National Urban Policies,* pp. 425-440, 2020.
[http://dx.doi.org/10.1007/978-981-15-3738-7_18]

[33]   D. Das, and J.J. Zhang, "Pandemic in a smart city: Singapore's COVID-19 management through technology & society", *Urban Geogr.,* vol. 42, no. 3, pp. 408-416, 2021.
[http://dx.doi.org/10.1080/02723638.2020.1807168]

[34]   S. Lim, "SMART CITIES: Big data, civic hackers, and the quest for a new Utopia (W. W. NORTON & Company, 2013)", *Korean Association of Space and Environment Research,* vol. 28, no. 2, pp. 212-217, 2018.
[http://dx.doi.org/10.19097/kaser.2018.28.2.212]

[35]   T. Yigitcanlar, and J.H. Han, "Ubiquitous eco cities", *Int. J. Adv. Pervasive Ubiquitous Comput.,* vol. 2, no. 1, pp. 1-17, 2010.
[http://dx.doi.org/10.4018/japuc.2010010101]

[36]   I. Mălăel, L. Moutet, and V. Drăgan, "Numerical simulation of a vertical Axis wind turbine for urban use", *Appl. Mech. Mater.,* vol. 811, pp. 333-338, 2015.
[http://dx.doi.org/10.4028/www.scientific.net/AMM.811.333]

[37]   "Making sense of smart city sensors", *Urban and Regional Data Management,* pp. 123-134, 2013.
[http://dx.doi.org/10.1201/b14914-15]

[38]   G. Rometty, "Message from the senior vice president, global business services", *IBM Syst. J.,* vol. 47, no. 1, pp. 1-2, 2008.
[http://dx.doi.org/10.1147/sj.471.0002]

[39]   J.R. Gil-García, and T.A. Pardo, "E-government success factors: Mapping practical tools to theoretical foundations", *Gov. Inf. Q.,* vol. 22, no. 2, pp. 187-216, 2005.
[http://dx.doi.org/10.1016/j.giq.2005.02.001]

[40]   E.P. Weber, and A.M. Khademian, "Wicked problems, knowledge challenges, and collaborative capacity builders in network settings", *Public Adm. Rev.,* vol. 68, no. 2, pp. 334-349, 2008.
[http://dx.doi.org/10.1111/j.1540-6210.2007.00866.x]

[41]   "Urban and rural population growth and world urbanization prospects", *World Urbanization Prospects: The 2018 Revision,* pp. 9-31, 2019.

[42]   R. Giffinger, and H. Kramar, "Benchmarking, profiling, and ranking of cities", *Performance Metrics for Sustainable Cities,* pp. 35-52, 2021.
[http://dx.doi.org/10.4324/9781003096566-4]

[43]   M. Schneider, "Smart waste management fur die smart city", *Smart City Made in Germany,* pp. 373-379, 2020.
[http://dx.doi.org/10.1007/978-3-658-27232-6_41]

[44]   J. André, "Von Der smart city zur learning city", *Smart City Made in Germany,* pp. 169-174, 2020.
[http://dx.doi.org/10.1007/978-3-658-27232-6_18]

[45]   N. Komninos, *Intelligent cities and the evolution toward technology-enhanced, global and user-driven territorial systems of innovation.pp. 187-200.Handbook on the Geographies of Innovation*pp. 187-200.
[http://dx.doi.org/10.4337/9781784710774.00022]

[46]   C. Kühnhold, "Smart city loop", *Smart City Made in Germany,* pp. 587-592, 2020.
[http://dx.doi.org/10.1007/978-3-658-27232-6_61]

[47]   "Sino-Singapore Tianjin eco-city, smart grid, smart city", *IEEE PES Innovative Smart Grid Technologies (ISGT).,* 2012.
[http://dx.doi.org/10.1109/ISGT.2012.6175618]

[48]   T. Alizadeh, "Crowdsourced smart cities versus corporate smart cities", *IOP Conf. Ser. Earth Environ. Sci.,* vol. 158, p. 012046, 2018.
[http://dx.doi.org/10.1088/1755-1315/158/1/012046]

[49]   A. Sircar, M. Shah, S. Sahajpal, D. Vaidya, S. Dhale, and A. Chaudhary, "Geothermal exploration in Gujarat: Case study from Dholera", *Geothermal Energy,* vol. 3, no. 1, p. 22, 2015.
[http://dx.doi.org/10.1186/s40517-015-0041-5]

[50]   A. Datta, "New urban utopias of postcolonial India", *Dialogues Hum. Geogr.,* vol. 5, no. 1, pp. 3-22, 2015.
[http://dx.doi.org/10.1177/2043820614565748]

[51]   C. Chakraborty, and B. Nandi, "'Mainline' telecommunications infrastructure, levels of development and economic growth: Evidence from a panel of developing countries", *Telecomm. Policy,* vol. 35, no. 5, pp. 441-449, 2011.

[http://dx.doi.org/10.1016/j.telpol.2011.03.004]

[52]   S. Allwinkle, and P. Cruickshank, "Creating smart-er cities: An overview", *J. Urban Technol.,* vol. 18, no. 2, pp. 1-16, 2011.
[http://dx.doi.org/10.1080/10630732.2011.601103]

[53]   J.V. Winters, "Why are smart cities growing? Who moves and who stays*", *J. Reg. Sci.,* vol. 51, no. 2, pp. 253-270, 2011.
[http://dx.doi.org/10.1111/j.1467-9787.2010.00693.x]

[54]   M. Deakin, "The intelcities community of practice", *Web-Based Learning Solutions for Communities of Practice,* pp. 263-284, 2010.
[http://dx.doi.org/10.4018/978-1-60566-711-9.ch018]

[55]   M. Deakin, P. Cruickshank, "SCRAN: The network", *Smart Cities,* pp. 162-182, 2013.
[http://dx.doi.org/10.4324/9780203076224-18]

[56]   V. Bush, "As we may think", *Interactions,* vol. 3, no. 2, pp. 35-46, 1996.
[http://dx.doi.org/10.1145/227181.227186]

[57]   R.R. Widner, "Physical renewal of the industrial city", *Ann. Am. Acad. Pol. Soc. Sci.,* vol. 488, no. 1, pp. 47-57, 1986.
[http://dx.doi.org/10.1177/0002716286488001004]

[58]   D.H. Shin, "Ubiquitous city: Urban technologies, urban infrastructure and urban informatics", *J. Inf. Sci.,* vol. 35, no. 5, pp. 515-526, 2009.
[http://dx.doi.org/10.1177/0165551509100832]

[59]   M. Xavier, and J. Meneses, *Dropout in Online Higher Education: A scoping review from 2014 to 2018.* eLearn Center, Universitat Oberta de Catalunya: Barcelona.
[http://dx.doi.org/10.7238/uoc]

[60]   V. Bush, "As we may think (an article that appeared in the atlantic monthly in 1945 predicting the electronic revolution)", *J. Electron. Publ.,* vol. 1, no. 1&2, 1995.
[http://dx.doi.org/10.3998/3336451.0001.101]

[61]   R.R. Widner, "Physical renewal of the industrial city", *Ann. Am. Acad. Pol. Soc. Sci.,* vol. 488, no. 1, pp. 47-57, 1986.
[http://dx.doi.org/10.1177/0002716286488001004]

[62]   C. Kühnhold, "Smart city loop", *Smart City Made in Germany,* pp. 587-592, 2020.
[http://dx.doi.org/10.1007/978-3-658-27232-6_61]

[63]   *Grußwort Wikimedia Deutschland* Wikipedia und Geschichtswissenschaft.
[http://dx.doi.org/10.1515/9783110376357-002]

[64]   W.H. Frey, "Black in-migration, white flight, and the changing economic base of the Central City", *Am. J. Sociol.,* vol. 85, no. 6, pp. 1396-1417, 1980.
[http://dx.doi.org/10.1086/227170]

[65]   J.K. Brueckner, "Lessons from urban economics", *Brookings-Wharton Papers on Urban Affairs,* vol. 2001, no. 1, pp. 65-97, 2001.
[http://dx.doi.org/10.1353/urb.2001.0003]

[66]   "Urban and rural population size and growth at the country level", *World Urbanization Prospects: The 2018 Revision,* pp. 33-53, 2019.
[http://dx.doi.org/10.18356/55f6b478-en]

[67]   M. Jindal, and A. Kazim, "Systematic review and deliberation of various multi-criteria decision-making techniques", *Multi-Criteria Decision Modelling,* pp. 189-204, 2021.*Systematic review and deliberation of various multi-criteria decision-making techniques.,* pp. 189-204, 2021.
[http://dx.doi.org/10.1201/9781003125150-11-11]

[68]   A. Chakraborty, M. Jindal, M.R. Khosravi, P. Singh, A. Shankar, and M. Diwakar, "A secure IoT-based cloud platform selection using entropy distance approach and fuzzy set theory", *Wirel. Commun. Mob. Comput.*, vol. 2021, pp. 1-11, 2021.
[http://dx.doi.org/10.1155/2021/6697467]

[69]   A. Kazim, M. Jindal, R. Sharma, R. Choudhary, V. Kumar Sharma, and E. Bajal, "Big data analytics and artificial intelligence in business and marketing: Cloud security and encryption influencing business", *SSRN Electr. J.*, 2021.
[http://dx.doi.org/10.2139/ssrn.3884455]

[70]   *Transforming management with AI, big-data, and IoT.* Springer, 2022.
[http://dx.doi.org/10.1007/978-3-030-86749-2] "Federated learning for IoT applications", In: *EAI/Springer Innovations in Communication and Computing.* Springer, 2022.
[http://dx.doi.org/10.1007/978-3-030-85559-8]

[71]   A. Chakraborty, M. Jindal, and S. Gupta, "Post-COVID-19 view of indian economy with emphasis on service sector: A regression implementation", *Pervasive Healthcare,* pp. 295-323, 2021.
[http://dx.doi.org/10.1007/978-3-030-77746-3_19]

[72]   C. Kühnhold, "Smart city loop", *Smart City Made in Germany,* pp. 587-592, 2020.
[http://dx.doi.org/10.1007/978-3-658-27232-6_61]

[73]   "indianexpress", Available at:https://images.indianexpress.com/2019/06/mumbai-waterloggin--759.jpg

[74]   "pinimg", Available at:https://i.pinimg.com/564x/82/bf/24/82bf24c00ad8e84846cfb616e68901db.jpg

[75]   "digitaloceanspaces", Available at:https://s01.sgp1.digitaloceanspaces.com/large/847483-3467--bjcdovwkix-1502939939.jpg

[76]   "A glimpse of timeline development of dholera sir and delhi mumbai industrial corridoR", Available at:https://www.meenakshikhurana.com/a-glimpse-of-timeline-development-of-dholera-sir--nd-delhi-mumbai-industrial-corridor/

[77]   "SMELTS Framework for smart city initiative", Available at:https://www.researchgate.net/figure/SMELTS-Framework-for-smart-city-initiative_fig1_306067950

CHAPTER 2

Pithy & Comprehensive Review of Practical and Literal Models

Debajit Mishra[1,*], **Muskan Jindal**[2] and **Dimitrios A. Karras**[3]

[1] Department of Ocean Studies & Marine Biology, Pondicherry University, Port Blair Campus, India

[2] Amity School of Engineering and Technology, Noida, Uttar Pradesh, India

[3] National and Kapodistrian University of Athens (NKUA), Hellas, Greece

Abstract: The development and success of various smart cities is contingent on the multiple models of expertise they employ and execute like a functional and smart infrastructure to handle traffic chaos, a sustainable water recycling system, a smart administration task manager, or an efficient waste management plant. The development and efficacy of various smart cities are directly dependent on the efficiency of multiple models it employees. Thus, the presented study aims to review, analyse and document the various models that perform mundane tasks "smartly", on the basis of key criteria namely: efficacy on the task in hand, power and time consumption, human interaction, upfront cost and operational task. These outcomes are then collated, and assayed by the application of various mathematical and statistical models to determine their performance as compared to the pre-existing non-technical approach of pursuing the same. Finally, the purpose of this study is to present a complete analysis of the performance of various models of smart cities to comprehend the profitability overall and provide suitable points to improve the same.

Keywords: Internet of Things, Smart Cities, Operational & Upfront Cost, Performance Quotient.

1. INTRODUCTION

With a growing global population and rapid industrialization, which is expected to increase by over 10% within the next three decades, culminating in three-quarters of the world's urban population by 2050, nations around the globe are opting to fortify their cities to cater to the citizen-centric requirements and the burnout this would put on existing urban services [1 - 3]. This will be done as per the United

* Corresponding author Debajit Mishra: Department of Ocean Studies & Marine Biology, Pondicherry University, Port Blair Campus, India; E-mail: debajitmishra6@gmail.com

Satya Prakash Yadav, Sansar Singh Chauhan, Sanjeev Kumar Pippal and Victor Hugo C. de Albuquerque (Eds.)

Nations Sustainable Development Goals '2030 [4]. As shown by the numerous public and commercial projects now underway, Smart Cities (SCs) have emerged as a significant endeavour by various governmental means in ensuring better accessibility and hospitability to the projected population growth and giving residents a better living standard [5 - 12]. It is indeed difficult to pin down an SC; though factually cities affirm to be "smart" depending on a range of metrics, such as incorporating novel e-governance initiatives, establishing social learning enterprises and community-based outreach programmes, reinforcing circular economy, and using web-based technologies for continuous improvement [1, 13]. In this study, we define SC concept as the use of a myriad of information and communication technologies (ICTs) to improve the quality of citizens' living experience. This includes the ICT application in all of the previously mentioned areas, such as administration, transportation, accommodation, entrepreneurship, sustainable packaging, social cognition, community mobilization, and opportunity provision, among others. In an ideal world, the SC concept extends beyond the traditionally defined limits of a conventional city's organizational and social structures by enabling connectivity between them, allowing it to function more cohesively and effectively. When opposed to a typical city environment, SCs have numerous benefits (in terms of value): SCs are at the forefront of a cutting-edge technology that will assist governments in meeting their climate goals. SCs are concerned with SC management, smart transportation systems, and SC administration, to lower cities' greenhouse gas emissions and enable innovative technology to flourish for healthier and cleaner living. By 2025, SC projects will be worth USD 1 trillion, providing a significant financial incentive for governments as well as private enterprises to actively contribute to the technological revampments that enable SC growth [1, 14]. The goal of an SC project is to improve the quality of life for city residents and to contribute to the development of an inclusive society in which all viewpoints are respected and equal opportunities are offered. In the framework of smart cities, ICTs are a critical component of providing public services through improving citizen interactions with the city environment and making life simpler. There is an instance of the application of the computing frameworks on various SC projects [15 - 36].

The purpose of this work is to examine, assess, and record numerous models that execute routine activities "smartly," based on important factors such as task productivity, resource and time consumed, interpersonal interaction, initial expense, and operating workload. These results are then compiled and analysed using a variety of modelling methods to assess their performance in comparison to a non-technical method to pursuing the same. Finally, the objective of this study is to give a comprehensive insight into the performance of several smart city models to understand their profitability from a broad perspective and to suggest ways to improve them.

2. COMPREHENSIVE ANALYSIS OF PREVIOUS WORKS

The continued success of various smart cities is dependent on the various models of expertise they employ and implement, such as a functional and smart infrastructure to handle traffic congestion, a sustainable water recycling system, a smart administration task manager, or an efficient waste management plant. The efficiency of numerous models employed by distinct smart cities is directly reliant on their development and efficacy. Comparative analysis of previous studies concerned with this perspective is tabulated in Table **1** as follows:

Table 1. Comparative Analysis of Previous Works.

Citation	Aim/Objective	Advantage	Drawback
Tsai, S. B., *et al.* (2021) [37]	The study concentrates on recent developments in advanced digital transport networks for IoT based SC applications, including both automated advancement and novel deployments.	Under blockchain technology, a long-term GCU implementation for transport systems is being established.	The fast railway sector's upstream marketplace has a pattern of inadequate enterprise participation.
Dahmane, W. M *et al.* (2021) [38]	The study intends to construct a competent modified methodology based on formal techniques and networking interpretations.	A system has been implemented that methodically creates a robust and stable Smart City Model (SCM) that can subsequently be incorporated and used by the building information model (BIM).	Realistic cases that are highly nonlinear have been used to demonstrate the efficacy of the proposed paradigm.
Kumar, N., *et al.* (2021) [39]	To optimize the flow of traffic, the study offers a traffic-light control framework built upon deep reinforcement learning.	It uses the real-time traffic environment's vehicle dynamics as input.	The efficacy of the cutoff guideline, which is implemented on the central site that creates traffic control signalling, has been questioned.
Viale, A., *et al.* (2021) [40]	The study intends to build a model that can achieve high performance with low latency in camera systems.	Using Dynamic Vision Sensors, the design consumes very little power than standard frame-based camera systems.	A low power setup is a must for the functioning of the model.

(Table 1) cont.....

Citation	Aim/Objective	Advantage	Drawback
Drakoulelis, M., *et al.* (2021) [41]	The work aims to use the virtualized IoT model to immerse and test daily applications under realistic settings and limitations.	It uses actual data from a selection of detectors to simulate a sensor's activities.	The proposed method might condense the activities to a simple computation.
Wang, B., *et al.* (2021) [42]	The installation of a commercial vehicle-road collaboration system derived from satellite navigation and location, as well as composite sensing technology, is proposed in this article.	It progressively enables vehicle-to-road cooperation and self-driving implementations.	The passage mapping for automated vehicles involves intense geolocation.
Xu, Y *et al.* (2021) [43]	The work delves into assessing the acceptability of the FCW system and to look into the elements that influence drivers' views.	The findings of this study may aid investigators in better understanding passenger vehicle driving patterns and developing more efficient vehicle FCW systems.	With increasing vehicular speed, passenger vehicle drivers' approval of an FCW system declines.
Shin, D. H., *et al.* (2012) [44]	By examining Korea's widespread urban planning scenarios, this study aims to offer an outline of the social-economic vision of interconnected devices.	This research shows how ubiquitous computing is understood and represented in policymaking in South Korea.	It is necessary to assess information technology infrastructure in the light of fluid social-economic developments.
Chen, X., *et al.* (2020) [45]	This paper tackles the topic by examining the influence of a modular framework for analysis on transport and traffic patterns to increase effective communication and the high bandwidth of the underpinning system design.	Times over the past decades, the adoption of mobile Connectivity and the use of portable devices has enabled ubiquitous traffic data.	The amount of route users has grown to be high enough to disrupt the existing traffic patterns as a result of the rising usage of distinct mobile applications.
De Falco, S., *et al.* (2019) [46]	The work aims to improve the effectiveness of urban spaces in a previously unexplored area.	It examines the idea of urban sustainability.	Peripheral urban spaces are overlooked.
Zhilin, S., *et al.* (2019) [47]	The goal of the research is to bring together disparate urban projects in a better knowledge of current self-governance methods.	It addresses from technical urban growth to socioeconomic issues projects.	There is no consensus on a holistic SC vision.
Angelidou, M. et al. (2017) [48]	The work throws light on ICTs' pivotal role in enhancing the operation of urban spaces.	It is shown expanding connections for knowledge sharing and advancement	The majority of SC initiatives do not use bottom-up techniques.

(Table 1) cont.....

Citation	Aim/Objective	Advantage	Drawback
Yang, J., *et al.* (2016) [49]	To use an adaptive local optimization technique, we present an effective object recognition tracking method.	Multi-source data in a greater fraction is collated and utilized intelligently for managing transport efficiently.	The updating technique is critical in determining the tracking findings' quality.
Puri, V., *et al.* (2016) [50]	Bicycling with multi-modal reciprocal network connectivity is the goal of the study.	It provides benefits for reducing road congestion and engine exhaust reduction.	As a precondition of the bike, bicycle sharing has its drawbacks, such as compromised confidential communications and driver safety precautions.
Kelley, S. B. *et al.* (2020) [51]	The research shows how early users of innovative automobile technology are induced to travel.	Cities' targeted areas for automatic guided internet-based technology varies significantly from the regular populace of each city.	The degree of connectivity and automation in autonomous and connected cars is complicated.

3. SMART CITY COMPONENTS

A smart city consists of several components (Fig. **1**). Data acquisition is the first part of smart city services, followed by data transmission, data curation; and analysis of the data, respectively. Data acquisition depends on the application and has been a driving force for the development of sensing systems in several sectors. The second aspect is data interchanging, which encompasses sending information from data gathering machinery to the data centre for warehousing and interpretation. This objective has been met in a myriad of areas. The use of 4G and 5G innovations, as well as network servers that may transport data locally or globally, is common in smart city efforts. The third phase is cloud-based, which involves using a variety of storage strategies to back up and restore data to use it in the final level, analysis of the data. The process involving identifying patterns and conclusions from the collected information to make an inference is known as data analysis. In certain circumstances, simple analysis, such as basic decision-making and aggregation, may suffice. The cloud's accessibility allows for not only large and diverse data collection, stockpiling, and handling, but also real-time supervised and unsupervised machine learning techniques for taking even more structured decisions [52].

3.1. Smart Agriculture

A major component of the United Nations Sustainable Development Goals for 2030 is food security. With a growing global population and severe climatic variability producing irregular weather in the world's food centres, the race to guarantee that food supply is made cost-effective and that finite inputs like water are used properly has become a top issue for governments all over the world. It involves the use of sensors placed in flora and landscapes to monitor various factors to aid in decision-making and in the prevention of diseases, pests and other problems. Smart agriculture is becoming increasingly popular. Precision agriculture is a component of the smart agriculture paradigm, and it entails the placement of sensors in plants to give focused measurements and, as a result, the deployment of targeted care mechanisms. Precision agriculture is a subset of smart agriculture. Precision agriculture would be required for food protection and security, and as such, it is a critical component of the battle for a sustainable farming today and in the future. The most significant uses of artificial intelligence (AI) in the Internet of Things (IoT) for agriculture include crop surveillance and early diagnosis of pathogens, as well as data-driven crop management and decision-making processes [53, 54].

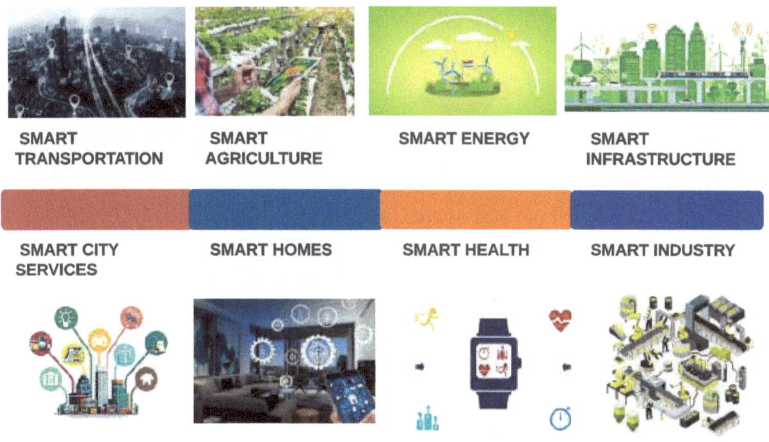

Fig. (1). Smart City Components.

3.2. Smart City Services

Smart City Services applications include municipal duties such as water distribution, wastewater treatment, and environmental maintenance. Water quality monitors may be placed to continuously monitor the condition of the water and identify leakages. Waste disposal is a common aspect of SC efforts, from shafts in Barcelona to bins fitted with cloud-connected sensors to not only alert the necessary personnel when they need to be emptied but also use AI to identify the optimal path to minimize costs. Sensors may also be used to monitor pollutant concentrations in cities and direct residents to the nearest available parking garage to conserve gasoline [55 - 58].

3.3. Smart Energy

Power comes from a primary generator, generally the impoundment facilities and nonrenewable fuel sources. The power production strategy utilised with these implementations demands that the output generated by such sites surpasses the requirement by a significant amount to assure uninterrupted power supply. Spotting and correcting problems in such setups take time. Furthermore, as clean energy systems become more affordable, the modern consumer not only receives but also generates their power. Smart Networks employ ICT to render existing and future grids more visible, enable distributed energy generation at both the customer and efficiency level, and provide self-healing characteristics. Smart grids provide true power information to providers at various locations on the system, from the supply convoys to the consumer. Smart grids give real-time information on consumer utilization, allowing for improved distributed generation control, incorporating many energy technologies, and self-healing to assure optimum amount [59].

3.4. Smart Health

Smart Health uses ICT to enhance healthcare coverage and efficacy [60 - 62]. With an expanding population and healthcare expenditures, academics and clinicians have been focusing on this issue. The conventional healthcare systems are overloaded and fail to meet rising public demands. In this sense, smart health systems strive to make healthcare accessible to as many users as possible *via* e-medicine and AI-assisted diagnostics depicted in Fig. (**1**). It is now feasible to use cloud computing to handle real-time health data while also tracking daily activities and identifying aberrant motions using inertial sensors. Overall expenses and stress on healthcare institutions are reduced.

3.5. Smart Home

The Smart Home is a significant component of SC applications because it is the hub of the occupants' lives. Smart Homes are equipped with sensing equipment that collects data about the residence and its residents. These sensors may include ambiance sensors, motion detectors, and power trackers.

3.6. Smart Industry

Industries worldwide are always striving to improve efficiency and production, and reduce costs. The Industry 4.0 concept envisions a linked workplace with interoperability of all transitional functions. The IoT makes this feasible. The application of IoT in design and processing procedures has resulted in faster and better advancement, streamlining of manufacturing strategies (strategies and competencies), improved efficiency, and increased machinery safety regulations. Nevertheless, dealing with such a diverse mix of sensors and equipment poses unique problems for IoT systems in Smart Enterprises. Industry 4.0 services are being developed and deployed using AI and IoT. Sensors integrated with types of machinery and other manufacturing processes offer data that may be used to improve functionality, improve marketing intelligence activities, and more. Many academics have postulated AI-IoT archetypes for Smart Industry. Data-driven condition-based proactive maintenance strategy, machinery health monitoring, and operation regulation are key industrial AI implementations [63 - 66].

3.7. Smart Infrastructure

Current infrastructure is critical to its residents' quality of life; municipal authorities must introduce new roadways, highways, and factories for their use, as well as undertake upkeep to ensure their continued use. Smart infrastructure assists communities in guaranteeing that their architecture is in good condition and useable by employing sensors for monitoring the seismic vulnerability of buildings/bridges *via* multiple sensors and nanodevices. The data obtained by these sensors enables the proactive repair of such vital metropolitan systems [67, 68].

3.8. Smart Transportation

Numerous metropolitan areas face traffic jams, greenhouse gas emissions, and rostering and cost-cutting challenges for public transportation. With the fast-widespread adoption of web-based technologies, connectivity between vehicles, infrastructural facilities, and pedestrians has become ingrained. Whether vehicle-to-vehicle (V2V), vehicle-to-infrastructure (V2I), vehicle-to-pedestrian (V2P), or pedestrian-to-infrastructure (P2I) communication, such technologies enable the creation of intelligent transport systems. For every car equipped with a Gps unit and every driver carrying a smartphone, several techniques rely on GPS to analyse driver behaviour and traffic characteristics. This real-time data is already being deployed for route planning in programmes *viz.* Waze and Google Maps, as well as for public transportation travel planning [69]. Sensor-equipped traffic control systems can also direct cars to the closest parking slot.

4. INTERNET OF THINGS (IOT) FOR SMART CITIES (SCS)

IoT is the main player in the SC efforts, facilitating ubiquitous digitalization notion. It inculcates to the pervasive networking of objects to the internet, allowing data communication to the cloud and perhaps receiving of instructions for completing tasks. IoT entails the collating of information and the use of predictive analytics to retrieve information that helps decision-making and legislation. Around 80 billion gadgets are inextricably tied to the world wide web by 2025 [70], spurring far more web applications. IoT enables monitors in SCs to accrue and intimate information on one end of the city to a centralized node, which is subsequently processed or digitised for pattern recognition and prediction.

4.1. IoT Architectures for SCs

After the acceptance of cloud amenities, the IoT combines data detection, routing, interpretation, and archiving processes. A typical IoT design is made up of five levels, each of which operates on the input from the preceding layer. Also, it depicts the 3 separate designs for IoT environments. The Sensing layer, also known as the Perception layer, is made up of detectors that might collect data on a wide range of parameters in any activity, along with actuators that may operate on material things, like RFID readers for decoding RFID tags as well as other similar technologies. Through wireless connection technologies such as Wi-Fi, cellular internet, Zigbee, and Bluetooth, the data acquired by the sensing layer is sent on to the Middleware layer *via* the networking layer. The Middleware layer offers a general interface between the sensing layer hardware and the Application layer, which uses the information which provides users with utilities through different APIs and data warehousing tools. The business layer is connected to the application layer and is utilized to create programs and strategies that aid in the overall functioning of the system.

SC platforms rely heavily on sensing. Sensors offer the information and expertise needed to develop SC solutions. Due to the heterogeneity of SC Initiatives and their various functionalities, a variety of sensors are employed as part of such ventures (Fig. **2**).

In the context of layouts, IoT configurations are generally classified according to the kind of operational duties assigned to various components of the IoT environment; this classification is mostly supported by the empirical computation functions which are depicted in Fig. (**2**). There are 3 designs for IoT applications based on the level of the IoT platform at which data processing may occur: cloud, fog, and edge approaches. The characteristics of each of the 3 tiers of the IoT environment are listed in Table **1**. These IoT designs don't show mutually exclusive characteristics; rather, the goal of this hierarchical system is to augment the upper layer by giving only meaningful information pertinent to the device's productivity and reliability. The objective for every IoT design engineer is to draw a line between both the competencies of the 3 tiers while bearing operating costs and needs in mind.

Fig. (2). Sensing technologies for smart cities from an IoT perspective.

Cloud Computing Model. It was the initial conceptual design for IoT applications and is predicated upon the concept that information processing from the various models of the IoT environment should occur in the clouds. Cloud enables unbroken shared resources (computer, storage and services) to be accessed through the network remotely. It ought to be able to attribute those resources as needed without human oversight, timeframe or pools as needed, and accessible from a range of platforms. The cloud offers both software and hardware for intelligent city operations. This has the benefit of providing a central administration interface for observing, controlling the IoT system and distributing control strategies depending upon the information recorded. Additionally, this standardization also permits cloud platforms to have big enough processing and stocking capacity to execute complicated tasks such as data retrieval, pattern identification and sensor readings in intelligent cities to make the most use of it. Nevertheless, the use of the IoT cloud computing environment is rather disadvantageous. First, the transfer of all collected information in the cloud raises the traffic of the network, however, this may have been not accurate for components where measured values are not quite regular. Furthermore, data outgoings may arise given the huge quantities of information that the numerous sensor nodes have to convey. Cloud computing technology also has the drawback of data lag, because sensor modules reside on the layer of the sensor and cloud decision-making/processing leads to data delay in the transfer of sensor information, especially if several devices simultaneously start transmitting data. When utilising this approach, network dependability can be a problem, because the bulk of encrypted traffic may not allow reliable data transfer techniques to be implemented as IoT devices grow [71].

Fog Computing Model. Because the majority of data generated in the IoT occurs at the sensory terminal of the system, also known as the edge, to address several of the issues with the cloud computing paradigm, Fog Computing was developed for the IoT. Fog computing offers a more varied redistribution of duties than the cloud technology dictates by transferring certain operations to local interfaces. Fog computing often focuses on data processing conducted by gateways and other access points on the IoT internet layer. As system components today provide improved cloud-based services, they may be utilized for simple data processes. Activities such as agglomeration and sensor readings acquisition, straightforward analysis and decisions may be conducted to decrease the transfer of knowledge to the upper cloud layer. The issues to be addressed during prediction comprise but are not restricted to, *e.g.* does the choice need an estimated return for one dimension and contemporaneous readings for another?? Can information obtained for one item be approximated and the presently recorded amount used for another magnitude? Based on prior data for a certain period, upper layers can offer decision-making alternatives instead of information, giving superior cloud layer quality data, and resulting in improved use of cloud services. Fog levels can locate decision-making, as they have access to a specific region's local state. It would be beneficial to build decentralized decision-making methods, that in some situations could be essential. It also allows local networking to be set up using non-internet technology (*e.g.* Zigbee, Bluetooth, RFID *etc.*) where sensors and other terminal devices broadcast data to the cloud-connected Fog layer (also known as the access points of the systems). Fog computing reduces the cost of deploying IoT systems, and improves resilience with decreased lag, congestion and transmission failures. This also increases efficiency level since faster judgments may be made about the acquired signals, which is crucial in crucial decision-making circumstances. In addition, Fog devices can not only collect input from comparable units on the perimeter but also gather information from a variety of other device kinds. This capacity to measure many characteristics in the contextual setting means an implementation of IoT system design. Data upstream from the Fog layer in the IoT architecture can be utilised to acquire a deeper understanding of dynamic systems and to drive new scheme operating regulations, generally in the cloud. Decision-making advice from the upper cloud system can be supplied for equipment in the Fog layer to ensure seamless system functioning. But the allocation of tasks between the cloud and the fog layer must be balanced, bearing in mind the expenses involved [72, 73].

Edge Computing Model. Fog Computing aimed to shift some decisions toward the edge of the network. In recent days, more competent gadgets that are linked to 'edge' nodes, standard decision and computation have been created on these machines, to further reduce network and device costs at the fog levels and ensure progressive spread of decisions. Edge computing is the exploitation of information at the "thing" level, *i.e.* by detectors and other IoT devices. Another notion of Edge Calculation describes the Edge computing layer, instead of key parameters, as an intermediate layer involving Fog and 'things.' In this instance, they vary from fog devices that offer smooth connection and information protection throughout the IoT environment as aggregation and decision-making units in a lower scale. The goal of the Fog and Edge frameworks is to decentralise the IoT data to reduce costs, increase scalability and increase stability [74, 75].

5. STATE OF THE ART: SMART CITY (SC) MODELS

A variety of conceptual models of the SC have resulted in varying subjectivity and hence different conceptualizations in recent times.

To emphasize the impact of stakeholders in the SC, several researchers have leveraged the triple helix conceptual framework [76 - 78]. The model was used to investigate the urban economy's knowledge and expertise, and Leydesdorff and Deakin [79] presented it as a tool for studying the meta-stabilizing prospects of urban technology in SCs. In a modified triple helix, Lombardi *et al.* [78] broadened their coverage to encompass civic society, and in the following study, this idea was combined with five city clusters (Governance, Economy, Human Capital, Living and Environment) [80]. Such interconnections are being utilized to frame a study of SC dynamic interaction and to derive policy recommendations.

The SC was operationalized by Nam and Pardo [81] as a paradigm that integrated organisational, technical, and human aspects. They used the approach to develop strategic recommendations for SC programmes' effectiveness. Several scholars enhanced the model's intricacy to further examine these themes, centralising SC implementations in its blueprint [82]. They identified three internal components that have a direct influence on the SC: technology, organisations, and policy. External elements (government, people and communities, natural environment, and infrastructure) have a secondary degree of influence. Assessing local authority recommendations and derive suggestions for practitioners and academicians was the goal of this approach.

Dameri [83] proposed a multiscale focus on the SC's imperatives instead of the means to achieve these targets, highlighting the necessity for a theoretical model for an SC concept derived from practical experience. It centered on a set of fundamental SC components (citizens, land, technology, and governance). Then came the spatial level, with impacts at the local, regional, city network, national, and global dimensions. Finally, the concept offered a third tier with SC goals, such as environmental sustainability, the standard of living and well-being, civic engagement, awareness, and intellectual assets. The concept aimed to assist local authorities and public agencies in implementing SC projects that were centered on these end goals.

As a consequence of the SC project experiences, the ASCIMER Project Team established a model for their research. The prototype interprets the SC as the conglomeration of the facets of "Governance," "Economy," "Environment," "Mobility," "People," and "Living" outlined by Information communication technology and high-performance engineering [84] and recommends a categorization of SC projects and their incorporation through a comprehensive and holistic approach inspired by the work of Giffinger *et al.* [85].

Current SC conceptual ideas have emphasised governance as a critical problem for the programmes' success [86]. Castelnovo *et al.* [87] offer a citizen-centric paradigm to Smart governance, with "Community Building and Management" at its core. There are four more elements to this idea (vision and strategic planning formulation, societal profitability, Capital Management, and Socio-economic stewardship), and suggested an integrated framework to evaluate participatory policy-making in cities.

Finally, Fernández-Güell *et al.* [88] offered a systems-based perspective on cities in their paper. It centres the framework on urban demands, which is encompassed by four domains (societal, economic, political and environmental). The city arises as a result of the spatial layer, which includes various infrastructure and services and amenities, as well as the technical layer that sustains the spatial layer. Economic, sociological, technical, and geopolitical developments all have an impact on the city and its layers. The model is envisioned as a predictive tool for explaining ongoing and prospective events.

To enable professionals to find strategies to effectively promote intelligent urban growth, researchers examined schemes from 60 metropolitan intelligent cities worldwide and highlighted 4 major kinds.

"The phrase 'smart city' persists mostly a motto than a clear-cut action programme," stated Penn State Professor of Telecommunications Krishna Jayakar. "Intelligent metro areas employ modern ICT to address critical issues like accommodation, infrastructure, and resources in industrial development and service delivery."

Jayakar's research team utilised clustering analysis to develop 4 intelligent city models by examining programmes executed. The aim was to discover the groupings of projects most commonly used as a method to create fundamental paradigms or systems in the creation of intelligent cities.

Cities that follow the essential services model are defined by their reliance on wireless services for disaster risk reduction and preventive care. Cities such as Tokyo and Copenhagen have robust communications infrastructure and have expanded in certain well-selected initiatives.

The smart transportation model refers to cities that reduce traffic congestions by utilising technology such as IT and communication, public transit, shared mobility and/or self-driving vehicles. This category includes Singapore and Dubai.

Cities that use the wide spectrum approach usually have a high degree of civic involvement and stress urban governance, such as irrigation, waste disposal management, as well as prevention of pollution.

The most prevalent approach is the business ecosystem model. It leverages technological innovation to strengthen economic output by leveraging digital training and supporting high-technology companies.

Cities seeking to put smart urban plans into practice may also examine the 4 models to evaluate urban areas which most closely fit their social and economic situations to help develop their own plans.

6. THE CASE OF VIENNA

In 2011, the Vienna SC initiative began. In 2013, the municipal council of Vienna launched the strategy implementation by engaging collaborators from several municipal agencies and numerous specialists in the area. This strategy results in the "Smart City Wien Framework Strategy" in 2014 [89], aiming at developing recommendations for the implementation of the SC initiatives and actions. This approach comprises three routes: "Standard of living", "Assets" and "Innovative thinking", which organize particular connected themes and aims. The procedure of major stakeholder participation continues *via* several discussions on issues related to the SC with various degrees of achievement. The operational efficiency and the degree of execution as well as the stakeholders' pivotal role led to the representation of Vienna case study as a pillar for this study.

In this case study, a two-and-a-half-year run conceptual model following the release of the strategy paper is illustrated, comparing the initiatives created in the SC Strategy with the viewpoints of the various players. Recommendations are then offered for a modification of the approach. These ideas do not only focus on meeting the goals, but also on expanding the participation of the internal and external parties as the crucial element in building future initiatives. The approach consequently contrasts the assessment of the SC initiatives executed in Vienna with the outputs of conducting interviews with 14 major stakeholders inside the city.

Given the ability to accurately assess the initiatives, the following procedures were followed to gather objective support and change the theoretical design:

In the first step, the archetype must be restructured to inculcate the metropolitan planning organizations. For every sub-system be it political, knowledge, social, or economic, greater contributors per program and the number of organizations addressed in the discussion are given.

It is pivotal to distinguish two facets, notably which parameters have been directly impacted by ongoing projects, and the essential aspects of an SC according to the relevant parties since they can be categorized into four metrics to divulge their relative strength. The initiatives influencing each variable is then contrasted with the words used in the definitions supplied by the stakeholders in their interviews, generating two alternative versions of the model.

The number of initiatives addressing each problem and trend was compared to the survey findings on their relevance in the case of Vienna. The findings of global trends will be evaluated clearly, and the outcomes of individual problems will be utilized to support the principles.

The changes in the model are explained from the centre to its outside bounds to facilitate its interpretation. The final phase offers a compilation of all the adjustments to the conceptual framework. This model integrates the three analyses (financiers, initiatives and demand functions, and constraints) and develops connections between the unexpected events. It is essential to note that this visualisation presents the relative weights of each of the three components of the study individually (financiers, initiatives and demand functions, and constraints), but it does not permit quantitative inferences between such sections.

6.1. Subsystems and Stakeholders in the Vienna Smart City Initiative

Across both systems, the public sector indisputably plays a major role in strategic planning. The sociopolitical subsystem's main operating group is made up of public corporations, local government agencies, and national competent authorities. Municipality jurisdictions are given nearly identical status as public enterprises in these groupings, even though public organisations were cited as significant stakeholders infrequently. Concerning the other stakeholders involved, there has been some controversy. Members of research institutes were mentioned more frequently by the stakeholders interrogated than representatives of commercial enterprises. However, a review of the programmes found that private firms are considerably more active than academic and research institutions. Civil society is not participating in the Vienna SC, according to both the implementation and discourses on the concept.

6.2. Vienna Smart City Projects and Dimensions

In regard to the relevance of the metrics, there are some similarities and variations between these two formats of the conceptual model. The majority of initiatives focus on the environmental factor, which is ranked fourth among the stakeholders' priorities. In these viewpoints, "Governance" is often the most significant dimension, followed by "People." Because these dimensions rank second and third in terms of project numbers, there is some overlap across discourses and implementation. "Living" follows in the discourses, and as per the range of initiatives impacting it, it is the fifth most crucial component. Mobility was not frequently mentioned by the experts questioned, even though it is an essential aspect of the Vienna SC Strategy. In both findings reveal that the "Economy" component has a lower weightage. This element's words are the least frequently cited by stakeholders, and that is the one handled by the fewest initiatives.

6.3. Global Trends and Urban Challenges for Vienna

The findings of both sets of patterns and conflicts reveal that "climate change" is the most significant international pattern, although there is a substantial difference between analysts' opinions and the number of jobs addressing "social polarisation" and "economic instability." This worldwide trend is endorsed by "global urbanisation" in the project auditing phase, whereas there are fewer initiatives to address "economic instability." "Social polarisation" and "need for new governance models" follow behind "climate change" in the polling data, while "technology-driven approaches" and "economic instability" are the least significant themes. The significance placed on "climate change" is reflected in the large number of initiatives that address the subject.

6.4. Global Vision and Guidelines

Although "social polarisation" and "economic instability" are major worldwide problems, there are few programmes that address them. The recommendations seek to bridge the gap between real SC implementation and shareholders' outlooks and to foster citizen and political participation.

In stakeholder discourses, SCs are not primarily viewed as technological entities. Only three of the stakeholders engaged explicitly state this vision. However, even though most projects make use of technological advancements, just 16 initiatives in the study make use of information and communication technologies. This is the third most crucial worldwide trend highlighted by the programmes. However, it is considered a minor global trend. Technology, while vital, is not the focus of the Vienna SC, and this should be preserved.

Effective stakeholder participation. The importance of public organizations, particularly municipal and free public businesses, is universally acknowledged. Nevertheless, the stakeholders' peripherals are imbalanced, and greater coordination amongt them might strengthen the initiative's performance. Fewer than four definitions referred to a citizen-centric Inclusive and socioeconomic stratification are some of the main worldwide trends and problems for Vienna. To bridge the gap between stakeholders' aspirations and standardisation, stakeholders must be made aware of the necessity to include civic members.

Increasing societal engagement in environmental initiatives. There is also agreement on the need for "tackling climate change" as a major global issue impacting Vienna, but there are some contradictions. The environment appears to be a minor component in the stakeholders' notions of the Smart City. While efforts should be made in this way, other features of the city were deemed more important. This implies raising awareness of certain climate change concerns.

Like the "Environment" factor, mobility initiatives generally contain an environmental component. So, there are many more initiatives influencing this aspect than stakeholders acknowledge in their descriptions. However, they believe mobility issues to be critical and must be solved. So should mobility projects.

Intensifying governance. The "Governance" factor is essential in the discussions and is the third in terms of initiatives. Unfortunately, there is still a huge disparity between the limited number of governance initiatives and the expansion of "Environment" projects. Expanding the number of governance initiatives would provide a more equitable endeavour. In any event, the number of governance projects is small. Increasing the strong emphasis on governance is so advised.

The promotion of social equity and human and social capital. Personnel is ranked second in terms of scope and approaches. A similar gap exists between the few programmes on "People" and "Environment", as in the instance of governance. In the stakeholder study, the second trend identified as having the greatest problems is "social polarisation". Increasing the number of social inclusion programmes will help address this conflict. Despite its relevance to investors, few programmes are promoting human and social capital. Endorsing quality human resources is thus critical for social inclusion.

Ratcheting up efforts to promote social and human capital in the "Economy" component It is evident that the economic aspect is imbalanced in the system, as indicated by the small number of programmes that address it. Most initiatives focus on the worldwide trend of "economic instability" and its problems. Collaborators perceive the trend as minor. However, one of the most important problems, according to stakeholders, is: Building human and social capital as a determinant of economic growth As a result, promoting social and human capital will help to bolster the system's monetary power.

Last but not least, the Vienna Smart City Strategy should emphasise by focusing on social and human capital. An important responsibility for governance is to promote stakeholder participation. The environmental and transportation elements would likely remain relevant. Human and social capital can help establish a better system equilibrium. An integrated and complete conceptual model for Smart Cities was proposed, as well as a technique to study Smart City implementation and discourses to extract a foundation for designing efforts in the sector. Several headline goals for the Vienna SC initiatives in major facets of its innovations should be more encouraged (Fig. **3**).

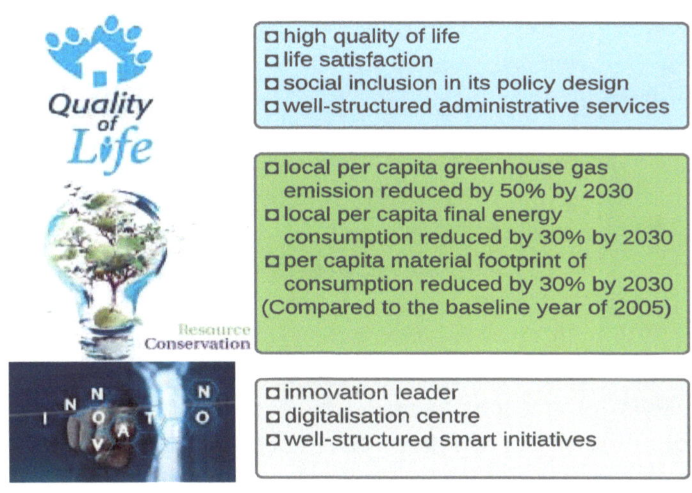

Fig. (3). Vienna sc headline goals.

CONCLUSION AND FUTURE SCOPE

All international cities have distinct characteristics that have a substantial impact on the implementation methods, cluster groupings, and recognized SC norms. A generic implementation framework for the administration of SCs, comparative analysis of SC standards, implementations, and clustered models around the globe are provided in the study. There is now a diverse perspective on not just the notion of an SC, but also the features and methods of its administration. The proper model determines the categorization into the clustering pattern, which influences the adoption of suitable archetypes for a certain SC. The following are the key results presented in this work:

- European frameworks are more vividly expressive but not particularly comprehensive; parts of feedback are lacking at all levels; and standards and regulations are not universal, allowing for misinformation to flourish.
- While North American city models fulfil the requirement for good governance and have a good reputation not only regionally but also internationally, they are not very accessible as a model for other megacities due to a lack of information and unique requirements that are only appropriate to local circumstances in North America.
- The authors propose the following for the efficient administration of SCs in Europe based on the findings of the article:
- Create a technical foundation; actively Engage stakeholders
- Provide input to all layers of management (strategy, tactics, and operations)
- Revamp current laws in the field of SC standards
- Update the model regularly, and
- Promote a bottom-up strategy.

This study emphasizes the need of viewing each city as a unique entity and understanding the interconnectedness of factors such as systems, components, archetypal, patterns, and rules that influence social, behavioural, and cultural characteristics as well as change acceptability. The quintessential suggested SC implementation model for the European area is a reference for diplomatic urban planning, including how to efficiently demonstrate, handle, and continue improving it to achieve the desired objectives and perks of implementation (sustainable development and standard of living), as well as how to adapt it to relevant regulations and particular city or region constraints. Future studies endeavours will be dependent on the model's deployment and validation in practice.

REFERENCES

[1]   A.S. Syed, D. Sierra-Sosa, A. Kumar, and A. Elmaghraby, "IoT in smart cities: A survey of technologies, practices and challenges", *Smart Cities,* vol. 4, no. 2, pp. 429-475, 2021. [http://dx.doi.org/10.3390/smartcities4020024]

[2]   H. Ahvenniemi, A. Huovila, I. Pinto-Seppä, and M. Airaksinen, "What are the differences between sustainable and smart cities?", *Cities,* vol. 60, pp. 234-245, 2017. [http://dx.doi.org/10.1016/j.cities.2016.09.009]

[3]   F. S. Nino, "Sustainable development goals—united nations", *United Nations Sustainable Development,* 2015.

[4]   P. Cardullo, and R. Kitchin, "Being a 'citizen' in the smart city: up and down the scaffold of smart citizen participation in Dublin, Ireland", *GeoJournal,* vol. 84, no. 1, pp. 1-13, 2019. [http://dx.doi.org/10.1007/s10708-018-9845-8]

[5]   J. Desdemoustier, N. Crutzen, and R. Giffinger, "Municipalities' understanding of the smart city concept: An exploratory analysis in belgium", *Technol. Forecast. Soc. Change,* vol. 142, pp. 129-141, 2019. [http://dx.doi.org/10.1016/j.techfore.2018.10.029]

[6]   M. Khan, M. Woo, K. Nam, and P. Chathoth, "Smart city and smart tourism: A case of Dubai", *Sustainability,* vol. 9, no. 12, p. 2279, 2017. [http://dx.doi.org/10.3390/su9122279]

[7]   S. Wu, T. Chen, Y. Wu, and M. Lytras, "Smart cities in Taiwan: A perspective on big data applications", *Sustainability,* vol. 10, no. 2, p. 106, 2018. [http://dx.doi.org/10.3390/su10010106]

[8]   W. Ejaz, and A. Anpalagan, "Internet of things for smart cities: overview and key challenges", *Internet of Things for Smart Cities,* pp. 1-15, 2019. [http://dx.doi.org/10.1007/978-3-319-95037-2_1]

[9]   M. Janssen, S. Luthra, S. Mangla, N.P. Rana, and Y.K. Dwivedi, "Challenges for adopting and implementing IoT in smart cities", *Internet Res.,* vol. 29, no. 6, pp. 1589-1616, 2019. [http://dx.doi.org/10.1108/INTR-06-2018-0252]

[10]   R. Sánchez-Corcuera, A. Nuñez-Marcos, J. Sesma-Solance, A. Bilbao-Jayo, R. Mulero, U. Zulaika, G. Azkune, and A. Almeida, "Smart cities survey: Technologies, application domains and challenges for the cities of the future", *Int. J. Distrib. Sens. Netw.,* vol. 15, no. 6, 2019. [http://dx.doi.org/10.1177/1550147719853984]

[11]   B.N. Silva, M. Khan, and K. Han, "Towards sustainable smart cities: A review of trends, architectures, components, and open challenges in smart cities", *Sustain Cities Soc.,* vol. 38, pp. 697-713, 2018. [http://dx.doi.org/10.1016/j.scs.2018.01.053]

[12]   R. Atat, L. Liu, J. Wu, G. Li, C. Ye, and Y. Yang, "Big data meet cyber-physical systems: A panoramic survey", *IEEE Access,* vol. 6, pp. 73603-73636, 2018. [http://dx.doi.org/10.1109/ACCESS.2018.2878681]

[13]   R.G. Hollands, "Will the real smart city please stand up?", *City,* vol. 12, no. 3, pp. 303-320, 2008. [http://dx.doi.org/10.1080/13604810802479126]

[14]   L.G. Anthopoulos, and C.G. Reddick, "Understanding electronic government research and smart city: A framework and empirical evidence", *Inf. Polity,* vol. 21, no. 1, pp. 99-117, 2016. [http://dx.doi.org/10.3233/IP-150371]

[15]   N. Chen, Y. Chen, Y. You, H. Ling, P. Liang, and R. Zimmermann, "Dynamic urban surveillance video stream processing using fog computing", *IEEE Second International Conference on Multimedia Big Data (BigMM),* 2016, pp. 105-112 Taipei, Taiwan. [http://dx.doi.org/10.1109/BigMM.2016.53]

[16]   J. Santos, T. Wauters, B. Volckaert, and F. De Turck, "Fog computing: Enabling the management and orchestration of smart city applications in 5G networks", *Entropy,* vol. 20, no. 1, p. 4, 2017.
[http://dx.doi.org/10.3390/e20010004] [PMID: 33265095]

[17]   R. K. Barik, H. Dubey, A. B. Samaddar, R. D. Gupta, and P. K. Ray, "FogGIS: Fog Computing for geospatial big data analytics", *IEEE Uttar Pradesh Section International Conference on Electrical, Computer and Electronics Engineering (UPCON),* 2016, pp. 613-618 Varanasi, India.
[http://dx.doi.org/10.1109/UPCON.2016.7894725]

[18]   W. Shi, J. Cao, Q. Zhang, Y. Li, and L. Xu, "Edge computing: Vision and challenges", *IEEE Internet Things J.,* vol. 3, no. 5, pp. 637-646, 2016.
[http://dx.doi.org/10.1109/JIOT.2016.2579198]

[19]   T. Taleb, S. Dutta, A. Ksentini, M. Iqbal, and H. Flinck, "Mobile edge computing potential in making cities smarter", *IEEE Commun. Mag.,* vol. 55, no. 3, pp. 38-43, 2017.
[http://dx.doi.org/10.1109/MCOM.2017.1600249CM]

[20]   X. Wang, L.T. Yang, X. Xie, J. Jin, and M.J. Deen, "A cloud-edge computing framework for cyber-physical-social services", *IEEE Commun. Mag.,* vol. 55, no. 11, pp. 80-85, 2017.
[http://dx.doi.org/10.1109/MCOM.2017.1700360]

[21]   Z. Ji, I. Ganchev, M. O'Droma, L. Zhao, and X. Zhang, "A cloud-based car parking middleware for IoT-based smart cities: Design and implementation", *Sensors,* vol. 14, no. 12, pp. 22372-22393, 2014.
[http://dx.doi.org/10.3390/s141222372] [PMID: 25429416]

[22]   E. Patti, and A. Acquaviva, "IoT platform for smart cities: Requirements and implementation case studies", *IEEE 2nd International Forum on Research and Technologies for Society and Industry Leveraging a better tomorrow (RTSI),* 2016, pp. 1-6 Bologna, Italy.
[http://dx.doi.org/10.1109/RTSI.2016.7740618]

[23]   B. Cheng, S. Longo, F. Cirillo, M. Bauer, and E. Kovacs, "Building a big data platform for smart cities: Experience and lessons from santander", *IEEE International Congress on Big Data,* 2015, pp. 592-599 New York, NY, US.
[http://dx.doi.org/10.1109/BigDataCongress.2015.91]

[24]   R. Petrolo, V. Loscri, and N. Mitton, "Towards a smart city based on cloud of things", *Proceedings of the 2014 ACM International Workshop on Wireless and Mobile Technologies for Smart Cities,* 2014, pp. 61-66.
[http://dx.doi.org/10.1145/2633661.2633667]

[25]   R. Lea, and M. Blackstock, "City hub: A cloud-based iot platform for smart cities", *IEEE 6th International Conference on Cloud Computing Technology and Science,* 2014, pp. 799-804 Singapore.
[http://dx.doi.org/10.1109/CloudCom.2014.65]

[26]   N. Mitton, S. Papavassiliou, A. Puliafito, and K. S. Trivedi, "Combining Cloud and sensors in a smart city environment", *EURASIP J. Wirel. Commun. Networ.,* vol. 1, 2012.
[http://dx.doi.org/10.1186/1687-1499-2012-247]

[27]   G. C. Fox, S. Kamburugamuve, and R. D. Hartman, "Architecture and measured characteristics of a cloud based internet of things", *International Conference on Collaboration Technologies and Systems (CTS),* 2012, pp. 6-12 Denver, CO, USA.
[http://dx.doi.org/10.1109/CTS.2012.6261020]

[28]   R. Mulero, A. Almeida, G. Azkune, P. Abril-Jiménez, M.T. Arredondo Waldmeyer, M. Paramo Castrillo, L. Patrono, P. Rametta, and I. Sergi, "An IoT-aware approach for elderly-friendly cities", *IEEE Access,* vol. 6, pp. 7941-7957, 2018.
[http://dx.doi.org/10.1109/ACCESS.2018.2800161]

[29]   J. Helbostad, B. Vereijken, C. Becker, C. Todd, K. Taraldsen, M. Pijnappels, K. Aminian, and S. Mellone, "Mobile health applications to promote active and healthy ageing", *Sensors,* vol. 17, no. 3, p. 622, 2017.

[http://dx.doi.org/10.3390/s17030622] [PMID: 28335475]

[30] S. Stavrotheodoros, N. Kaklanis, K. Votis, and D. Tzovaras, "A smart-home IoT infrastructure for the support of independent living of older adults", In: *IFIP International Conference on Artificial Intelligence Applications and Innovations.* Springer: Cham, 2018, pp. 238-249.
[http://dx.doi.org/10.1007/978-3-319-92016-0_22]

[31] V. Djaja-Josko, and J. Kolakowski, "UWB positioning system for elderly persons monitoring", *23rd Telecommunications Forum Telfor (TELFOR),* 2015, pp. 169-172 Belgrade, Serbia.
[http://dx.doi.org/10.1109/TELFOR.2015.7377440]

[32] D. Bonino, M.T.D. Alizo, A. Alapetite, T. Gilbert, M. Axling, and H. Udsen, "Almanac: Internet of things for smart cities", *3rd International Conference on Future Internet of Things and Cloud,* 2015, pp. 309-316 Rome, Italy.

[33] E. Psomakelis, F. Aisopos, A. Litke, K. Tserpes, M. Kardara, and P.M. Campo, "Big IoT and social networking data for smart cities: Algorithmic improvements on Big Data Analysis in the context of RADICAL city applications", *Proceedings of the 6th International Conference on Cloud Computing and Services Science,* vol. 1, pp. 396-405, 2016.
[http://dx.doi.org/10.5220/0005934503960405]

[34] Y. Zheng, T. Liu, Y. Wang, Y. Zhu, Y. Liu, and E. Chang, "Diagnosing New York city's noises with ubiquitous data", *Proceedings of the 2014 ACM International Joint Conference on Pervasive and Ubiquitous Computing,* 2014, pp. 715-725.
[http://dx.doi.org/10.1145/2632048.2632102]

[35] F. Longo, D. Bruneo, S. Distefano, G. Merlino, and A. Puliafito, "Stack4Things: A sensing-an--actuation-as-a-service framework for IoT and cloud integration", *Ann. Telecommun.,* vol. 72, no. 1-2, pp. 53-70, 2017.
[http://dx.doi.org/10.1007/s12243-016-0528-5]

[36] B. Tang, Z. Chen, G. Hefferman, T. Wei, H. He, and Q. Yang, "A hierarchical distributed fog computing architecture for big data analysis in smart cities", *Proceedings of the ASE Big Data & Social Informatics,* 2015, pp. 1-6.
[http://dx.doi.org/10.1145/2818869.2818898]

[37] S. B. Tsai, B. B. Gupta, D. P. Agrawal, W. Wu, and A. Liu, "Recent advances in intelligent transportation systems for cloud-enabled smart cities", *J Adv Transp,* 2021.
[http://dx.doi.org/10.1155/2021/9792543]

[38] W.M. Dahmane, S. Ouchani, and H. Bouarfa, "Towards a reliable smart city through formal verification and network analysis", *Comput. Commun.,* vol. 180, pp. 171-187, 2021.
[http://dx.doi.org/10.1016/j.comcom.2021.09.006]

[39] N. Kumar, S. Mittal, V. Garg, and N. Kumar, "Deep reinforcement learning-based traffic light scheduling framework for sdn-enabled smart transportation system", *IEEE Trans. Intell. Transp. Syst.,* vol. 22, no. 8, pp. 4919-4928, 2021.
[http://dx.doi.org/10.1109/TITS.2020.2984033]

[40] A. Viale, A. Marchisio, M. Martina, G. Masera, and M. Shafique, "CarSNN: An efficient spiking neural network for event-based autonomous cars on the loihi neuromorphic research processor", *Neur. Evolu. Comp.,* 2021, pp. 1-10 Shenzhen, China.
[http://dx.doi.org/10.1109/IJCNN52387.2021.9533738]

[41] M. Drakoulelis, G. Filios, V.G. Ninos, I. Katsidimas, and S. Nikoletseas, "Virtual sensors: An industrial application for illumination attributes based on machine learning techniques", *Ann. Telecommun.,* vol. 76, no. 7-8, pp. 529-535, 2021.
[http://dx.doi.org/10.1007/s12243-021-00856-w]

[42] B. Wang, C. Chen, and T. Zhang, "Commercial Vehicle Road Collaborative System Based on 5G-V2X and Satellite Navigation Technologies", In: *China Satellite Navigation Conference (CSNC 2021) Proceedings* Springer: Singapore, 2021, pp. 274-282.

[43]   Y. Xu, Z. Ye, C. Wang, and K. Gao, "Modeling commercial vehicle drivers' acceptance of forward collision warning system", In: *Smart Transportation Systems 2021*. Springer: Singapore, 2021, pp. 167-180.
[http://dx.doi.org/10.1007/978-981-16-2324-0_17]

[44]   D.H. Shin, and T. Kim, "Enabling the smart city: The progress of u-city in Korea", *Proceedings of the 6th International Conference on Ubiquitous Information Management and Communication*, 2012, pp. 1-7.
[http://dx.doi.org/10.1145/2184751.2184872]

[45]   X. Chen, S. Zhang, X. Ding, S.N. Kadry, and C.H. Hsu, *IoT cloud platform for information processing in smart city*. Wiley, 2020.*Comput. Intell.* Wiley, 2020.

[46]   S. de Falco, M. Angelidou, and J.P.D. Addie, "From the "smart city" to the "smart metropolis"? Building resilience in the urban periphery", *Eur. Urban Reg. Stud.,* vol. 26, no. 2, pp. 205-223, 2019.
[http://dx.doi.org/10.1177/0969776418783813]

[47]   S. Zhilin, B. Klievink, and M. De Jong, "Community self-governance in the smart city: Towards a typology", In: *E-Participation in Smart Cities: Technologies and Models of Governance for Citizen Engagement*. Springer: Cham, 2019, pp. 81-97.
[http://dx.doi.org/10.1007/978-3-319-89474-4_5]

[48]   M. Angelidou, "The role of smart city characteristics in the plans of fifteen cities", *J. Urban Technol.,* vol. 24, no. 4, pp. 3-28, 2017.
[http://dx.doi.org/10.1080/10630732.2017.1348880]

[49]   J. Yang, R. Xu, J. Cui, and Z. Ding, "Robust visual tracking using adaptive local appearance model for smart transportation", *Multimedia Tools Appl.,* vol. 75, no. 24, pp. 17487-17500, 2016.
[http://dx.doi.org/10.1007/s11042-016-3285-6]

[50]   V. Puri, C. Van Le, R. Kumar, and S.S. Jagdev, "Fruitful synergy model of artificial intelligence and internet of thing for smart transportation system", *IJHIoT,* vol. 4, no. 1, pp. 43-57, 2020.
[http://dx.doi.org/10.4018/IJHIoT.2020010104]

[51]   S.B. Kelley, B.W. Lane, B.W. Stanley, K. Kane, E. Nielsen, and S. Strachan, "Smart transportation for all? A typology of recent US smart transportation projects in midsized cities", *Ann. Assoc. Am. Geogr.,* vol. 110, no. 2, pp. 547-558, 2020.

[52]   Z. Khan, A. Anjum, K. Soomro, and M.A. Tahir, "Towards cloud based big data analytics for smart future cities", *J. Clou. Comp.,* vol. 4, no. 1, pp. 1-11, 2015.
[http://dx.doi.org/10.1186/s13677-015-0026-8]

[53]   A. Koubaa, A. Aldawood, B. Saeed, A. Hadid, M. Ahmed, A. Saad, H. Alkhouja, A. Ammar, and M. Alkanhal, "Smart Palm: An IoT framework for red palm weevil early detection", *Agronomy,* vol. 10, no. 7, p. 987, 2020.
[http://dx.doi.org/10.3390/agronomy10070987]

[54]   M.J. O'Grady, D. Langton, and G.M.P. O'Hare, "Edge computing: A tractable model for smart agriculture?", *Artif.Int. Agric.,* vol. 3, pp. 42-51, 2019.
[http://dx.doi.org/10.1016/j.aiia.2019.12.001]

[55]   I. Rojek, and J. Studzinski, "Detection and localization of water leaks in water nets supported by an ICT system with artificial intelligence methods as a way forward for smart cities", *Sustainability,* vol. 11, no. 2, p. 518, 2019.
[http://dx.doi.org/10.3390/su11020518]

[56]   K. Pardini, J.J.P.C. Rodrigues, S.A. Kozlov, N. Kumar, and V. Furtado, "IoT-based solid waste management solutions: A survey", *J. Sen. Actu. Netw.,* vol. 8, no. 1, p. 5, 2019.
[http://dx.doi.org/10.3390/jsan8010005]

[57]   J. Dutta, C. Chowdhury, S. Roy, A.I. Middya, and F. Gazi, "Towards smart city: Sensing air quality in city based on opportunistic crowd-sensing", *Proceedings of the 18th International Conference on*

Distributed Computing and Networking, 2017, pp. 1-6.
[http://dx.doi.org/10.1145/3007748.3018286]

[58]   F. Al-Turjman, and A. Malekloo, "Smart parking in IoT-enabled cities: A survey", *Sustain Cities Soc.,* vol. 49, p. 101608, 2019.
[http://dx.doi.org/10.1016/j.scs.2019.101608]

[59]   E. Shirazi, and S. Jadid, "Autonomous self-healing in smart distribution grids using agent systems", *IEEE Trans. Industr. Inform.,* vol. 15, no. 12, pp. 6291-6301, 2019.
[http://dx.doi.org/10.1109/TII.2018.2889741]

[60]   R.V. Andreão, M. Athayde, J. Boudy, P. Aguilar, I. de Araujo, and R. Andrade, "Raspcare: A telemedicine platform for the treatment and monitoring of patients with chronic diseases", In: *Assistive Technologies in Smart Cities* intechopen, 2018.
[http://dx.doi.org/10.5772/intechopen.76002]

[61]   P. A. Keane, and E. J. Topol, "With an eye to AI and autonomous diagnosis", *npj Digital Med,* vol. 1, p. 40, 2018.
[http://dx.doi.org/10.1038/s41746-018-0048-y]

[62]   G. Trencher, and A. Karvonen, "Stretching "smart": Advancing health and well-being through the smart city agenda", *Local Environ.,* vol. 24, no. 7, pp. 610-627, 2019.
[http://dx.doi.org/10.1080/13549839.2017.1360264]

[63]   B.R. Haverkort, and A. Zimmermann, "Smart industry: How ICT will change the game!", *IEEE Internet Comput.,* vol. 21, no. 1, pp. 8-10, 2017.
[http://dx.doi.org/10.1109/MIC.2017.22]

[64]   F. Tao, J. Cheng, and Q. Qi, "IIHub: An industrial internet-of-things hub toward smart manufacturing based on cyber-physical system", *IEEE Trans. Industr. Inform.,* vol. 14, no. 5, pp. 2271-2280, 2018.
[http://dx.doi.org/10.1109/TII.2017.2759178]

[65]   P. Trakadas, P. Simoens, P. Gkonis, L. Sarakis, A. Angelopoulos, A.P. Ramallo-González, A. Skarmeta, C. Trochoutsos, D. Calvo, T. Pariente, K. Chintamani, I. Fernandez, A.A. Irigaray, J.X. Parreira, P. Petrali, N. Leligou, and P. Karkazis, "An artificial intelligence-based collaboration approach in industrial iot manufacturing: Key concepts, architectural extensions and potential applications", *Sensors,* vol. 20, no. 19, p. 5480, 2020.
[http://dx.doi.org/10.3390/s20195480] [PMID: 32987911]

[66]   J. Wan, J. Yang, Z. Wang, and Q. Hua, "Artificial intelligence for cloud-assisted smart factory", *IEEE Access,* vol. 6, pp. 55419-55430, 2018.
[http://dx.doi.org/10.1109/ACCESS.2018.2871724]

[67]   S. Konovalov, D. Mayorov, Y. Ponomarev, and T. Soloveva, "High-precision smart system on accelerometers and inclinometers for Structural Health Monitoring: Development and applications", *12th France-Japan and 10th Europe-Asia Congress on Mechatronics,* 2018, pp. 52-57 Tsu, Japan.
[http://dx.doi.org/10.1109/MECATRONICS.2018.8495730]

[68]   S.G. Farag, "Application of smart structural system for smart sustainable cities", *4th MEC International Conference on Big Data and Smart City (ICBDSC),* 2019, pp. 1-5 Muscat, Oman.
[http://dx.doi.org/10.1109/ICBDSC.2019.8645582]

[69]   Y. Wang, S. Ram, F. Currim, E. Dantas, and L. A. Sabóia, "A Big Data approach for Smart Transportation Management on Bus Network", In: *IEEE International Smart Cities Conference (ISC2),* 2016, pp. 1-6.Trento, Italy.
[http://dx.doi.org/10.1109/ISC2.2016.7580839]

[70]   A. Lele, *Strategic technologies for the military: Breaking new frontiers.* SAGE Publications India, 2009.
[http://dx.doi.org/10.4135/9788132108122]

[71]   P. Mell, and T. Grance, "The NIST definition of cloud computing", *Computer security resource center,* 2011.
[http://dx.doi.org/10.6028/NIST.SP.800-145]

[72]   J. Bar-Magen Numhauser, *Fog computing introduction to a new cloud evolution.* University of Alcalá, 2012.

[73]   M. Aazam, S. Zeadally, and K.A. Harras, "Fog computing architecture, evaluation, and future research directions", *IEEE Commun. Mag.,* vol. 56, no. 5, pp. 46-52, 2018.
[http://dx.doi.org/10.1109/MCOM.2018.1700707]

[74]   H. El-Sayed, S. Sankar, M. Prasad, D. Puthal, A. Gupta, M. Mohanty, and C.T. Lin, "Edge of things: The big picture on the integration of edge, IoT and the cloud in a distributed computing environment", *IEEE Access,* vol. 6, pp. 1706-1717, 2018.
[http://dx.doi.org/10.1109/ACCESS.2017.2780087]

[75]   A. Yousefpour, C. Fung, T. Nguyen, K. Kadiyala, F. Jalali, A. Niakanlahiji, J. Kong, and J.P. Jue, "All one needs to know about fog computing and related edge computing paradigms: A complete survey", *J. Systems Archit.,* vol. 98, pp. 289-330, 2019.
[http://dx.doi.org/10.1016/j.sysarc.2019.02.009]

[76]   M. Deakin, "Smart cities: The state-of-the-art and governance challenge", *Triple Helix,* vol. 1, no. 1, p. 7, 2014.
[http://dx.doi.org/10.1186/s40604-014-0007-9]

[77]   H. Etzkowitz, and C. Zhou, "Triple helix twins: Innovation and sustainability", *Sci. Public Policy,* vol. 33, no. 1, pp. 77-83, 2006.
[http://dx.doi.org/10.3152/147154306781779154]

[78]   P. Lombardi, S. Giordano, A. Caragliu, C. Del Bo, M. Deakin, P. Nijkamp, K. Kourtit, and H. Farouh, "An advanced triple-helix network model for smart cities performance", In: *Green and Ecological Technologies for Urban Planning: Creating Smart Cities.,* O. Ercoskun, Ed., IGI Global, 2012, pp. 59-73.
[http://dx.doi.org/10.4018/978-1-61350-453-6.ch004]

[79]   L. Leydesdorff, and M. Deakin, "The triple helix model and the meta-stabilization of urban technologies in smart cities", *arXiv,* 2010.

[80]   P. Lombardi, S. Giordano, H. Farouh, and W. Youse, "Modelling the smart city performance", *Innovation,* vol. 25, no. 2, pp. 137-149, 2012.
[http://dx.doi.org/10.1080/13511610.2012.660325]

[81]   T. Nam, and T.A. Pardo, "Smart city as Urban Innovation: Focusing on management, policy, and context", *Proceedings of the 5th International Conference on Theory and Practice of Electronic Governance,* 2011, pp. 185-194.
[http://dx.doi.org/10.1145/2072069.2072100]

[82]   H. Chourabi, T. Nam, S. Walker, J.R. Gil-Garcia, S. Mellouli, and K. Nahon, "Understanding smart cities: An integrative framework", *45th Hawaii International Conference on System Sciences,* 2012, pp. 2289-2297 Maui, HI, USA.

[83]   R.P. Dameri, "Searching for smart city definition: A comprehensive proposal", *Int. J. Comput. Technol.,* vol. 11, no. 5, pp. 2544-2551, 2013.
[http://dx.doi.org/10.24297/ijct.v11i5.1142]

[84]   M. Jindal, and A. Kazim, "11 Systematic review and deliberation of various multi-criteria decision-making techniques", *Multi-Criteria Decision Modelling,* pp. 189-204, 2021.

[85]   A. Chakraborty, M. Jindal, M.R. Khosravi, P. Singh, A. Shankar, and M. Diwakar, "A Secure IoT-based cloud platform selection using entropy distance approach and fuzzy set theory", *Wirel. Commun. Mob. Comput.,* vol. 2021, pp. 1-11, 2021.
[http://dx.doi.org/10.1155/2021/6697467]

[86]   A. Kazim, M. Jindal, R. Sharma, R. Choudhary, V. Kumar Sharma, and E. Bajal, "Big data analytics and artificial intelligence in business and marketing: Cloud security and encryption influencing business", *SSRN,* p. 3884455, 2021.
[http://dx.doi.org/10.2139/ssrn.3884455]

[87]   F. Al-Turjman, S.P. Yadav, M. Kumar, V. Yadav, and T. Stephan, *Transforming Management with AI, Big-Data, and IoT* Springer, 2022.

[88]   S. P. Yadav, B. S. Bhati, D. P. Mahato, and S. Kumar, *Federated Learning for IoT Applications.* Springer, 2022.
[http://dx.doi.org/10.1007/978-3-030-85559-8]

[89]   A. Chakraborty, M. Jindal, and S. Gupta, "Post-COVID-19 view of indian economy with emphasis on service sector: A regression implementation", In: *Pervasive Healthcare.* Springer: Cham, 2022, pp. 295-323.
[http://dx.doi.org/10.1007/978-3-030-77746-3_19]

CHAPTER 3

Categorizing Obstacles in the Implementation of Smart Cities with Probable Solution Models

Debajit Mishra[1,*], Sumedha Jain[2], Muskan Jindal[3] and Satya Prakash Yadav[4]

[1] *Department of Ocean Studies & Marine Biology, Pondicherry University, Port Blair Campus, India*

[2] *Chandigarh College of Engineering and Technology, Chandigarh, India*

[3] *Department of Computer Science, Amity School of Engineering and Technology, Amity University, Noida, Uttar Pradesh, India*

[4] *Department of Computer Science and Engineering, G.L. Bajaj Institute of Technology and Management, Greater Noida, U.P, India*

Abstract: The development and implementation of smart cities can be a complex and challenging task as it becomes difficult to implement the notional concepts of smart cities that do not directly cater to the on-site problems. This study aims to identify and classify the various obstacles occurring in the development, planning & budget discussion of smart cities. It will deliberate wide purview of problems including standard difficulties like budget development that includes both capital upfront cost or Capex and operational cost or Opex, geographical & climatic challenges endemic to the city of development, employment & administration challenges like government permits, vendor availabilities, and technology troubles from IoT perspective. This study aims to categorize various issues into major five gradations namely: technical purview, location endemic purview, administration or employment troubles, pecuniary or financial issues and miscellaneous issues. Moreover, this study also provides a heads-up and detailed recommended steps to avoid the identified problems but presents specific case studies to show the significance and application of recommended solutions in multiple smart cities around the globe.

Keywords: Administration or Employment Troubles, Internet of Things, Pecuniary or Financial Issues, Smart Cities.

1. INTRODUCTION

Since the inception of the Smart City (SC) approach, various scholars have attempted to develop the most appropriate Information and Communication

* **Corresponding author Debajit Mishra:** Department of Ocean Studies & Marine Biology, Pondicherry University, Port Blair Campus, India; E-mail: debajitmishra6@gmail.com

Satya Prakash Yadav, Sansar Singh Chauhan, Sanjeev Kumar Pippal and Victor Hugo C. de Albuquerque (Eds.)

Technologies (ICTs)-based framework [1 - 6]. Because of the demands and practical circumstances in cities that have developed SC systems, all such applications have not followed a standardization and hence have specific attributes. Therefore, there is no one-size-fits-all framework for SCs; nonetheless, there exist a few prevalent archetypes that cater to the needs of cities [7]. The properties of the components in command of amassing, analyzing, and utilising data distinguish different configurations [8]. The most common ones are (1) cloud computing, (2) fog computing, and (3) edge computing, to name a few. These structures are modular and could be used in various sectors within the same city [9, 10]. Architectonic resolutions should be thoroughly examined in assessing their impact on the overall framework, as illustrated by Almeida *et al.* [11].

1.1. Cloud Computing

Cloud computing is a concept for providing on-demand networking accessibility to a virtualized environment element (*e.g.*, platforms, processors, memory, algorithms, and functions) that could also be swiftly supplied and dispersed with negligible administrative intervention or network operator contact [12]. The framework can be divided into multiple strata. Reciprocity has been observed within multiple strata of the same archetype. The dissemination and simulation of relevant data are the foundations of the framework, which have been partitioned into categories. Kaur and Maheshwari [13] postulated a wellness programme as per the proffered paradigm when it came to the enterprises that utilised it. Biswas and Muthukkumarasamy [14] introduced a system for smart city authentication that leverages a cloud environment to combine blockchain with the Internet of things (IoT). Mazza *et al.* [15] provide a mobile cloud services paradigm for representing metadata concerning smart cities. Khanna and Anand [16] present a Cloud-based IoT-modulated supervised security system.

1.2. Fog Computing

As an outgrowth of Big data analytics, Fog computing was conceptualised by Bar-Magen Numhauser [17] in CISCO. The functionality and accountability of the program's base are improved significantly through this expansion. Additionally, the changes are due to the placement of data acquisition and interpretation units in the same access point as the data acquisition modules, resulting in reduced connectivity. The framework is deployed in systems having low power consumption, globally disparate platforms, or activities where sending information to the server and waiting for it to be processed is impractical. Bruneo *et al.* [18] provide a global telecommunications usage scenario employing the fog computing approach in terms of initiatives that utilised this framework. Chen *et al.* [19] devised a fog computing-based vibrant video feed computation technique that allows for reliable data analysis and accountability. To exchange interface signals between devices, Santos *et al.* [20] designed a truly operational nodal tracking system. Barik *et al.* [21] developed a fog computing-moduled platform enabling the collation of spatiotemporal predictive analyses.

1.3. Edge Computing

Edge computing is a framework based on the idea that if the information is captured at the program's interface, it ought to be more effective to interpret that information there as well. This one is analogous to fog computing, except that the fog sheds light on the architecture and edge on other aspects. This is vital to remember that the edges of the networks might not be the teensiest sensor, but rather the link between the centralised internet connection and cloud computing. Shi *et al.* [22] illustrate how this approach is distinct from the others and when it would be useful to adopt it all in the ventures that employed it. Taleb *et al.* [23] recommend a scheme that enables electronic edge computing to improve viewers' online streaming quality in SCs. Wang *et al.* [24] offer a surveillance platform that relies on powerful cloud topology. Fig. **1** is organized using the set of disseminating various implemented SC projects using fog [19 - 21, 39, 40], edge [22 - 24] and cloud computing [25 - 38] architecture.

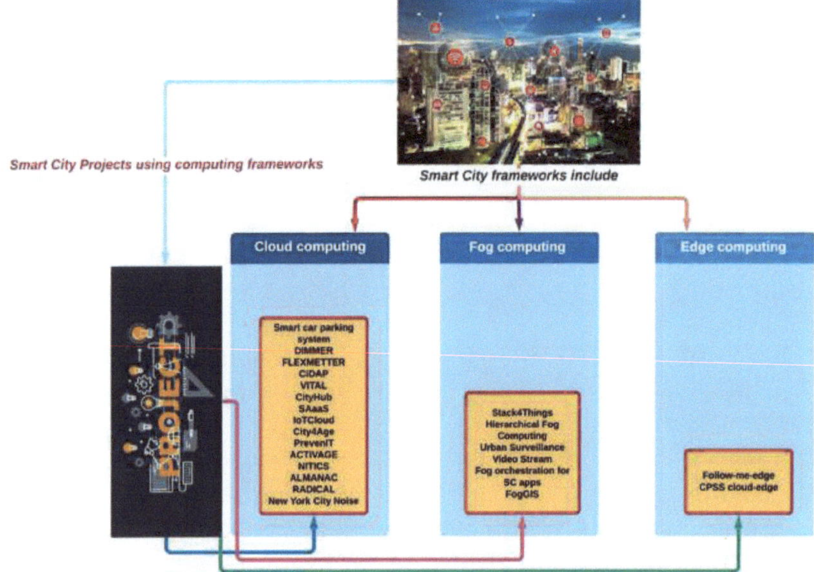

Fig. (1). SC projects using various computing architecture.

The study will discuss a myriad of challenges, which include typical impediments such as budget management including both capital expense (Capex) and operating expenses (Opex), climatological challenges unique to the area of expansion, occupational and administrative issues such as permits, vendor availability, and technical constraints from an IoT viewpoint. Technological purview, site-specific purview, administrative purview, financial purview, and miscellaneous issues are the five primary gradations that this study tries to categorise diverse challenges under. Furthermore, this work includes not only a forewarning and thorough recommendations for avoiding the identified issues, but also particular case studies to demonstrate the importance and applicability of proposed solutions in numerous smart cities across the world.

2. COMPREHENSIVE ANALYSIS OF PREVIOUS WORKS

The design and implementation of SCs may be a daunting and time-consuming process, as it is difficult to apply theoretical SC principles that do not immediately address on-site issues. This study seeks to explore and categorize the different challenges and barriers that arise throughout the creation, strategizing, and budgeting of smart cities. Comparative analysis of previous studies concerned with this perspective is tabulated in Table **1** as follows:

Table 1. Comparative analysis of previous works.

Author	Aim/Objective	Advantage	Drawback
Monzon, A. (2015) [6]	The study aims to provide a platform for developing dynamic and multifaceted solutions to city challenges.	A methodology is created that analyses SC initiatives in the South and East Mediterranean Region.	The difficulty igovernance models would be to become more adaptable, enabling them to integrate top-down initiatives with bottom-up policies with spontaneity.
Zhang, K., *et al.* (2017) [41]	The work intends to present most prospective SC applications and design, characterizing their security and privacy concerns.	Consequent to the objectives, research initiatives are taken for smart health and smart energy.	It does not apply to a limited range of SC initiatives.
Bawany, N. Z., (2015) *et al.* [42]	The goal of this article is to outline significant difficulties in smart city information system management and provide a framework to resolve these issues.	A smart city open-source architecture that allows for third-party enterprise applications is accentuated.	The suggested approach does not address socio-technical factors such as access, social determinants, competence, and so on.

(Table 1) cont.....

Author	Aim/Objective	Advantage	Drawback
Eckhoff, D., (2017) *et al.* [43]	The study addresses current private information technologies, examine the state-of-art in real-life cities worldwide, and identify potential future research paths.	The study may be used as a roadmap to help build privacy-friendly SCs.	A lack of comprehensive information security can result in bias and social stratification, resulting in an essentially unequal society.
Trencher, G. (2019) [44]	The Aizuwakamatsu SC in Fukushima, Japan, is examined in this study to show how an SC may be conceptualised and executed as a solution for addressing endogenous societal issues.	It testifies to the need to move beyond polarised discourses about various SC concepts.	The coexistence of opposing yet complementary perspectives and approaches is established.
Hasija, S., (2020) *et al.* [45]	The work intends to concentrate on the user-centric research problems in SC efforts.	The study examines some of the most modern improvements in SC efforts around the globe to highlight the potential and problems that such approaches present.	Instructions as to how production and manufacturing systems integration researchers may assist the worldwide SC movement have been met with scepticism.
Wenge, R., (2014) *et al.* [46]	From the standpoint of data, this paper offers a new framework that underlies all of the SCs' functioning.	The suggested framework is explored, along with design problems and insights into SC implementations.	Because of the enormous breadth of SCs, their definitions have not been defined, resulting in a wide range of suggested frameworks.
Law, K. H., (2019) *et al.* [47]	This article examines some of the technological improvements in SC initiatives and explores some of the concerns with computer security, confidentiality, and structural reforms.	While rapid urbanisation, which is the foundation for SC, helps drive employment and economic advancement, it also has major effects on a society's socio-cultural elements.	Notwithstanding the right planning, bias in the information gathered, the analytics used, and the digital advances deployed might result in unexpected consequences that harm particular community populations.
Scuotto, V., (2016) *et al.* [48]	The study illustrates how the usage of IoT in conjunction with the adoption of the Open Innovation (OI) model in SCs has altered the growth of urban regions and influenced the innovativeness of businesses.	The work a) has a coherent plan of SCs and IoT; b) takes a global OI perspective to SCs; c) develops specialized strategies and ad hoc OI Units for SC initiatives.	The assessment given has been developed solely on one instance of global enterprise operating in SC settings, which is a key drawback of this study.

(Table 1) cont.....

Author	Aim/Objective	Advantage	Drawback
Khan, H. H., (2020) *et al.* [49]	The goal of this research is to provide a theoretical foundation that addresses the fundamental problems that corporate and state organizations face.	Professionals can use the suggested theoretical foundation as a practice guideline to plan for long-term SC development.	More study is required to provide greater insight into the importance of the integration of sustainability into the implementation of SCs.
Kogan, N., (2014) *et al.* [50]	Based on established policy initiatives and pilot programs, the work aims to highlight major challenges and impediments to SC Monitoring and evaluation and give ideas and solutions.	The study adds to our understanding of SCs and ICT infusion for solving urban challenges.	The role of intellectual capital is underestimated.
Van den Bergh, J., (2016) *et al.* [51]	The work examines the instance of Ghent, Belgium, and the major obstacles it has faced in its quest to become an SC.	As an example of IT-enabled transition in the state sector, the study has contributed to a more competent quest of the SC idea and expands the scholastic volume of data on SC implementation.	It is far more difficult to come up with a reliable definition as to what it requires to become an SC and how that activity affects a municipal government.
Al-Azzam, M., (2019) *et al.* [52]	The research intends to provide a snapshot of smart health, which is described as context-aware and backed by mobile health in SCs.	It concentrates on the key potential and difficulties that s-health implies.	It is time-consuming to list all of the possibilities for incorporating the concept and the confidence and skills of s-health.
Nam, K., (2021) *et al.* [53]	The focus of this research is to illustrate the essential features of the blockchain system concerning the SC framework.	Major difficulties and drawbacks linked to technology, as well as certain misunderstandings, are explored.	Making predictions about how technologies will thrive and impact the industry is a difficult task.
Yadav, S. P., (2022) *et al.* [54]	This article intends to use a mix of quantitative and qualitative approaches to examine the application of economic growth and telecommunication services environment in the Brussels City and Province.	Brussels' present lagging status might be a chance to advance in the realm of wireless services.	To validate the study, subjective interview sessions with field organisations are required.

3. WIDE PURVIEW OF PROBLEMS IN SMART CITY

Today, every city is aiming to become the "Smart city of tomorrow", however, there are many challenges faced in its implementation that should be focused on while discussing the opportunities and the benefits of smart city initiatives for better development of smart city plans (Fig. (**2**)). These challenges can be addressed as the combination of technical, pecuniary, or financial aspects, the collaboration between public and private participants, governance, location of endemic and other miscellaneous issues, as deciphered in Fig. (**2**).

Fig. (2). A flowchart showing various iot challenges in smart city.

Technical challenges lead to challenges in privacy, security, and interoperability. Different intercity/intracity data management techniques between already existing smart devices and to be installed future smart devices bring their technical challenges. It becomes challenging to invest billions of USD in implementing these smart cities when the return on investments (ROI) is unsure, which gives rise to financing/funding issues. For any city to become a smart city, government and its citizens' involvement is of utmost importance. Since a smart city can only be successful when its citizens are "smart" enough to engage themselves and show active participation in knowing about all these new technologies being used to make a city smart. Also, the thing here to be taken care of is that smart city planning should be done while considering all groups of people, not just the technologically advanced people. Now, this chapter covers these above-mentioned issues and other miscellaneous obstacles that are faced while implementing the smart city concept in detail.

3.1. Technical Challenges in Smart City Plan

Development and implementation of a smart city follow the technology-centered approach which mostly leads to challenges in privacy, security, and interoperability [55]. A smart city aims at improving and easing everybody's day to day life by implementing smart transportation, smart health, smart traffic management, pre-weather monitoring, smart governance, smart waste management, smart governance and citizen welfare. From the perspective of real-time data gathering, smart city embeds ICT within a city infrastructure including the diffusion of a wireless sensor network. An effective and strongly coupled integration among complex city systems including infrastructures, civil engineering, societal and financial networks, *etc.* is the key challenge as many heterogeneous technologies must be taken into consideration together [45, 55]. Also, each city differs from the other so along with implementing smart cities to justify solutions to day-to-day problems faced, also consider how these technologies used are affecting the people that get to use them.

Overcoming interoperability *i.e.*, the ability of different devices to share and make use of the information is critical for smart city development. It can be said future addition of more systems must fulfil the requirements of previously made architecture. Smart city plans can threaten the security and privacy of the residents, intruding the individual integrity of the citizens. Implementations of smart city plans endanger physical and cyber security. The collection of big data, its analysis and accessibility are urgent requirements for smart city transformation.

Many of the startups and technology companies with a data-as-a-service business model sharing crowd sourced input with third parties ensure data privacy protection with methodologies like depersonalization and anonymization of data sets. Since awareness of data sharing risks is rising, it is not clear whether end-users trust such assurances and will provide their consent to share their data, especially when it comes to city authorities. Developing effective data governance and operating models for balancing the private rights of the end-users with data accessibility assurance for building smart city solutions is the biggest challenge. The lack of full-scale testbeds hampers realistic operational conditionals causing a technology lock-in effect. With rapidly developing technologies, planning is tough as technology ages fast.

To summarize, huge data stored in clouds (owned, managed and operated by businesses, universities and government organizations like AWS, Google Cloud, Microsoft Azure), challenges faced while connecting the devices with the already existing ecosystem of tools, redistributing control to private sector people, and system and service interoperability bring issues related to security and interoperability. Sensor monitoring being done every time and everywhere leads to privacy issues since nowadays everything is getting captured in cameras installed, though they are for record purposes, but define a sense of fear in everyone's mind of getting monitored every time. Preserving citizens' privacy and data security are factors affecting privacy.

3.2. Financial Challenges in Smart City Plan

As cities aim to implement smart technologies, investing in such projects on a wide-scale basis presents a significant challenge. There are some concerns with regard to measuring cost benefits and return on investments (ROI), due to the huge cost associated with implementation and deployment mechanisms along with facilitating smart city initiatives. It is difficult to get financing/funding for a smart city project where it is hard to devise the benefits or returns of the project.

It is well observed by researchers and various analytical organizations that any smart city initiative can help in asset digitalization, and bring about a whole world of opportunities by providing new data insights, increased efficiency, and new revenue streams/business models. For gaining access to all these possible advantages, we need to identify all the critical challenges lying in between and try finding solutions or alternatives to them [45].

To summarize, difficulties concerning the financing of smart city initiatives, tight budget constraints, disparate financing structures, bounded funding, lack of understanding of possible business models, high startup price, and uncertain return on investment are identified issues affecting smart city's integration. All the above-stated issues fall under the umbrella of financial or pecuniary challenges as depicted in Fig. (3).

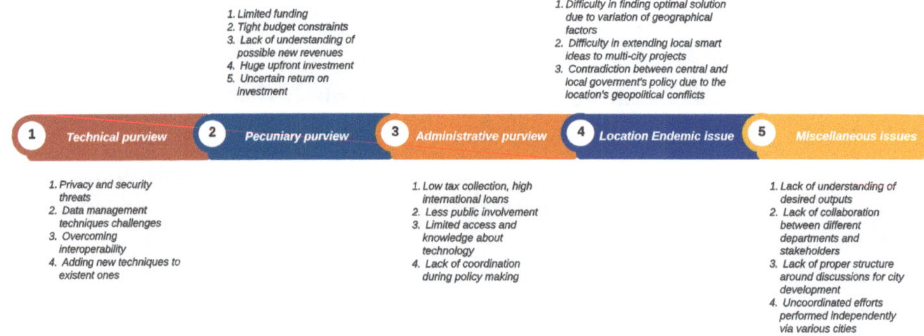

Fig. (3). Wide purview of problems in smart city.

Challenges for Smart City Funding [56]:

1. Every city has its geography, thus geographic constraints. Each project would have different impacts and challenges on different cities. Thus, keeping these geographic constraints in mind, project testing needs to be done, thus cost investment varies from location to location, and city to city. For this, pre-implementation analysis is a must.

2. Adopting the most suitable and efficient technology is again a huge task, here, gain cost plays a critical role in deciding the technology that can be used.

3. To gain positive returns, investors use investment vehicles that are of either low risk (certificates of deposit or bonds) or high risk (stocks, mutual funds). The appropriate selection is also really important for a project to be successful with minimal expenses.

4. Once funding is arranged, it also depends on investors and public participants involved. The more active is the participation, the higher is the success rate of the project.

3.3. Administrative and Governance Challenges in Smart City Plan

If the challenges are viewed with respectto politics, not only fast-evolving technologies but also huge upfront investment cost is an issue of concern [45]. A well-implemented technology itself does not make a city smart, however institutional changes and a new socio-technical form of governance are the need of the hour.

Smart cities' mission is an innovative initiative by the government to help improve the city's economic growth and quality of life of people with the efficient use of technologies, collecting data and bringing it to use to determine various factors. Smart cities not only target smart transportation, and smart health but would also focus on traffic management, pre-weather monitoring, smart governance, and smart waste management.

Smart governance is a key factor that plays a key role in analyzing the successful implementation of smart techniques [57]. Hereby determining and analyzing various factors consumed to measure smart city governance, various gaps and inconsistencies in the entire system comprising government and citizens, can also be brought to light.

The government also faces some challenges, some of which are listed as follows:

1. Funding: Huge investments need to be made to bring each individual's data on public clouds (like AWS, GooCloudloud, Microsoft Azure) and the government is already running low on budgets due to various developments going on. Tax collected is also insufficient to hold its funding, heavy international loans, trading costs, *etc* [57].

2. Less public involvement: Although public participation is better than governance, the government can't include the public in every matter due to security and political reasons.

3. Limited access and technology knowledge: Not everyone in a city are affiliated and have access to advanced technologies/internet, smart city solutions should be implemented considering people from all walks of life. E-learning should be made accessible to such people *via* various training programs.

4. Political impact: Policymaking procedures should be collective. Previous experiences and strategies used in particular situations in the past may fasten up new policies decision while keeping the suggestions of people of multiple cities into considerations. This may also alleviate the differences between cities of bigger and smaller sizes.

Solutions to these challenges can be the use of computer and information technology, instant messaging in banking, E-consultation *i.e* bridging the communication gap between government and citizen where citizens have easy access to all public information, knowledge of the funds being provided by the government, insights into the expenses done at the development of the city. Citizens should also be allowed to keep their points and give valuable feedback.

3.4. Location Endemic Purview

Depending on location and geographical factors, since each area in a city, is affected, differently, finding an overall optimal solution satisfying the majority of cities and areas might be difficult to achieve [58]. The major issues in the location endemic purview are pointed out as follows:

1. Difficulty in finding optimal solutions due to variation in geographical factors.

2. Difficulty in extending local smart ideas to multi-city projects.

3. Contradiction between central and local government's policies.

It becomes difficult to extend local smart city idea to multiple cities due to the idea being localized and more suitable for people of a particular locality only. Here, the willingness of local government also plays a critical role [58]. No matter how strong the central government is, it can conflict with the local government's rules if a smart city setup is to be done in a region where policies have been made by the local government.

3.5. Miscellaneous Issues

Apart from the issues accentuated above, there lie several other issues:

1. No clear understanding of desired output.

2. Communication gap and lack of collaboration between different departments and stakeholders (creditors, directors).

3. Lack of proper structure around discussions for city development.

4. Uncoordinated efforts performed independently *via* various cities.

5. Widening inequalities and dispossession of land and livelihoods, outdated rules and regulations.

6. Lack of expertise, knowledge and technology awareness hampers smart city initiatives.

4. CASE STUDIES

These are the specific situation of something used or examined to support a claim or idea about a smart city.

4.1. Fujisawa

Fujisawa Smart Town (a residential neighbourhood inside Fujisama City, Japan) is an SC collaboration between the corporate and state sectors (Fujisawa's City Council) (https://fujisawasst.com/EN/project/). Its objective is to create a smart community that is both sustainable and lifestyle-oriented. To this end, they have concentrated on enhancing environmental, governmental, and citizen services.

In Fujisawa Smart Town, every family has a solar power producing system and storing battery cells. Furthermore, a technology known as Smart HEMS (Home Energy Management System) is in charge of energy usage. Furthermore, because each building's energy usage is controlled, assistance is offered to those households that use an exorbitant amount in improving energy productivity and effectiveness.

To maintain the town's security, they are working on numerous projects such as a disaster preventive push notification TV system, surveillance cameras, lighting, and human patrols. In addition, the municipality has sponsored LED street lights. When a passer-by or an automobile is recognised, these lights adjust their brightness.

In terms of citizen initiatives, Fujisawa smart town offers a Wellness Square, which encourages social contact. Several facilities are provided in this neighbourhood, including pharmacies, clinics, nurseries, libraries, after-school care centres, and a location where residents may share their expertise. In addition, a community platform known as SOY LINK is utilised to interact with other residents of the area.

4.2. Santander

Cheng *et al.* [27] undertook one of the most significant SC research initiatives in Santander (Spain) from 2012 to 2014.

Around 2000 environmental sensors and 400 parking sensors, as well as 2000 RFID tags and QR codes and 60 traffic monitoring devices, were put in Santander as part of this project (http://www.smartsantander.eu/index.php/testbeds/item/132 -santander-summary). This effort helped to promote new SC initiatives that are now being implemented in Santander.

Santander City Brain (https://www.santanderci tybrain.com/) is an open platform where residents may post their ideas for improving the city, as well as review and comment on those of other citizens. Santander City Council promotes citizen participation in this manner.

The Santander Open Data Portal (http://datos.santander.es/) has 90 datasets in a variety of formats. The site also encourages the development of apps by promoting those that make use of the data available.

Pulso de la Ciudad (http://maps.smartsantan der. EU/#page3) is an open platform where residents can use their smartphones to report incidents in the city. Those incidents that necessitate City Council involvement are forwarded to the appropriate department. (https://sede.santander.es/) Portal of Electronic Adminis- tration

4.3. Vienna

The suggested developed framework mentioned in [59] addresses the three highlighted topics: (a) the significance of governance and stakeholders, (b) the integration of aspects related to the projects and initiatives executed, and (c) the linkage of these components to the cities' issues. The concept emphasizes the necessity of a holistic vision of the Smart City that includes all these facets. This intricacy necessitates a step-by-step approach to extracting and integrating results.

The conceptual model helped evaluate the present status of implementation and stakeholders' point of views of the Vienna Smart City Strategy, highlighting commonalities and contrasts, as illustrated in Fig. (4). It also showed the tool's use in showing the conceptual model's interconnected parts and deriving recommendations to bridge the two views. The model accurately represents the initiative's contributors and their engagement. However, future studies should focus on public engagement and future collaborative planning visions. Stakeholders' views on Smart Cities' problems reveal a more balanced perspective of the many components. This notion is both documented and implemented. An uneven progression of the considerations is highlighted by the conceptual model.

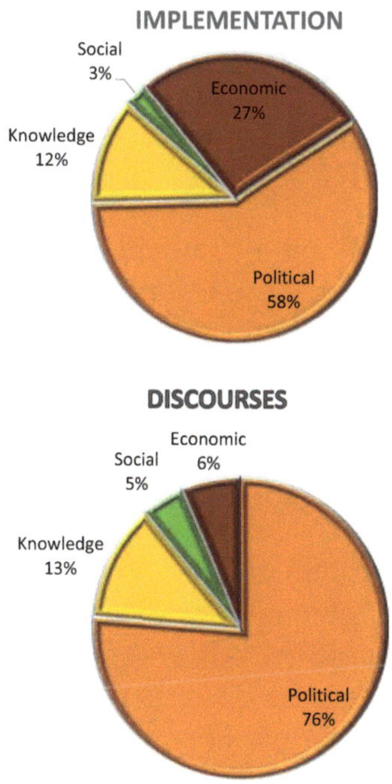

Fig. (4). Conceptual smart city model for vienna showing various stakeholders' involvement in its implementation and discourses.

The model effectively represented a complicated vision to the questioned stakeholders. It helped guide the study of a highly complicated issue and aided in the stakeholder controversy. It was notably useful for local authorities and business enterprises who collaborate with the Smart City system. They agreed that the conceptual framework accurately portrays their interconnected vision and may aid them to communicate their thoughts to others.

To attract more demographics, the model must be made more sophisticated. For technologists, it should incorporate new tool-focused dimensions. It may be used as a reference point for study to address further degree of complexity. Finally, it should be streamlined for information dissemination by civil society organizations.

Finally, these findings must be backed up with inferential evidence. To allow wider application of the conceptual model, the additional study must first systematise its relationship with data processing. This study's text processing code will be utilised to construct textual programming. The study was conceptualized using a quantification method to evaluate the external and internal benefits of Smart City projects. The model's features and agglomerations have been designed to integrate with other contemporary evaluation techniques [2, 6]. Internalised and statistical data connections will allow correlational case studies of cities implementing Smart City strategies as shown in Fig. (4).

CONCLUSION AND FUTURE SCOPE

More work can be done on making a strategic approach to smart city integration. Vision/benefits after implementing a particular smart technology should be clear to all the citizens abiding in the city. Proper goals and strategies should smart set. A smart city plan should be made keeping people from all walks of life in mind. People who are not much aware of the technology or have limited access to it should be given educational lessons so that technology implemented comes to use of all and is efficiently utilized.

Note of financial goals, business model, organization structure, and policies should be deployed before implementation. Flexible policies should be made for the available tools and technology. All core processes and procedures for the development of smart cities must be described. A smart city can open to a whole new world as it can help us give insights into all the new data. Besides reorganizing the existing structurally well-implemented smart city using the Internet of Things, asset tracking, Machine learning, and Artificial Intelligence can trigger various new revenue streams.

Experienced funders should be brought along and all available funding resources should be taken into consideration. Various new business models can be incorporated into some funding issues. Businesses model can be created where instead of investing for the entire asset or system, one can just pay for the time a particular asset has been used and according to what outcome it has produced for the consumer. The asset sharing concept can also be implemented where the asset can be circulated in the market quickly, by renting it to a customer for a certain time and then passing it to the next customer once the previous one finishes. Here IoT can make this asset sharing secure by connecting them to the internet and tracking its usage. Blockchain also plays a vital role in making a city smart. It revolves around concepts like decentralization, immutability, and transparency. Blockchain technology always exchanges crypto currencies without involving any third party. Assets monitoring in a supply chain helps keep a track of all theft points, timely monitor inventory stock amount, maintain training the right supply of goods, noticing any delay in assets reaching their destination due to various parameters like theft, and weather conditions.

A smart city is a concept that focuses on solving the city's developing problems with the help of technology. Maintaining smart street lights (to save light cost and energy by using it when and where required), smart healthcare (nowadays everybody has a smartwatch, which can monitor a person's daily health and routine, making them attentive to their bodily requirements), smart waste management (to smartly differentiate between wet and dry waste and help to locate bins at places), smart speed monitoring (which can help reduce the rate of accidents happening).

If people, stakeholders and government start doing factual listening *i.e* trying to accept new ideas and differences when they get to know about something new, then the smart city concept can reach a higher success rate. Detailed information and strategic plans should be shared with stakeholders for better implementation.

Strategies like planning, design, technical review and implementation tests should be developed. And experienced designers should be involved in the entire integration process.

Alone technology and its integration cannot make a city smart; the citizens should also be smart and active enough to make the best use of it. So that the output is much greater than the investments made. Thus, people should be invited to volunteer for any smart city-related work, which will encourage them to be a part of the progress.

Smart governance plays a key role for successful implementation of a smart city, thus to build one, global goals should be set, processes should be planned while considering available resources; stepwise suggestions should be taken from expertise so that they can not only understand the smart city concept but also can lead to smart governance formation.

REFERENCES

[1]   G.C. Lazaroiu, and M. Roscia, "Definition methodology for the smart cities model", *Energy,* vol. 47, no. 1, pp. 326-332, 2012.
[http://dx.doi.org/10.1016/j.energy.2012.09.028]

[2]   R. Giffinger, C. Fertner, H. Kramar, and E. Meijers, *City-ranking of European medium-sized cities.* Cent. Reg. Sci: Vienna, UT, 2007, pp. 1-12.

[3]   R. Sánchez-Corcuera, A. Nuñez-Marcos, J. Sesma-Solance, A. Bilbao-Jayo, R. Mulero, U. Zulaika, G. Azkune, and A. Almeida, "Smart cities survey: Technologies, application domains and challenges for the cities of the future", *Int. J. Distrib. Sens. Netw.,* vol. 15, no. 6, 2019.
[http://dx.doi.org/10.1177/1550147719853984]

[4]   R. Moss Kanter, and S.S. Litow, "Informed and interconnected: A manifesto for smarter cities", *Harvard Business School General Management Unit Working Paper,* pp. 9-141, 2009.

[5]   R.P. Dameri, "Searching for Smart City definition: A comprehensive proposal", *Int. J. Comput. Technol.,* vol. 11, no. 5, pp. 2544-2551, 2013.
[http://dx.doi.org/10.24297/ijct.v11i5.1142]

[6]   A. Monzon, "Smart cities concept and challenges: Bases for the assessment of smart city projects", *International conference on smart cities and green ICT systems (SMARTGREENS),* 2015, pp. 1-11 Lisbon, Portugal.

[7]   R. Petrolo, V. Loscrì, and N. Mitton, "Towards a smart city based on cloud of things, a survey on the smart city vision and paradigms", *Trans. Emerg. Telecommun. Technol.,* vol. 28, no. 1, p. e2931, 2017.
[http://dx.doi.org/10.1002/ett.2931]

[8]   M. Al-Hader, A. Rodzi, A.R. Sharif, and N. Ahmad, "Smart city components architicture", *2009 International Conference on Computational Intelligence, Modelling and Simulation,* 2009, pp. 93-97 Brno, Czech Republic.
[http://dx.doi.org/10.1109/CSSim.2009.34]

[9]   S. Yamamoto, S. Matsumoto, and M. Nakamura, "Using cloud technologies for large-scale house data in smart city", *4th IEEE International Conference on Cloud Computing Technology and Science Proceedings,* 2012, pp. 141-148 Taipei, Taiwan.
[http://dx.doi.org/10.1109/CloudCom.2012.6427546]

[10]   F. Longo, A. Puliafito, and O. Rana, "Guest editors' introduction to the special issue on fog, edge, and cloud integration for smart environments", *ACM Trans. Internet Technol.,* vol. 19, no. 2, 2019.

[11]   A. Almeida, R. Mulero, P. Rametta, V. Urošević, M. Andrić, and L. Patrono, "A critical analysis of an IoT—aware AAL system for elderly monitoring", *Future Gener. Comput. Syst.,* vol. 97, pp. 598-619, 2019.
[http://dx.doi.org/10.1016/j.future.2019.03.019]

[12]   P. Mell, and T. Grance, "The NIST definition of cloud computing", *Computer security resource center,* 2011.
[http://dx.doi.org/10.6028/NIST.SP.800-145]

[13]   M.J. Kaur, and P. Maheshwari, "Building smart cities applications using IoT and cloud-based architectures", *International Conference on Industrial Informatics and Computer Systems (CIICS),* 2016, pp. 1-5 Sharjah, United Arab Emirates.

[http://dx.doi.org/10.1109/ICCSII.2016.7462433]

[14]   K. Biswas, and V. Muthukkumarasamy, "Securing smart cities using blockchain technology", *IEEE 18th International Conference on High Performance Computing and Communications; IEEE 14th International Conference on Smart City; IEEE 2nd International Conference on Data Science and Systems (HPCC/SmartCity/DSS)*, 2016, pp. 1392-1393 sydney, NSW, Australia.
[http://dx.doi.org/10.1109/HPCC-SmartCity-DSS.2016.0198]

[15]   D. Mazza, D. Tarchi, and G.E. Corazza, "A unified urban mobile cloud computing offloading mechanism for smart cities", *IEEE Commun. Mag.*, vol. 55, no. 3, pp. 30-37, 2017.
[http://dx.doi.org/10.1109/MCOM.2017.1600247CM]

[16]   A. Khanna, and R. Anand, "IoT based smart parking system", *International Conference on Internet of Things and Applications (IOTA)*, 2016, pp. 266-270 Pune, India.
[http://dx.doi.org/10.1109/IOTA.2016.7562735]

[17]   J. Bar-Magen Numhauser, *Fog Computing Introduction to a New Cloud Evolution.* University of Alcalá, 2012.

[18]   D. Bruneo, S. Distefano, F. Longo, G. Merlino, A. Puliafito, and V. D'Amico, "Stack4Things as a fog computing platform for Smart City applications", *IEEE Conference on Computer Communications Workshops (INFOCOM WKSHPS)*, 2016, pp. 848-853 San Francisco, CA, USA.
[http://dx.doi.org/10.1109/INFCOMW.2016.7562195]

[19]   N. Chen, Y. Chen, Y. You, H. Ling, P. Liang, and R. Zimmermann, "Dynamic urban surveillance video stream processing using fog computing", *IEEE Second International Conference on Multimedia Big Data (BigMM)*, 2016, pp. 105-112 Taipei, Taiwan.
[http://dx.doi.org/10.1109/BigMM.2016.53]

[20]   J. Santos, T. Wauters, B. Volckaert, and F. De Turck, "Fog computing: Enabling the management and orchestration of smart city applications in 5G networks", *Entropy,* vol. 20, no. 1, p. 4, 2017.
[http://dx.doi.org/10.3390/e20010004] [PMID: 33265095]

[21]   R.K. Barik, H. Dubey, A.B. Samaddar, R.D. Gupta, and P.K. Ray, "FogGIS: Fog Computing for geospatial big data analytics", In: *IEEE Uttar Pradesh Section International Conference on Electrical, Computer and Electronics Engineering (UPCON)*, 2016, pp. 613-618.Varanasi, India.

[22]   W. Shi, J. Cao, Q. Zhang, Y. Li, and L. Xu, "Edge computing: Vision and challenges", *IEEE Internet Things J.,* vol. 3, no. 5, pp. 637-646, 2016.
[http://dx.doi.org/10.1109/JIOT.2016.2579198]

[23]   T. Taleb, S. Dutta, A. Ksentini, M. Iqbal, and H. Flinck, "Mobile edge computing potential in making cities smarter", *IEEE Commun. Mag.*, vol. 55, no. 3, pp. 38-43, 2017.
[http://dx.doi.org/10.1109/MCOM.2017.1600249CM]

[24]   X. Wang, L.T. Yang, X. Xie, J. Jin, and M.J. Deen, "A cloud-edge computing framework for cyber-physical-social services", *IEEE Commun. Mag.*, vol. 55, no. 11, pp. 80-85, 2017.
[http://dx.doi.org/10.1109/MCOM.2017.1700360]

[25]   Z. Ji, I. Ganchev, M. O'Droma, L. Zhao, and X. Zhang, "A cloud-based car parking middleware for IoT-based smart cities: Design and implementation", *Sensors,* vol. 14, no. 12, pp. 22372-22393, 2014.
[http://dx.doi.org/10.3390/s141222372] [PMID: 25429416]

[26]   E. Patti, and A. Acquaviva, "IoT platform for Smart Cities: Requirements and implementation case studies", *IEEE 2nd International Forum on Research and Technologies for Society and Industry Leveraging a better tomorrow (RTSI)*, 2016, pp. 1-6 Bologna, Italy.

[27]   B. Cheng, S. Longo, F. Cirillo, M. Bauer, and E. Kovacs, "Building a big data platform for smart cities: Experience and lessons from santander", *IEEE International Congress on Big Data,* 2015, pp. 592-599 New York, NY, USA.
[http://dx.doi.org/10.1109/BigDataCongress.2015.91]

[28]   R. Petrolo, V. Loscri, and N. Mitton, "Towards a smart city based on cloud of things", *Proceedings of the 2014 ACM International Workshop on Wireless and Mobile Technologies for Smart Cities,* 2014, pp. 61-66.
[http://dx.doi.org/10.1145/2633661.2633667]

[29]   R. Lea, and M. Blackstock, "City hub: A cloud-based iot platform for smart cities", *IEEE 6th International Conference on Cloud Computing Technology and Science,* 2014, pp. 799-804.
[http://dx.doi.org/10.1109/CloudCom.2014.65]

[30]   N. Mitton, S. Papavassiliou, A. Puliafito, and K. S. Trivedi, "Combining cloud and sensors in a smart city environment", *J Wireless Com Network,* vol. 2012, p. 247, 2012.
[http://dx.doi.org/10.1186/1687-1499-2012-247]

[31]   G.C. Fox, S. Kamburugamuve, and R.D. Hartman, "Architecture and measured characteristics of a cloud based internet of things", In: *International conference on Collaboration Technologies and Systems (CTS),* 2012, pp. 6-12.Denver, CO, USA.
[http://dx.doi.org/10.1109/CTS.2012.6261020]

[32]   R. Mulero, A. Almeida, G. Azkune, P. Abril-Jiménez, M.T. Arredondo Waldmeyer, M. Paramo Castrillo, L. Patrono, P. Rametta, and I. Sergi, "An IoT-aware approach for elderly-friendly cities", *IEEE Access,* vol. 6, pp. 7941-7957, 2018.
[http://dx.doi.org/10.1109/ACCESS.2018.2800161]

[33]   J. Helbostad, B. Vereijken, C. Becker, C. Todd, K. Taraldsen, M. Pijnappels, K. Aminian, and S. Mellone, "Mobile health applications to promote active and healthy ageing", *Sensors,* vol. 17, no. 3, p. 622, 2017.
[http://dx.doi.org/10.3390/s17030622] [PMID: 28335475]

[34]   S. Stavrotheodoros, N. Kaklanis, K. Votis, and D. Tzovaras, "A smart-home IoT infrastructure for the support of independent living of older adults", In: *IFIP International Conference on Artificial Intelligence Applications and Innovations.* Springer: Cham, 2018, pp. 238-249.
[http://dx.doi.org/10.1007/978-3-319-92016-0_22]

[35]   V. Djaja-Josko, and J. Kolakowski, "UWB positioning system for elderly persons monitoring", *23rd Telecommunications Forum Telfor (TELFOR),* 2015, pp. 169-172 Belgrade, Serbia.
[http://dx.doi.org/10.1109/TELFOR.2015.7377440]

[36]   D. Bonino, M.T.D. Alizo, A. Alapetite, T. Gilbert, M. Axling, and H. Udsen, "Almanac: Internet of things for smart cities", *3rd International Conference on Future Internet of Things and Cloud,* 2015, pp. 309-316 Rome, Italy.

[37]   E. Psomakelis, F. Aisopos, A. Litke, K. Tserpes, M. Kardara, and P.M. Campo, "Big IoT and social networking data for smart cities: Algorithmic improvements on big data analysis in the context of radical city applications", *arXiv,* vol. 1607, p. 00509, 2016.
[http://dx.doi.org/10.5220/0005934503960405]

[38]   Y. Zheng, T. Liu, Y. Wang, Y. Zhu, Y. Liu, and E. Chang, "Diagnosing New York city's noises with ubiquitous data", *Proceedings of the 2014 ACM International Joint Conference on Pervasive and Ubiquitous Computing,* 2014, pp. 715-725.
[http://dx.doi.org/10.1145/2632048.2632102]

[39]   F. Longo, D. Bruneo, S. Distefano, G. Merlino, and A. Puliafito, "Stack4Things: A sensing-an--actuation-as-a-service framework for IoT and cloud integration", *Ann. Telecommun.,* vol. 72, no. 1-2, pp. 53-70, 2017.
[http://dx.doi.org/10.1007/s12243-016-0528-5]

[40]   B. Tang, Z. Chen, G. Hefferman, T. Wei, H. He, and Q. Yang, "A hierarchical distributed fog computing architecture for big data analysis in smart cities", *Proceedings of the ASE BigData & Social Informatics,* vol. 2015, pp. 1-6, 2015.
[http://dx.doi.org/10.1145/2818869.2818898]

[41]   K. Zhang, J. Ni, K. Yang, X. Liang, J. Ren, and X.S. Shen, "Security and privacy in smart city applications: Challenges and solutions", *IEEE Commun. Mag.*, vol. 55, no. 1, pp. 122-129, 2017.
[http://dx.doi.org/10.1109/MCOM.2017.1600267CM]

[42]   N.Z. Bawany, and J.A. Shamsi, "Smart city architecture: Vision and challenges", *Int. J. Adv. Comput. Sci. Appl.*, vol. 6, no. 11, 2015.

[43]   D. Eckhoff, and I. Wagner, "Privacy in the smart city—applications, technologies, challenges, and solutions", *IEEE Commun. Surv. Tutor.*, vol. 20, no. 1, pp. 489-516, 2018.
[http://dx.doi.org/10.1109/COMST.2017.2748998]

[44]   G. Trencher, "Towards the smart city 2.0: Empirical evidence of using smartness as a tool for tackling social challenges", *Technol. Forecast. Soc. Change*, vol. 142, pp. 117-128, 2019.
[http://dx.doi.org/10.1016/j.techfore.2018.07.033]

[45]   S. Hasija, Z.J.M. Shen, and C.P. Teo, "Smart city operations: Modeling challenges and opportunities", *Manuf. Serv. Oper. Manag.*, vol. 22, no. 1, pp. 203-213, 2020.
[http://dx.doi.org/10.1287/msom.2019.0823]

[46]   R. Wenge, X. Zhang, C. Dave, L. Chao, and S. Hao, "Smart city architecture: A technology guide for implementation and design challenges", *China Commun.*, vol. 11, no. 3, pp. 56-69, 2014.
[http://dx.doi.org/10.1109/CC.2014.6825259]

[47]   K.H. Law, and J.P. Lynch, "Smart city: Technologies and challenges", *IT Prof.*, vol. 21, no. 6, pp. 46-51, 2019.
[http://dx.doi.org/10.1109/MITP.2019.2935405]

[48]   V. Scuotto, A. Ferraris, and S. Bresciani, "Internet of Things", *Bus. Process. Manag. J.*, vol. 22, no. 2, pp. 357-367, 2016.
[http://dx.doi.org/10.1108/BPMJ-05-2015-0074]

[49]   H.H. Khan, M.N. Malik, R. Zafar, F.A. Goni, A.G. Chofreh, J.J. Klemeš, and Y. Alotaibi, "Challenges for sustainable smart city development: A conceptual framework", *Sustain. Dev.*, vol. 28, no. 5, pp. 1507-1518, 2020.
[http://dx.doi.org/10.1002/sd.2090]

[50]   N. Kogan, and K.J. Lee, "Exploratory research on the success factors and challenges of smart city projects", *Asia Pacific Journal of Information Systems*, vol. 24, no. 2, pp. 141-189, 2014.
[http://dx.doi.org/10.14329/apjis.2014.24.2.141]

[51]   J. Van den Bergh, and S. Viaene, "Unveiling smart city implementation challenges: The case of Ghent", *Inf. Polity*, vol. 21, no. 1, pp. 5-19, 2016.
[http://dx.doi.org/10.3233/IP-150370]

[52]   M.K. Al-Azzam, and M. Bader, "Smart city and smart-health framework, challenges and opportunities", *Int. J. Adv. Comput. Sci. Appl.*, vol. 10, no. 2, pp. 171-176, 2019.
[http://dx.doi.org/10.14569/IJACSA.2019.0100223]

[53]   K. Nam, C.S. Dutt, P. Chathoth, and M.S. Khan, "Blockchain technology for smart city and smart tourism: latest trends and challenges", *Asia Pac. J. Tour. Res.*, vol. 26, no. 4, pp. 454-468, 2021.
[http://dx.doi.org/10.1080/10941665.2019.1585376]

[54]   S. P. Yadav, B. S. Bhati, D. P. Mahato, and S. Kumar, "Federated learning for iot applications", In: *EAI/Springer Innovations in Communication and Computing (EAISICC)* Springer, 2022.
[http://dx.doi.org/10.1007/978-3-030-85559-8]

[55]   F. Al-Turjman, S.P. Yadav, M. Kumar, V. Yadav, and T. Stephan, *Transforming management with ai.big-data, and IoT* Springer, 2022.

[56]   C. Vadgama, A. Khutwad, M. Damle, and S. Patil, "Smart funding options for developing smart cities: A proposal for India", *Indian J. Sci. Technol.*, vol. 8, no. 1, pp. 1-12, 2015.
[http://dx.doi.org/10.17485/ijst/2015/v8i34/85418]

[57] M. Jindal, and A. Kazim, "Systematic review and deliberation of various multi-criteria decision-making techniques", *Multi-Criteria Decision Modelling,* pp. 189-204, 2021.

[58] A. Chakraborty, M. Jindal, M.R. Khosravi, P. Singh, A. Shankar, and M. Diwakar, "A secure iot-based cloud platform selection using entropy distance approach and fuzzy set theory", *Wirel. Commun. Mob. Comput.,* vol. 2021, pp. 1-11, 2021.
[http://dx.doi.org/10.1155/2021/6697467]

[59] A. Kazim, M. Jindal, R. Sharma, R. Choudhary, V. Kumar Sharma, and E. Bajal, "Big data analytics and artificial intelligence in business and marketing: Cloud security and encryption influencing business", *SSRN,* p. 3884455, 2021.
[http://dx.doi.org/10.2139/ssrn.3884455]

CHAPTER 4

Understanding the Future of Smart Cities from Technological and Commercial Point of View

Arushi Kapoor[1,*], **Vartika Agarwal**[2], **Muskan Jindal**[3] and **Shashank Awasthi**[4]

[1] *Robert R Mcormick School of Engineering and Applied Science, Northwestern University, Illinois, United States*

[2] *Department of Biotechnology, Savitribai Phule Pune University, Pune, Maharashtra, India*

[3] *Amity School of Engineering and Technology, Noida, Uttar Pradesh, India*

[4] *Department of Computer Science and Engineering, G.L. Bajaj Institute of Technology and Management, Greater Noida, U.P., India*

Abstract: While the development of smart cities is not an alien concept and in the last few decades, an increasing amount of investment both in terms of time and money is done, the pecuniary or financial benefit of this investment is still much uncharted. Like any other investment made, the return on investment plans and models are essential for further development. This research aims to explore, comprehend, analyse and further develop the return on investment in smart cities and various adjunct IoT and IoE-based models. The presented study primarily analyses and explores various possible financial benefits by deliberating multiple case studies of various smart cities and IoT-based projects worldwide. Additionally, a complete and detailed framework for each assayed case study is presented to comprehend the concept of RoI or return on investments which are distinct for every analysed case study contingent on numerous factors like investment, operational cost, area of application, *etc*. The presented study also aims to provide a comprehensive and comparative study between various plans of RoI for numerous case studies of smart cities and IoT-based projects.

Keywords: Internet of Things, Internet of Everything, Operational cost, Return on Investment (RoI), Smart cities.

1. INTRODUCTION

A smart city is a term that is used to describe a city that provides a better standard of living to its inhabitants by offering better public services and judicially uses the resources available thus reducing its environmental impacts. A formal definition

---

* **Corresponding author Arushi Kapoor:** Robert R Mcormick School of Engineering and Applied Science, Northwestern University, Illinois, United States; E-mail: kapoorarushi31@gmail.com

Satya Prakash Yadav, Sansar Singh Chauhan, Sanjeev Kumar Pippal and Victor Hugo C. de Albuquerque (Eds.)

of a smart city is an innovative sustainable city that uses various data and technologies together to improve the quality of life of its citizens and improve the efficiency of urban services [1].

Smart cities have become a necessity with a significant increase in the world's population in the past few decades and expectations for a better quality of life have also become a norm. By 2050, it is estimated that about seventy percent of the world's population will reside in urban areas. Urban cities currently consume more than seventy-five percent of the resources and energy available in the world and account for 80% of greenhouse gas production [2]. This emission along with other sources causes environmental pollution. The development of smart cities is a possible solution to this problem of rapid urbanization ad high population growth rates. The implementation of smart cities can help reduce water consumption, energy consumption, and carbon emissions and fulfil transport requirements [3].

All over the globe, smart cities are very different depending on their requirements, characteristics and components. Organizations like the International Organization for Standardization provide specific standards that are to be followed to maintain efficiency and safety. These standards help in the development of smart cities and can act as a guide for monitoring the functional performance of the cities [4]. For issues like security, climate change and transportation, these standards can act as guides for the development of potential solutions. Different factors are taken into account like resource management and business practices before these standards are formulated. By following them, we assess the performance of smart cities globally [5].

1.1. Components and Characteristic of Smart Cities

There are 9 important characteristics of smart cities. These characteristics include smart cities, buildings, smart transportation, smart infrastructure, smart governance, smart education and smart healthcare, and smart citizens as depicted in (Fig. **1**). The attributes of smart cities include urbanization and quality of life. Urbanization aspects for defence-related smart cities include technology, infrastructure and governance. The goal of a smart city is to improve the economic, social and environmental standards of a city as well as the people living in it [6].

Fig. (1). Components of a smart city Image Source [1].

There are four core themes of a smart city: economic infrastructure, physical infrastructure, social infrastructure and institutional infrastructure as depicted in Fig. (**2**). The economic infrastructure signifies that the city can provide continuous job opportunities and economic growth for its citizens by using the best practices of e-commerce and e-business. It also includes novel innovations in manufacturing and industry [7]. As well as integration of new technologies to enhance the performance of existing systems. The physical infrastructure signifies that the city can sustain and function for future generations also. The institutional infrastructure includes the governance of cities and is associated with the participation of citizens in decision making, and the quality of public and social services that are available. To maximize the benefits available to the citizens regional and central governments must work in sync with each other. The physical infrastructure includes both natural as well as manufactured infrastructure that can help sustain the lives of present and future generations. Social themes include human capital and intellectual capabilities. Citizen responsibility plays an important role in sustaining a smart city and helps in the evolution of a city. In comparison with normal cities, the citizens of smart cities can grow to their potential to live a quality life [8].

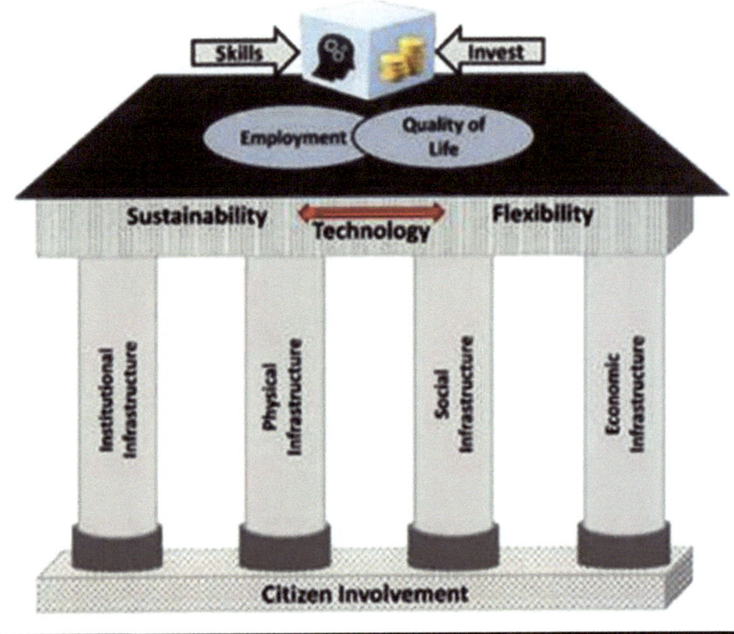

Fig. (2). Four core themes of smart cities [10].

Some of the other parameters that are important for the development of thriving smart cities are open data networks, flexible monetization schemes and security as well as wireless connectivity. These components help to integrate IOT technologies into smart cities [9].

1.2. Internet of Things and its Application in Smart Cities

The Internet of things (IoT) is a communication network that allows devices to communicate with each other and users using microcontrollers and transceivers. These devices are connected to a network that facilitates this communication process. Cloud-based IoT technologies receive, analyse and manage data in real-time to help communities make informed decisions that can improve the standard of living by using technology that can make tasks much easier such as streamlined trash collection systems, a decrease of traffic congestion and improvement in the air quality of their city. The citizens can use smartphones and other mobile devices to engage with smart city ecosystems. To reduce cost and improve sustainability it is a good idea to pair devices and data with the physical infrastructure of a city [11].

IoT technology along with secure wireless connectivity can change the traditional elements of life and transform them as depicted in Fig. (**3**). Some examples of real-world applications of IoT include-Transformation of normal street lights into high power embedded EDS'c can help commuters with traffic issues and provide weather and natural calamity warnings. These could also detect free parking spaces and alert drivers where to find a parking space. Some smart cities like New York are using IOT technology to reduce traffic congestion by applying a congestion management system that has improved the travel time avenues by ten percent. Communication networks across different areas of the city have replaced pay phones and provide free super fast wifi, phone call and device charging booths are available. Tablets displaying city services, maps and directions are also installed [12]. In Denmark Copenhagen sensors are being used to monitor the traffic in real-time this data can help to improve traffic management and help reduce travel time for commuters. In London, smart parking projects are being implemented to allow drivers to quickly find vacant spots for car parking.

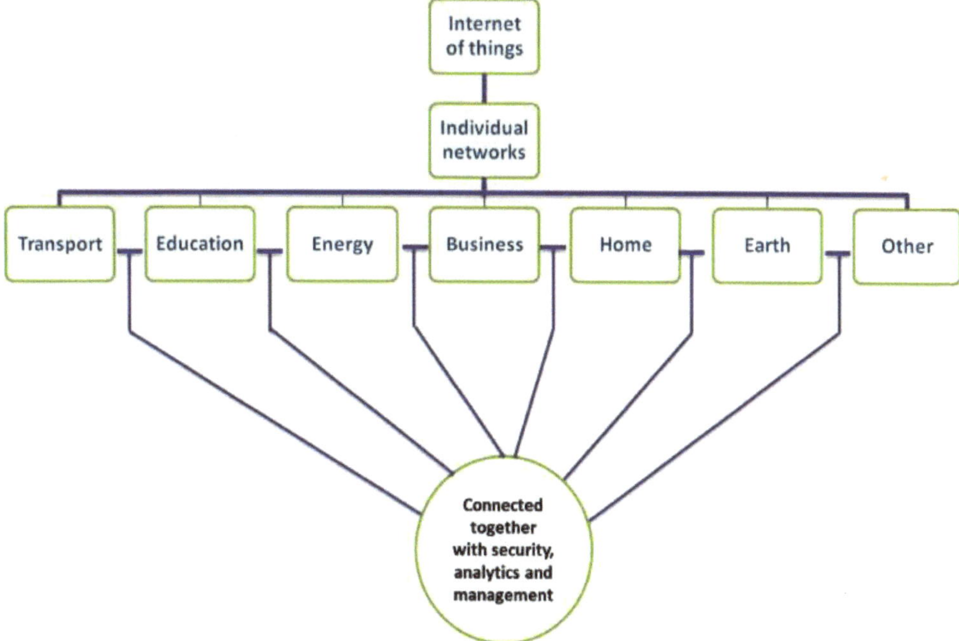

Fig. (3). Internet of Things is a network of networks [11].

1.3. The Age of Smart Cities

The early phase of the twenty-first century marks a time of significant technological development. For instance, Uber, a software company, is presently giving the world's largest taxi service. Companies like Amazon and Ali Baba have become the largest retailers. The AI and IT systems have disrupted the conventional ideas of operating and investing in the concept of 'Smart City as shown in Fig. (4). These technologies are indeed powerful for the development of a digital world that leads to urbanization [17].

BENEFITS
- Better Planning & Economic Growth
- Less Pollution and Reduced Energy Consumption
- Better and Faster Infrastructure
- Less Commuting & Better Transportation Systems
- Reduced Traffic Accidents
- Better Crime Control
- Responsive Government Action
- Cost-Efficiencies & Competitiveness

CONCERNS
- Cyber-attacks
- Techno-Terrorists
- Vulnerable Industrial Controls
- Human-Machine Interface Weaknesses
- Maintenance & Updating
- Reduced Human Interaction
- Natural Disasters
- Reduced Privacy
- Trolling and Distortion of Democratic Processes

Fig. (4). Enlisting several benefits and concerns of a smart city (Image Adapted from [17]).

The coming age of Smart cities would also be characterized by a few significant changes like:

· Challenges to privacy in individuals.

· A major part of life would be devoted to education and retraining.

· Health care and fitness would be challenging issues.

· There would be an enormous need for cybersecurity as threats of cybercrime would increase considerably.

· Major problems like changes in climate and global demographics would be observed leading to mass immigration and migration.

· Increasing dependency on automated systems and AI.

Despite the increased comfort that 'smart cities would provide us with, it is necessary to evaluate at what cost would it do so? Lack of care in using technologies may impose potential threats to core values like freedom and pursuit of happiness and also curtail our privacy in the longer run and depicted in Fig. (**5**).

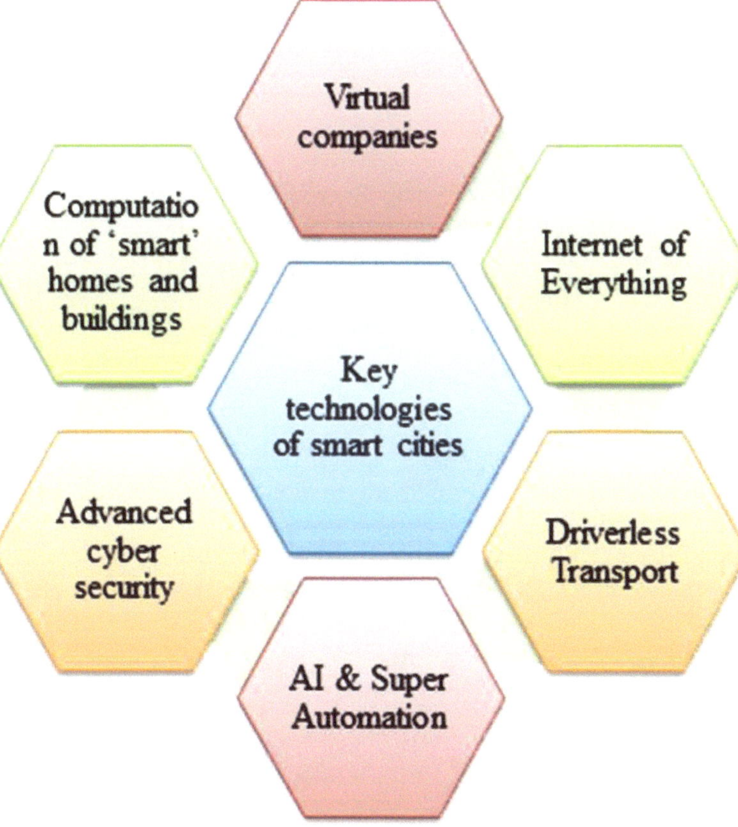

Fig. (5). The key technologies of a smart city.

Among the most critical and frequently discussed concepts of urban cities, lies the multidimensional smart city concept [19]. Several studies have been reported over a decade that account for the technological advances due to smart cities [20]. However, the commercial benefits that result from smart cities is a lesser-discussed aspect so far [21].

We are mostly aware of the benefits of converting a contemporary city to a smart city [22]. Development into a smart city is characterized by an increasing shift towards i) e-shopping ii) e-work iii) e- maintenance and iv) e- leisure. All of these factors would converge and primarily lead to the development of e-commerce [13]. With an increasing number of cities being converted into smart cities across the globe, it becomes considerably important to analyse and discuss factors that potentially encourage investors to invest in smart city development [23].

The conventional wisdom of e-commerce suggests that in the first decade of the 21st century itself, approximately ninety percent of population growth occurred in the US metropolitan jurisdictions [13]. The suburban era has significantly evolved to become self-sufficient and attract activities for urban and business residents [24].

Besides the obvious development, the fact that 'smart cities' do widen the gap between rural and urban populations cannot be ignored completely [25]. City, therefore, becomes of immense importance that the goals of what we call a 'smart city' are extremely well-defined [26]. People living in a 'smart city' would undoubtedly have access to better-equipped technologies [17]. The key element of a smart city would include:

   i. Fulfilment of business needs and of individual needs.
  ii. More job opportunities.
 iii. Improved infrastructure and resources.
 iv. Better technology and use of Artificial Intelligence.
  v. Support of citizens for better planning of a smart city.
 vi. Provide a safe and secure atmosphere for living.
 vii. Creating a sustainable environment.
viii. Circular economy preferred over disposal economy.

1.4. Smart Cities Mission of India

A Smart Cities Mission was introduced in India to improve the quality of life of people and drive economic growth by enabling the development of local areas and harnessing technology, especially one that leads to Smart outcomes. (Government of India - 2016) The mission targets a hundred cities in the period of 2015-16 to 2019-20 [14].

According to this mission, an Indian smart city is required to have an adequate water supply, sanitation facilities, affordable housing, good IT connectivity, a sustainable environment, electric supply, e-governance, safety and security of citizens and health and education of the residents.

Despite having an agenda designed so elaborately, a major shortcoming of the Indian Smart cities is the lack of an inclusive and efficient financial system. A good financial system would allow people to invest in important activities like business, education, and health to increase their standards of living [14].

The need for a potent financial system in the creation of a smart city was underlined for the first time by Huston *et al.* in 2015 [27]. As smart cities encourage the use of cutting-edge technology, they might act as potential hotspots for business and technological advancements [28]. The inadequacy in the management of financial matters has constrained the growth of smart cities in developed countries as well [14].

1.5. Internet of Things (IoT)

With the advent of the design of Internet Connectivity to a wide range of products and services like automotive vehicles, ships and aircraft, washing machines, ovens and refrigerators, it has become increasingly important for manufacturers to improve the reliability and effectiveness of performance in their products [29]. It is now possible to monitor the performance of their products *via* the Internet [30].

This type of design was initially confined to monitoring defence-related performance and efficiency of operation but is now used throughout the world. This technology indeed has unlimited potential to improve performance, but the misuse of technology would lead to cyber security abuses. It is ironic that the technology developed by the U. S Defense Advanced Research Agency, DRAPA, may become a major threat to the smart defence system of the U.S [17].

1.6. Framework for ROI

In the present time, where people are heavily investing in smart cities, it becomes increasingly essential to know and evaluate the returns and benefits of investments [31]. With the advent of 5G, the process of collecting data has become more efficient and easier [32].

People already residing in a 'Smart city' might not notice the small developments even though they indirectly contribute towards improving their lifestyle [33]. However, for people migrating into this city from a small town, life in a smart city is more attractive, the change is considered defence structure-related significant [34].

"451 Research forecasts" have estimated that the investment towards the digital infrastructure of Smart cities would show a steep rise in the years to come as shown in Fig. (6). They have proposed that from 36.6 billion dollars in the year 2019, it may significantly rise to about forty-seven billion dollars in the year 2025. The increased interest to invest in 'Smart City' infrastructure would enable companies to develop better solutions for the market [16].

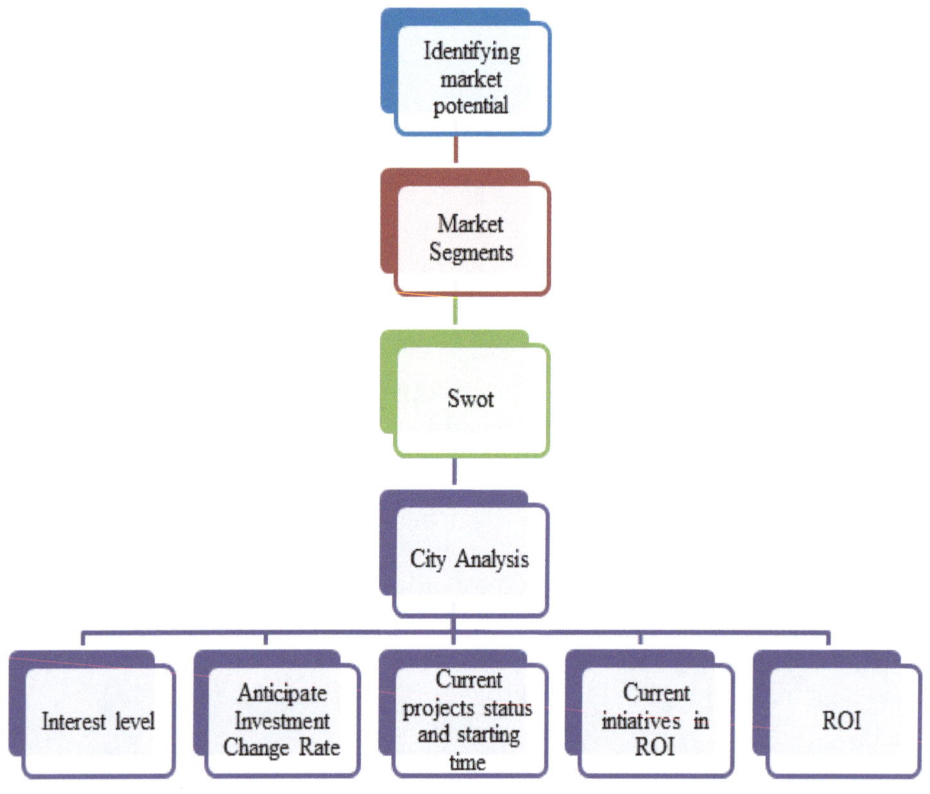

Fig. (6). Conceptual frameworks of ROI (Image adapted from [16]).

A thesis was published that primarily focused on the near-market opportunities of the Smart Cities present in Europe [35]. The European Commission: Smart City, 2016 describes the Smart City as a place where the existing traditional services and networks have been made comparatively more efficient with the help of telecommunication and digital technologies for the benefit of both its inhabitants and businesses [36]. A Smart City would include the use of modern technologies in most of its different functions depicted in Fig. (7) like waste management, logistics, ways of energy production, *etc.* the development of these ideas would require the implementation of a smart technology in different areas and interconnecting them later [37]. Few of the cities have initiated the implementation of Smart technologies and IoT sensors in their operations [38]. However, most of the projects are in an early stage and short-term data is only available as of now [39].

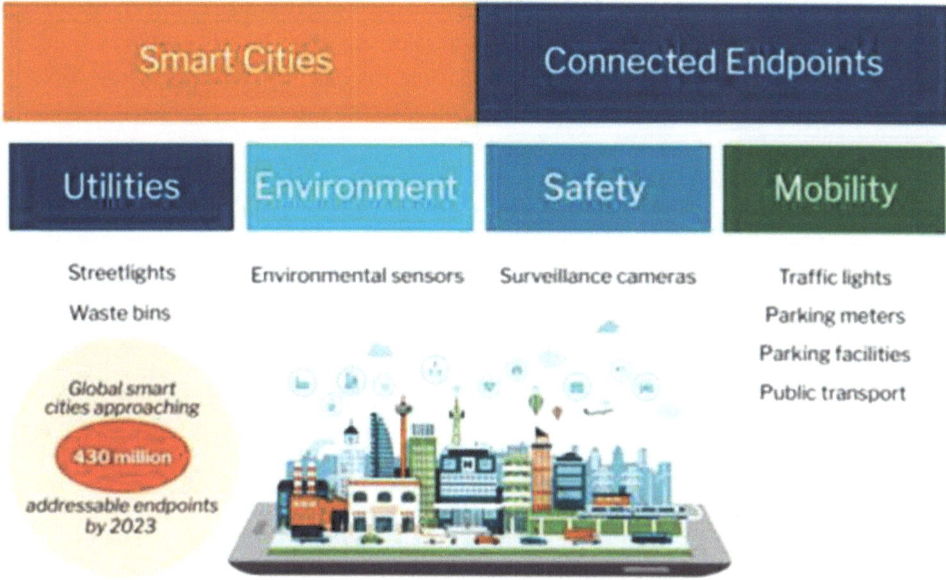

Fig. (7). Smart City I a structure (ESI, 2019). (Adapted from *Alec Boman, Market Opportunities in Smart Cities*).

Being in the middle of a data revolution that provides new insights into cities enables us to better understand the expectations of citizens regarding smart buildings and cities [40]. Also, the return-on-investment needs to be analyzed for creating smart environments. Several questions need to be addressed like: How does the public respond when there is a traffic gridlock? What are the major tourist attractions? What are the variations in energy consumption from weekends to weekdays? What do people enjoy in their leisure time? How could we better protect their privacy [15]?

Understanding the multifaceted nature of smart cities and how the different views improve the quality of urban life would be fundamental in designing better urban infrastructures and services and quantifying investments in smart cities [15].

A survey by manufacturing executives of CISCO reports a few major challenges in the development of smart factories that include the inability to justify ROI and insufficient funds or investments to modernize.

1.6.1. Compare ROI of IoT based Projects

The IoT market is huge in terms that it harbours a broad range of customers [41]. An individual might purchase an IoT solution for enhancing their comfort, for entertainment and in business cases. Whatever might be the purpose, all the consumers would initially evaluate the return on investment and then decide if the purchase would be worth it or not [18].

The most common approach to realize IoT- based cost reductions is condition monitoring. The optimization of product cost and reduction of the structure cost would require analyzing parameters critical to the production process [42]. Another approach might include the optimization of supply chain IoT. For instance, in a warehouse, the application of RFID technology would lead to a much more detailed observation of the actual inventories of the raw material involved [18].

1.6.2. Comparing ROI for Different European Countries

The market potential of smart cities in different European countries was evaluated using SWOT analysis and market segmentation [43]. The baseline details of several countries were collected that would include the population, position of cities in the hyperconnected cities ranking database, 5G availability, operating budget and the GDP of the city [44].

A major part of the analysis was about identifying risks in Smart project implementation [45]. A few major risks would include playing with the existing technologies employed in the city, the increasing shift towards data and analytics as well as the telecommunication/IT infrastructure [46]. Studying these parameters is essential as implementing these technologies into cities having poorly developed infrastructure is comparatively more difficult than in cities with a well-developed infrastructure [16].

Further, a comparative aspect of the study ranked these Smart cities from best to worst [47]. The current initiatives of these Smart Cities were then ranked from best to worst. These initiatives were sorted at five different stages in the database development that would include Piloting, Not Pursuing, Planning, Partial deployment and Wide-Scale deployment [16].

1.7. Copenhagen

The capital of Denmark ranks seventh in the list of hyper-connected cities. The present IT- infrastructure initiatives taken in Copenhagen have reached stage two-level [16]. Nevertheless, when it comes to data analytics, it is in an improved stage as compared to other cities [48]. Data is used for the improvement of operations of the city and is also given to the stakeholders for future use [52]. The technologies that are in use now include Blockchain, Robots, Drones and Artificial intelligence. Further, the 5G network is soon to be introduced here [49].

1.8. Helsinki

The capital city of Finland is reportedly the most advanced form of smart city with several smart technologies in use like Facial recognition, Artificial Intelligence, *etc.* The data collection system here has reached Stage 4 which enables better usage of available data [16]. The availability of 5G networks on a commercial scale indicates better connectivity. However, a few major challenges have been identified for the implementation of Smart projects that include climate change, risks involved in digital security, income inequality and skill gaps [50].

1.9. Brussels

With a population of one million, Brussels is the capital city of the European Union. The technology here is in the developing stage [16]. The major challenges faced here include financial and budget constraints [53]. Further, the lack of 5G availability restricts the fast development of Smart projects in the city. The major area of focus here is transportation and mobility [51]. For this purpose, several initiatives have been taken like developing a Smart Parking App and building up intelligent traffic signals [51].

1.10. Vienna

Being the capital city of Austria, Vienna is the cultural, political and economic centre of Austria. With a ranking of fifty in the hyperconnected cities list, it is at an advanced stage in terms of Smart technologies. The challenges in the development of Vienna as a Smart City include an increase in crime rates, issues related to public safety and major gaps in skills and talent development [16].

1.11. Contribution of Smart Cities in Urbanisation

Smart cities use information and digital technology to make more informed choices and decisions that help to improve the standard of living of the citizens. Smart cities apply digital intelligence to the urban cities and help to apply it to solve public problems as depicted in Fig. (**8**). Smart city technologies have helped potential to impact all spheres of life in a city and have a positive effect [54]. Some of the benefits of smart cities are as follows:

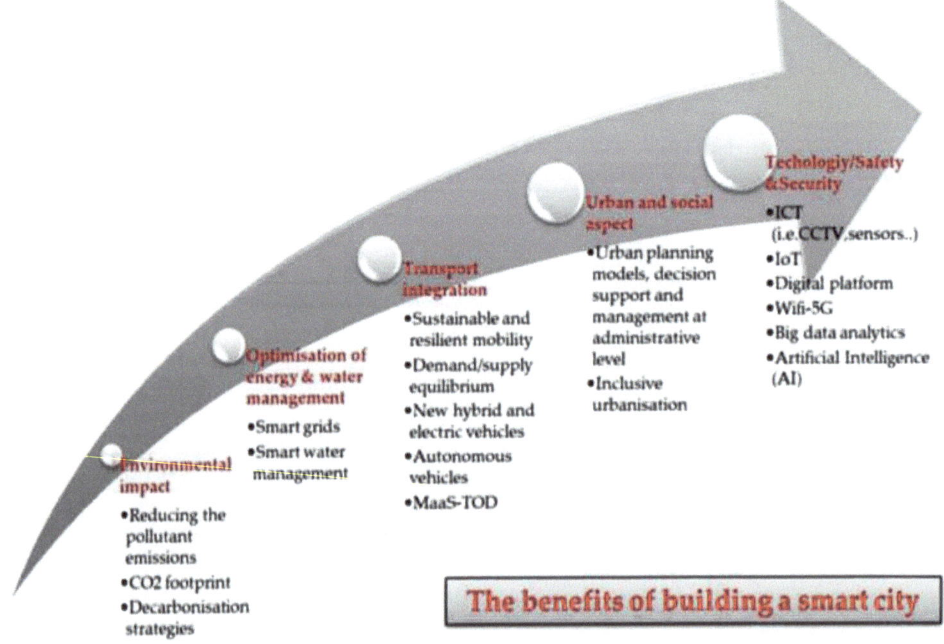

Fig. (8). Benefits linked with smart cities such as lower environmental impact, optimum use of energy and water, sustainable transport modes, better urban city planning and improved cybersecurity [54].

1.11.1. Better Public Security

For all cities, the security of their citizens is of utmost priority. Smart cities have municipal families that can monitor their citizens better by using CCTV cameras with facial recognition. Services such as smoke detectors and fire alarms are also used in smart cities to make all homes safer. It has been seen that by using various technologies, the fatalities due to incidents such as homicide, road traffic and fires can be dramatically reduced by about 8 to 10%. Reports of assault, burglary and car thefts have reduced dramatically to about 30 to 40 percent [55]. This also gives the residents of the city a sense of safety and freedom of movement in the city. By using this technology in smart cities, authorities can use the resources and personnel more effectively. For example, central-time crime mapping uses statistical analysis information to identify patterns, and using this information, the police can identify potential high-risk areas of crime and take effective measures to prevent any incidents. Smart systems increase the efficiency of call centres and field operations. The application of these types of technologies has greatly reduced the emergency response time by about twenty to thirty-five percent. In a city where the average response time is fifty minutes, this reduces it by more than seventeen minutes [56]. The overall impact of smart city applications in improving the quality of life of its citizens is depicted in Fig. (9).

Fig. (9). Impact of smart city applications on improving the standard of living of its residents [54].

1.11.2. Reducing Travel Time

To optimize mobility, many cities are now using smart technologies for the clean and efficient transportation of goods, services and people. Smart cities that use smart mobility applications can potentially cut down the travel time by about fifteen to twenty percent by the year 2025. In more developed cities, the use of such technologies can help save up to fifteen minutes while in a relatively newer developing city, the time reduced could be between twenty to thirty minutes every day. Cities with well-built transit systems are the ones that benefit the most from these technologies. By using mobile applications such as Mobility as a service and Transport on Demand (TOD), people can have access to information such as the best mode of transport, the best possible route and this helps to reduce traffic congestion and produce cost-effective solutions [57]. By installing IoT sensors on transit infrastructure such as roads, it can help the authorities to fix any damages or problems before breakdowns. Intelligent syncing of traffic signals to coordinate them perfectly can reduce the average commutes by five percent in cities where buses are a popular mode of transport. Smart parking applications can also direct drivers to available spots which reduces a lot of time often spent on finding a parking spot. To optimize mobility, many cities are now using smart technologies for the clean and efficient transportation of goods, services and people. An example of a smart city that has optimised its traffic is Los Angeles where intelligent transport technologies have helped to control the traffic flow. Sensors sends real-time information and data about traffic flow to a central traffic management platform that analyses the data and information and accordingly adjusts the traffic signal lights depending on the traffic situation within a few minutes [58].

1.11.3. Better Health Care Facilities

Cities with dense populations need to monitor and provide effective healthcare services to their citizens. Health companion applications have helped in the monitoring of chronic diseases like asthma and diabetes. These applications collect real-world patient information and this is then used to improve treatment protocols and drug development. These remote patient monitoring systems can reduce the number of patients in high-income households by about four percent. The information that is collected can also be sent to healthcare practitioners for early interventions [59]. The use of such technologies in smart cities can lead to data generation that can help to identify people who are predisposed or at a higher risk and appropriate steps can be taken. By using the internet, important messages about vaccinations, sanitation and new treatment regimens can be circulated among the public leading to increased access to correct verifiable information [60]. By using data-based interventions for maternal and child healthcare, the mortality rates can be reduced by 5 percent. The use of infectious disease surveillance systems in smart cities that monitor infections can help to contain any epidemic. The technology like telemedicine has provided easier access to the general public of doctors through video conferencing features. This, in turn, reduces time and expense associated with travel and can be lifesaving in instances where there is a shortage of doctors in low-income cities [61].

1.11.4. Lower Environmental Impact

With an increase in the population, there has also been an increase in industrialisation and consumption of natural resources that has led to high environmental pressure. Technological innovations such as automation systems for buildings along with dynamic electricity pricing can cut down emissions by about 5 to 10 percent. To reduce water consumption, efficient systems such as water tracking systems that provide digital feedback to the user can help make people more aware about the water consumption per day and can help in conservation by about 15 percent in metropolitan cities. Another reason for water shortage is the water wastage due to faulty pipers by using sensors and analytics. This loss can be reduced by twenty-five percent. Applications that monitor the waste disposal of each household can be optimised for better waste collection practices [62]. Most challenges are faced during the waste collection stage, a solution to this could be the use of waste containers that contain a sensor that can detect the amount of garbage collected and when the threshold is reached, the system sends a notification to the sanitation workers. Thus this will help in efficient waste collection [63]. Smart cities are using tools to collect data related to pollution. Technological innovations such as air quality sensors to predict air pollution allow faster identification of the cause of the problem and steps can be taken to rectify it; for instance, Beijing is a city that uses a technology to track the sources of airborne pollutants which have been reduced by about twenty percent in a year by regulating the traffic and construction activity [64].

1.11.5. Smart Cities Can Create Urban Communities

Residents of smart cities can be connected using applications like Meetup and Nextdoor. These digital applications and software allow real-world interactions between people. By using these applications, residents can feel being in sync with the government as well as other residents of the cities as they receive information in real-time. Efficient two-way communication channels between the citizens and local authorities lead to the general public being more responsive to new initiatives [65]. City governing bodies also maintain social media sites, some have also created applications for the citizens to voice their concerns and help in better decision-making. For instance, Paris has come up with a participatory budget where citizens can share their ideas and views on an online platform, and then online voting is done to decide the one that secures funding [66].

1.12. Smart Cities as a Way of Improving Commercial and Technological Development

1.12.1. Smart Can Provide Better Employment Opportunities to Its Citizens

Smart technologies can lead to the creation of new jobs such as maintenance and installation jobs. Platforms such as E career centres draw unemployed people into the workforce. Online retraining programs and data-driven formal education can help <u>make people skilled</u>. By digitalising important government functions, like business licensing and tax filing, the local business can save time with easier access to information. To provide affordable living accommodations to its residents in smart cities, the supply of housing is being expanded [67]. To remove the influence of bureaucracy that slows the process, the entire process is being digitised to reduce delays, thus leading to more construction and driving down the prices of housing. By using smart systems, land that is not being utilised can be identified to create more houses for people [68].

1.12.2. Smart Cities Open New Avenues for Partnerships Between Government and Private Entities and also Increase Private Sector Participation

In smart cities, smart technologies can allow opportunities than in a conventional city. Investment in infrastructure can be capital-intensive. In smart cities, a combination of traditional construction and a smart technology can respond to the demand of the changing world. For instance, in a neighbourhood adding a subway can take a lot of time, but instead using a privately operated bus service can be a much faster and more effective solution to the demand. In smart cities, the government needs not be the only funder and operator of all public services and infrastructures. For example, in Amsterdam, a public-private partnership is being followed that connects educational institutes, nonprofits and private sector companies [69] as depicted in Fig. (**10**).

1.12.3. Increased Digital Equity

Smart cities provide the residents with the best technology resources to create a more equitable environment for the citizens with services that are cost-effective and rapid such as public Wifi hotspots that are present throughout the city [70].

1.12.4. Better Infrastructure

By correlating data from BIM (Building Information Modeling), smart cities can use smart technologies for predictive analysis to identify areas that require repairs. This allows to save a great sum of money as funds can be managed better and infrastructure failures can be prevented.

1.12.5. Increasing Workforce Engagement

A productive city requires a highly effective workforce. By increasing the use of smart technologies, the burden of manual tasks can be reduced thus increasing the time available to the workforce for more productive tasks [71].

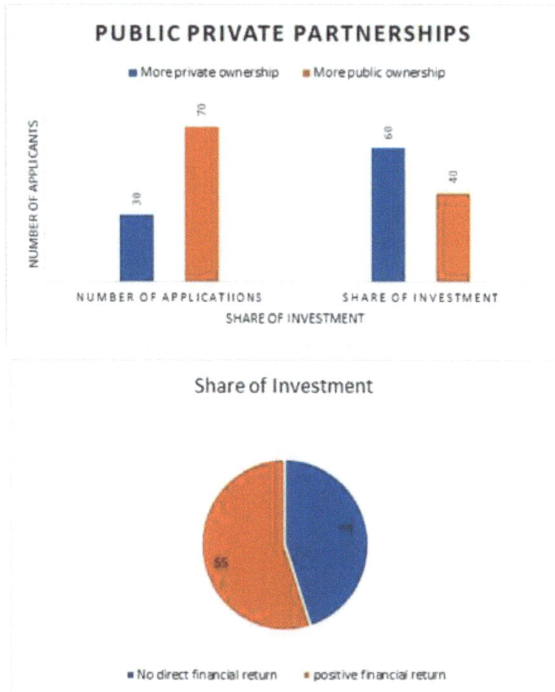

Fig. (10). The public sector can be the owner is most applications but the majority of investment could come from the private sector and public sector applications can generate returns.

2. FUTURE TRENDS OF SMART CITIES

It has been predicted that smart cities can generate economic benefits of $20 trillion by the year 2026 [72]. Companies are also given incentives to fund smart city projects through stimulus packages. By changing urban infrastructure, smart city development can be accelerated. Four key investment areas in the future can provide growth opportunities [73]. Four smart infrastructure investments for the future development of smart cities are shown in Fig. (**11**).

2.1. Enabling Technologies

New technologies like artificial intelligence and cloud computing can drive the evolution of smart cities and create new opportunities [74].

Smart Cities: Four infrastructure investment opportunities

Enabling technologies	Buildings & construction	Energy	Water & waste management

Fig. (11). Four infrastructure investment opportunities for the future in smart cities [75].

2.2. Building and Construction

Smart solutions can help to convert these buildings into much more energy-efficient and sustainable infrastructure and save up to 20% energy using innovations such as seasonal thermal storage in buildings that can be used depending on the need [75].

2.3. Improving Energy Source Management

Urban cities consume about two-thirds of the world's energy. To reduce this investment, smart energy systems are required. Investment is needed in smart grids and distribution networks that can better monitor energy flows to adjust supply according to the demand.

2.4. Smart Water and Waste Management

To effectively manage water resources and reduce wastage due to leakage and old drainage systems, it is important to upgrade the systems by using smart technology to detect leakage and pollution and help in proper maintenance planning [76].

CONCLUSION

The concept of smart cities has evolved as an application of the internet of things. Smart cities are an aggregate of all the other urban environment management strategies. This paper presented a primary analysis and the various possible financial benefits by deliberating multiple case studies of various smart cities and IoT based projects around the world. Smart cities are the solution to all urban challenges being faced today. Even though these cities are sustainable, some challenges are associated with smart cities due to the high data processing demands linked to them and the different types of networks and smart devices that are connected can lead to complex problems. This is to be ensured that these challenges are identified and improvements are made to develop efficient smart cities.

REFERENCES

[1]   S.P. Mohanty, U. Choppali, and E. Kougianos, "Everything you wanted to know about smart cities: the internet of things is the backbone", *IEEE Consum. Electron. Mag.,* vol. 5, no. 3, pp. 60-70, 2016.
[http://dx.doi.org/10.1109/MCE.2016.2556879]

[2]   A.J. Jara, D. Genoud, and Y. Bocchi, "Big data in smart cities: From poisson to human dynamics", *28th International Conference on Advanced Information Networking and Applications Workshops.,* 2014, pp. 785-790 Victoria, BC, Canada.
[http://dx.doi.org/10.1109/WAINA.2014.165]

[3]   A. Zanella, N. Bui, A. Castellani, L. Vangelista, and M. Zorzi, "Internet of things for smart cities", *IEEE Internet Things J.,* vol. 1, no. 1, pp. 22-32, 2014.
[http://dx.doi.org/10.1109/JIOT.2014.2306328]

[4]   E. Mardacany, "Smart cities characteristics: Importance of built environment components", *IET Conference on Future Intelligent Cities,* 2014, London.
[http://dx.doi.org/10.1049/ic.2014.0045]

[5]   O. Vermesan, and P. Friess, "Digitising the industry; Internet of things connecting the physical", *Digital and Virtual Worlds,* pp. 1-364, 2016.
[http://dx.doi.org/10.13052/rp-9788793379824]

[6]   S. Harris, "Securing big data in our future intelligent cities", *IET Conference on Future Intelligent Cities,* 2014, London, UK.
[http://dx.doi.org/10.1049/ic.2014.0049]

[7]   H. Chourabi, T. Nam, S. Walker, J.R. Gil-Garcia, S. Mellouli, K. Nahon, T.A. Pardo, and H.J. Scholl, "Understanding smart cities: An integrative framework", *45th Hawaii International Conference on System Sciences.,* 2012, Maui, HI, USA.
[http://dx.doi.org/10.1109/HICSS.2012.615]

[8]   B.N. Silva, M. Khan, and K. Han, "Towards sustainable smart cities: A review of trends, architectures, components, and open challenges in smart cities", *Sustain Cities Soc.,* vol. 38, pp. 697-713, 2018.
[http://dx.doi.org/10.1016/j.scs.2018.01.053]

[9]   M.H. Miraz, M. Ali, P.S. Excell, and R. Picking, "A review on Internet of things (IoT), internet of everything (IoE) and internet of Nano things (IoNT)", *Internet Technologies and Applications.,* 2015, Wrexham, UK.
[http://dx.doi.org/10.1109/ITechA.2015.7317398]

[10]   K.M. Nahiduzzaman, M. Holland, S.K. Sikder, P. Shaw, K. Hewage, and R. Sadiq, "Urban transformation toward a smart city: An E-commerce–induced path-dependent analysis", *J. Urban Plann. Dev.,* vol. 147, no. 1, p. 04020060, 2021.
[http://dx.doi.org/10.1061/(ASCE)UP.1943-5444.0000648]

[11]   R.U. Arora, "Financial sector development and smart cities: The Indian case", *Sustain Cities Soc.,* vol. 42, pp. 52-58, 2018.
[http://dx.doi.org/10.1016/j.scs.2018.06.013]

[12]   A. Crooks, K. Schechtner, A.K. Dey, and A. Hudson-Smith, "Creating smart buildings and cities", *IEEE Pervasive Comput.,* vol. 16, no. 2, pp. 23-25, 2017.
[http://dx.doi.org/10.1109/MPRV.2017.23]

[13]   P. Andras, L. Esterle, M. Guckert, T.A. Han, P.R. Lewis, K. Milanovic, T. Payne, C. Perret, J. Pitt, S.T. Powers, N. Urquhart, and S. Wells, "Trusting intelligent machines: Deepening trust within socio-technical systems", *IEEE Technol. Soc. Mag.,* vol. 37, no. 4, pp. 76-83, 2018.
[http://dx.doi.org/10.1109/MTS.2018.2876107]

[14]   R. Krishnamurthi, A. Nayyar, and A. Solanki, "Innovation opportunities through Internet of things (IoT) for smart cities", *Green and Smart Technologies for Smart Cities,* pp. 261-292, 2019.
[http://dx.doi.org/10.1201/9780429454837-13]

[15]   E. Ackerman, and E. Strickland, "Medical delivery drones take flight in east africa", *IEEE Spectr.,* vol. 55, no. 1, pp. 34-35, 2018.
[http://dx.doi.org/10.1109/MSPEC.2018.8241731]

[16]   M.A. Ahad, S. Paiva, G. Tripathi, and N. Feroz, "Enabling technologies and sustainable smart cities", *Sustain Cities Soc.,* vol. 61, p. 102301, 2020.
[http://dx.doi.org/10.1016/j.scs.2020.102301]

[17]   H. Ahvenniemi, A. Huovila, I. Pinto-Seppä, and M. Airaksinen, "What are the differences between sustainable and smart cities?", *Cities,* vol. 60, pp. 234-245, 2017.
[http://dx.doi.org/10.1016/j.cities.2016.09.009]

[18]   V. Albino, U. Berardi, and R.M. Dangelico, "Smart cities: Definitions, dimensions, performance, and initiatives", *J. Urban Technol.,* vol. 22, no. 1, pp. 3-21, 2015.
[http://dx.doi.org/10.1080/10630732.2014.942092]

[19]   M. Angelidou, A. Psaltoglou, N. Komninos, C. Kakderi, P. Tsarchopoulos, and A. Panori, "Enhancing sustainable urban development through smart city applications", *J. Sci. Tech. Policy Manag.,* vol. 9, no. 2, pp. 146-169, 2018.
[http://dx.doi.org/10.1108/JSTPM-05-2017-0016]

[20]   M. Batty, "Big data, smart cities and city planning", *Dialogues Hum. Geogr.,* vol. 3, no. 3, pp. 274-279, 2013.
[http://dx.doi.org/10.1177/2043820613513390] [PMID: 29472982]

[21]   D. Belanche, L.V. Casaló, and C. Orús, "City attachment and use of urban services: Benefits for smart cities", *Cities,* vol. 50, pp. 75-81, 2016.
[http://dx.doi.org/10.1016/j.cities.2015.08.016]

[22]   K. Benouaret, R. Valliyur-Ramalingam, and F. Charoy, "CrowdSC: Building smart cities with large-scale citizen participation", *IEEE Internet Comput.,* vol. 17, no. 6, pp. 57-63, 2013.
[http://dx.doi.org/10.1109/MIC.2013.88]

[23]   M. Blanck, and J.L.D. Ribeiro, "Smart cities financing system: An empirical modelling from the European context", *Cities,* vol. 116, p. 103268, 2021.
[http://dx.doi.org/10.1016/j.cities.2021.103268]

[24]   A. Buallay, R. El Khoury, and A. Hamdan, "Sustainability reporting in smart cities: A multidimensional performance measures", *Cities,* vol. 119, p. 103397, 2021.
[http://dx.doi.org/10.1016/j.cities.2021.103397]

[25]   C. Cantuarias-Villessuzanne, R. Weigel, and J. Blain, "Clustering of European smart cities to understand the cities' sustainability strategies", *Sustainability,* vol. 13, no. 2, p. 513, 2021.
[http://dx.doi.org/10.3390/su13020513]

[26]   C. Cantuarias-Villessuzanne, R. Weigel, and J. Blain, "Clustering of European smart cities to understand the cities' sustainability strategies", *Sustainability,* vol. 13, no. 2, p. 513, 2021.
[http://dx.doi.org/10.3390/su13020513]

[27]   M. Cavada, C. Rogers, and D. Hunt, "Smart cities: Contradicting definitions and unclear measures", *Proceedings of The 4th World Sustainability Forum,* 2014, Basel, Switzerland . [http://dx.doi.org/10.3390/wsf-4-f004]

[28]   M. Centenaro, L. Vangelista, A. Zanella, and M. Zorzi, "Long-range communications in unlicensed bands: The rising stars in the IoT and smart city scenarios", *IEEE Wirel. Commun.,* vol. 23, no. 5, pp. 60-67, 2016. [http://dx.doi.org/10.1109/MWC.2016.7721743]

[29]   A. Chakraborty, M. Jindal, and S. Gupta, "Post-COVID-19 view of Indian economy with emphasis on service sector: A regression implementation", *Pervasive Healthcare,* pp. 295-323, 2021. [http://dx.doi.org/10.1007/978-3-030-77746-3_19]

[30]   A. Chakraborty, M. Jindal, M.R. Khosravi, P. Singh, A. Shankar, and M. Diwakar, "A secure IoT-based cloud platform selection using entropy distance approach and fuzzy set theory", *Wirel. Commun. Mob. Comput.,* vol. 2021, pp. 1-11, 2021. [http://dx.doi.org/10.1155/2021/6697467]

[31]   C.C. Chan, C. Chen, S. Delaney, and A. Ferworn, "A Markerless high resolution structural health monitoring framework for smart cities", In: *IEEE Technology & Engineering Management Conference - Europe.,* 2021.Dubrovnik, Croatia. [http://dx.doi.org/10.1109/TEMSCON-EUR52034.2021.9488617]

[32]   A. Chaudhuri, "Internet of things, for things, and by things", *IoT-enabled smart cities,* pp. 103-123, 2018. [http://dx.doi.org/10.1201/9781315200644-5]

[33]   T.C.T. Chen, "Ubiquitous clinic recommendation by predicting a patient's preferences", *Electron. Commerce Res. Appl.,* vol. 23, pp. 14-23, 2017. [http://dx.doi.org/10.1016/j.elerap.2017.04.003]

[34]   F. De Filippi, C. Coscia, and R. Guido, "From smart-cities to smart-communities", *Int. J. E-Plan. Res.,* vol. 8, no. 2, pp. 24-44, 2019. [http://dx.doi.org/10.4018/IJEPR.2019040102]

[35]   J.C.F. De Guimarães, E.A. Severo, L.A. Felix Júnior, W.P.L.B. Da Costa, and F.T. Salmoria, "Governance and quality of life in smart cities: Towards sustainable development goals", *J. Clean. Prod.,* vol. 253, p. 119926, 2020. [http://dx.doi.org/10.1016/j.jclepro.2019.119926]

[36]   H.A. El Zouka, "An authentication scheme for wireless healthcare monitoring sensor network", *14th International Conference on Smart Cities: Improving Quality of Life Using ICT & IoT (HONET-ICT),* 2017, Irbid/Amman, Jordan. [http://dx.doi.org/10.1109/HONET.2017.8102205]

[37]   S. Escamilla Solano, P. Plaza Casado, and S. Flores Ureba, "undefined", *Innovation, Technology, and Knowledge Management,* pp. 65-77, 2016. [http://dx.doi.org/10.1007/978-3-319-40895-8_5]

[38]   "Federated learning for IoT applications", In: *EAI/Springer Innovations in Communication and Computing* Springer, 2022. [http://dx.doi.org/10.1007/978-3-030-85559-8]

[39]   "Future directions for smart cities", In. *Smart Cities* MIT Press, 2020. [http://dx.doi.org/10.7551/mitpress/11426.003.0007]

[40]   X. Gao, P. Pishdad-Bozorgi, D.R. Shelden, and S. Tang, "Internet of things enabled data acquisition framework for smart building applications", *J. Constr. Eng. Manage.,* vol. 147, no. 2, p. 04020169, 2021. [http://dx.doi.org/10.1061/(ASCE)CO.1943-7862.0001983]

[41]   R. Giffinger, and H. Kramar, "Benchmarking, profiling, and ranking of cities", *Performance Metrics for Sustainable Cities,* pp. 35-52, 2021.
[http://dx.doi.org/10.4324/9781003096566-4]

[42]   A. Homaifar, M. Jamshidi, Y. Seong, E.A. Doucette, A. Karimoddini, B.A. Erol, M.A. Khan, E. Tunstel, R.L. Roberts, R.F. Young, K. Snyder, and R.S. Swanson, "Operationalizing autonomy: A transition from the innovation space to real-world operations", *IEEE Syst. Man. Cybern. Mag.,* vol. 5, no. 4, pp. 23-32, 2019.
[http://dx.doi.org/10.1109/MSMC.2019.2935928]

[43]   *Intelligent Internet of things.* Springer, 2020.
[http://dx.doi.org/10.1007/978-3-030-30367-9]

[44]   M. Jindal, and A. Kazim, "Systematic review and deliberation of various multi-criteria decision-making techniques", *Multi-Criteria Decision Modelling,* pp. 189-204, 2021.
[http://dx.doi.org/10.1201/9781003125150-11-11]

[45]   A. Kazim, M. Jindal, R. Sharma, R. Choudhary, V. Kumar Sharma, and E. Bajal, "Big data analytics and artificial intelligence in business and marketing: Cloud security and encryption influencing business", *SSRN,* 2021.
[http://dx.doi.org/10.2139/ssrn.3884455]

[46]   N. Komninos, C. Bratsas, C. Kakderi, and P. Tsarchopoulos, "Smart City Ontologies: Improving the effectiveness of smart city applications", *J. Smart Cities,* vol. 1, no. 1, 2016.
[http://dx.doi.org/10.18063/JSC.2015.01.001]

[47]   K. Kotobi, and M. Sartipi, "Efficient and secure communications in smart cities using edge, caching, and blockchain", *2018 IEEE International Smart Cities Conference (ISC2),* 2018, Kansas City, MO, USA.
[http://dx.doi.org/10.1109/ISC2.2018.8656946]

[48]   R. Krishnamurthi, A. Nayyar, and A. Solanki, "Innovation opportunities through Internet of things (IoT) for smart cities", *Green and Smart Technologies for Smart Cities,* pp. 261-292, 2019.
[http://dx.doi.org/10.1201/9780429454837-13]

[49]   N. Kumar, D. Puthal, T. Theocharides, and S.P. Mohanty, "Unmanned aerial vehicles in consumer applications: New applications in current and future smart environments", *IEEE Consum. Electron. Mag.,* vol. 8, no. 3, pp. 66-67, 2019.
[http://dx.doi.org/10.1109/MCE.2019.2892278]

[50]   K. Kuru, and D. Ansell, "TCitySmartF: A comprehensive systematic framework for transforming cities into smart cities", *IEEE Access,* vol. 8, pp. 18615-18644, 2020.
[http://dx.doi.org/10.1109/ACCESS.2020.2967777]

[51]   K. Kuru, and W. Khan, "A framework for the synergistic integration of fully autonomous ground vehicles with smart city", *IEEE Access,* vol. 9, pp. 923-948, 2021.
[http://dx.doi.org/10.1109/ACCESS.2020.3046999]

[52]   A. Kylili, and P.A. Fokaides, "European smart cities: The role of zero energy buildings", *Sustain Cities Soc.,* vol. 15, pp. 86-95, 2015.
[http://dx.doi.org/10.1016/j.scs.2014.12.003]

[53]   Z. Li, R. Al Hassan, M. Shahidehpour, S. Bahramirad, and A. Khodaei, "A hierarchical framework for intelligent traffic management in smart cities", *IEEE Trans. Smart Grid,* vol. 10, no. 1, pp. 691-701, 2019.
[http://dx.doi.org/10.1109/TSG.2017.2750542]

[54]   F.Y. Liu, C.C. Chen, C.T. Cheng, C.T. Wu, C.P. Hsu, C.Y. Fu, S.C. Chen, C.H. Liao, and M.S. Lee, "Automatic hip detection in Anteroposterior pelvic radiographs—A Labelless practical framework", *J. Pers. Med.,* vol. 11, no. 6, p. 522, 2021.
[http://dx.doi.org/10.3390/jpm11060522] [PMID: 34200151]

[55]   E. Mardacany, "Smart cities characteristics: Importance of built environment components", *IET Conference on Future Intelligent Cities,* 2014.
[http://dx.doi.org/10.1049/ic.2014.0045]

[56]   M.L. Marsal-Llacuna, J. Colomer-Llinàs, and J. Meléndez-Frigola, "Lessons in urban monitoring taken from sustainable and livable cities to better address the Smart Cities initiative", *Technol. Forecast. Soc. Change,* vol. 90, pp. 611-622, 2015.
[http://dx.doi.org/10.1016/j.techfore.2014.01.012]

[57]   D. Miorandi, S. Sicari, F. De Pellegrini, and I. Chlamtac, "Internet of things: Vision, applications and research challenges", *Ad Hoc Netw.,* vol. 10, no. 7, pp. 1497-1516, 2012.
[http://dx.doi.org/10.1016/j.adhoc.2012.02.016]

[58]   M.H. Miraz, M. Ali, P.S. Excell, and R. Picking, "A review on Internet of things (IoT), internet of everything (IoE) and internet of Nano things (IoNT)", *Internet Technologies and Applications.,* 2015, Wrexham, UK.
[http://dx.doi.org/10.1109/ITechA.2015.7317398]

[59]   S. D. Mohamed Pero, "Summitry and leadership in regional organisations: Comparing ASEAN Summit and the European Council summit", *Leadership in Regional Community-Building,* pp. 185-220, 2019.
[http://dx.doi.org/10.1007/978-981-13-7976-5_6]

[60]   M. Molefi, E.D. Markus, and A. Abu-Mahfouz, "Wireless power transfer for IoT devices: A review", *2019 International Multidisciplinary Information Technology and Engineering Conference (IMITEC),* 2019, Vanderbijlpark, South Africa.
[http://dx.doi.org/10.1109/IMITEC45504.2019.9015869]

[61]   P. Neirotti, A. De Marco, A.C. Cagliano, G. Mangano, and F. Scorrano, "Current trends in smart city initiatives: Some stylised facts", *Cities,* vol. 38, pp. 25-36, 2014.
[http://dx.doi.org/10.1016/j.cities.2013.12.010]

[62]   A. Oliveira, and M. Campolargo, "From smart cities to human smart cities", *48th Hawaii International Conference on System Sciences,* 2015, Kauai, HI, USA.
[http://dx.doi.org/10.1109/HICSS.2015.281]

[63]   M.R. Palattella, M. Dohler, A. Grieco, G. Rizzo, J. Torsner, T. Engel, and L. Ladid, "Internet of things in the 5G era: Enablers, architecture, and business models", *IEEE J. Sel. Areas Comm.,* vol. 34, no. 3, pp. 510-527, 2016.
[http://dx.doi.org/10.1109/JSAC.2016.2525418]

[64]   K. Paskaleva, J. Evans, and K. Watson, "Co-producing smart cities: A Quadruple Helix approach to assessment", *Eur. Urban Reg. Stud.,* vol. 28, no. 4, pp. 395-412, 2021.
[http://dx.doi.org/10.1177/09697764211016037]

[65]   J. N. Pelton, and I. B. Singh, "Smart cities of today and tomorrow", In: *Better Technology, Infrastructure and Security* Springer, 2019.
[http://dx.doi.org/10.1007/978-3-319-95822-4]

[66]   D. Popescul, and L. D. Radu, "Data security in smart cities: Challenges and solutions", *Informatica Economica,* pp. 29-38, 2016.
[http://dx.doi.org/10.12948/issn14531305/20.1.2016.03]

[67]   N. Rocha, A. Dias, G. Santinha, M. Rodrigues, A. Queirós, and C. Rodrigues, "A systematic review of smart cities' applications to support active ageing", *Procedia Comput. Sci.,* vol. 160, pp. 306-313, 2019.
[http://dx.doi.org/10.1016/j.procs.2019.11.086]

[68]   L. Su, "Ecosystem energy analysis of Ningxia, China", *2011 International Conference on Electronics, Communications and Control (ICECC),* 2011.
[http://dx.doi.org/10.1109/ICECC.2011.6068024]

[69]   V. Sukhwani, R. Shaw, S. Deshkar, B.K. Mitra, and W. Yan, "Role of smart cities in optimizing water-energy-Food nexus: Opportunities in Nagpur, India", *Smart Cities,* vol. 3, no. 4, pp. 1266-1292, 2020.
[http://dx.doi.org/10.3390/smartcities3040062]

[70]   *Sustainable smart cities and smart villages research.* mdpi book, 2020.
[http://dx.doi.org/10.3390/books978-3-03928-219-7]

[71]   A. Tantau, and A.M.I. Şanta, "New energy policy directions in the European Union developing the concept of smart cities", *Smart Cities,* vol. 4, no. 1, pp. 241-252, 2021.
[http://dx.doi.org/10.3390/smartcities4010015]

[72]   "Transforming management with AI, big-data, and IoT", 2022.
[http://dx.doi.org/10.1007/978-3-030-86749-2]

[73]   M. Umair, M.A. Cheema, O. Cheema, H. Li, and H. Lu, "Impact of COVID-19 on IoT adoption in healthcare, smart homes, smart buildings, smart cities, transportation and industrial IoT", *Sensors,* vol. 21, no. 11, p. 3838, 2021.
[http://dx.doi.org/10.3390/s21113838] [PMID: 34206120]

[74]   X. Xia, X. Wu, S. BalaMurugan, and M. Karuppiah, "Effect of environmental and social responsibility in energy-efficient management models for smart cities infrastructure", *Sustain. Energy Technol. Assess.,* vol. 47, p. 101525, 2021.
[http://dx.doi.org/10.1016/j.seta.2021.101525]

[75]   C. Xu, X. Liao, J. Tan, H. Ye, and H. Lu, "Recent research progress of unmanned aerial vehicle regulation policies and technologies in urban low altitude", *IEEE Access,* vol. 8, pp. 74175-74194, 2020.
[http://dx.doi.org/10.1109/ACCESS.2020.2987622]

[76]   P. Xu, G. Dherbomez, E. Hery, A. Abidli, and P. Bonnifait, "System architecture of a driverless electric car in the grand cooperative driving challenge", *IEEE Intell. Transp. Syst. Mag.,* vol. 10, no. 1, pp. 47-59, 2018.
[http://dx.doi.org/10.1109/MITS.2017.2776135]

[77]   I. Yaqoob, I.A.T. Hashem, Y. Mehmood, A. Gani, S. Mokhtar, and S. Guizani, "Enabling communication technologies for smart cities", *IEEE Commun. Mag.,* vol. 55, no. 1, pp. 112-120, 2017.
[http://dx.doi.org/10.1109/MCOM.2017.1600232CM]

[78]   A. Zanella, N. Bui, A. Castellani, L. Vangelista, and M. Zorzi, "Internet of things for smart cities", *IEEE Internet Things J.,* vol. 1, no. 1, pp. 22-32, 2014.
[http://dx.doi.org/10.1109/JIOT.2014.2306328]

[79]   O. Zedadra, A. Guerrieri, N. Jouandeau, G. Spezzano, H. Seridi, and G. Fortino, "Swarm intelligence and IoT-based smart cities: A review", In: *The Internet of Things for Smart Urban Ecosystems Internet of Things,* F. Cicirelli, A. Guerrieri, C. Mastroianni, G. Spezzano, A. Vinci, Eds., Springer: Cham, 2018, pp. 177-200.
[http://dx.doi.org/10.1007/978-3-319-96550-5_8]

[80]   Z. Zhang, T. Jing, J. Han, Y. Xu, X. Li, and M. Gao, "ROI-based video transmission in heterogeneous wireless networks with multi-homed terminals", *IEEE Access,* vol. 5, pp. 26328-26339, 2017.
[http://dx.doi.org/10.1109/ACCESS.2017.2748138]

CHAPTER 5

Dynamic Involvement of Deep Learning and Big Data in Smart Cities

Nidhi Shah[1,*], **Arushi Kapoor**[2], **Namith Gupta**[3], **Vartika Agarwal**[4] and **Muskan Jindal**[4]

[1] *Department of Life Sciences, University of Mumbai, Mumbai, India*

[2] *Department of Biotechnology, Amity Institute of Biotechnology, Amity University, Noida, India*

[3] *Amity School of Engineering and Technology, Amity University, Noida, India*

[4] *Amity School of Engineering and Technology, Noida, Uttar Pradesh, India*

Abstract: Deep learning is an extension of Artificial Intelligence (AI) or cognitive learning that is used to optimize performance *via* the application of neural networks. And, big data analytics includes managing a plethora of continuous streams of data while obtaining valuable insights from them. Deep learning and Big Data analytics have been implemented in various avenues to obtain real-time optimized results, like biomedical applications, Computer Vision, and enhancing results for Internet of Things applications. This study aims to provide a deep insight into the application, performance, and values provided by Deep learning and Big-data analytics in the various intricacies of smart cities, smart governance and workflows in the same. Firstly, we provide applications or areas of smart cities that create Big-data, then provide techniques and literature where Big-data analytics is used to handle the same. Then, we present the different computing infrastructures used for IoT big data analytics, which include cloud, fog, and edge computing. Finally, we provide insights into various Deep learning modules that are successfully implemented in smart cities.

Keywords: Big Data Analytics, Deep Learning, Edge Computing and Neural Networks, Internet of Things.

INTRODUCTION

Recent times have observed a rapid growth in several new technologies like the smart grid, smart energies, and smart transportation. Among the major domains that take a leading role in information technology (ICT) include Big-data and the Internet of things (IoT) and Cloud computing (BIC). Without the evolution of IoT and big data analytics, the idea of a Smart City would have not been converted

---

* **Corresponding author Nidhi Shah:** Department of Life Sciences, University of Mumbai, Mumbai, India; E-mail: shahnidhi121@gmail.com

Satya Prakash Yadav, Sansar Singh Chauhan, Sanjeev Kumar Pippal and Victor Hugo C. de Albuquerque (Eds.)

into reality [1]. A major tool towards this transition was Deep Learning (DL), a machine learning technique that was used for understanding and classifying data. The usage of Deep Learning was further extended to urban modelling and infrastructure of Smart Cities. Today, the concept of Deep Learning is majorly used in Smart Education and Smart Health Solutions.

IoT enables the people of smart cities to be connected with the help of Smartphones and other sophisticated gadgets that significantly help in upgrading their quality of lifestyle. Deep learning rapidly changes the way people operate by facilitating better transportation, connectivity, healthcare, and education [1].

Geographic information system (GIS) is used for improving the road network. It includes the software, hardware and other arrangements for the purpose of accumulating, storing and disseminating significant information regarding different places on Earth [2].

The implementation of machine learning and deep learning in smart cities promises a bright prospect for the development of smart cities. With the help of a training model that can provide correct results with similar features, the concept of deep learning can be implemented in a better way [2]. The researchers would also focus on integrating such technologies in smart cities that would significantly enable improved interactions of smart devices. In the days to come, deep learning will have a huge impact on several different aspects like smart education, smart governance, transportation, health management, security and privacy [3].

Deep learning uses a network of multiple hidden layers interacting with each other. It is an effective way to detect and identify different human activities that go on in smart homes. The devices used in smart cities are usually portable and allow the users to use them anywhere and carry them during travel. However, they may not be as handy for senior citizens. It is therefore evident that deep learning will bring drastic changes in the way the cities operate but people might take some time to get accustomed to it. The datasets that are used to develop deep learning applications are not readily available mostly [3].

INTERNET OF THINGS (IOT)

IoT Architecture: It consists of 4 stages: Hardware, connectivity and communication middleware, big data storage, and analysis and IoT applications. Wearable and wireless sensors create and capture data that is later transformed Fig. (1) into actions by the actuators. The collected data from wireless sensors are saved in the cloud which is then transferred from the hardware stage to analytics tools *via* communication middleware and network connection. The valuable information is extracted after the analysis of the big data generated by IoT [4].

Characteristics of IoT generated Big Data: The characteristics of big data generated from IoT devices with five V's features are as follows Fig. (**2**):

i. Volume: Novel methods are in need for the processing of a humongous amount of generated data to draw out some useful insights.
ii. Variety: IoT data can be either unstructured, quasi-structured, semi-structured, or structured type formats.
iii. Velocity: Different IoT sensors and DL devices can be used to generate, save and move the data at high speed *via* internet procedures.
iv. Veracity: The obtained data from IoT devices must be corrected and validated.
v. Value: The importance and analysis of the obtained big data represent Value.

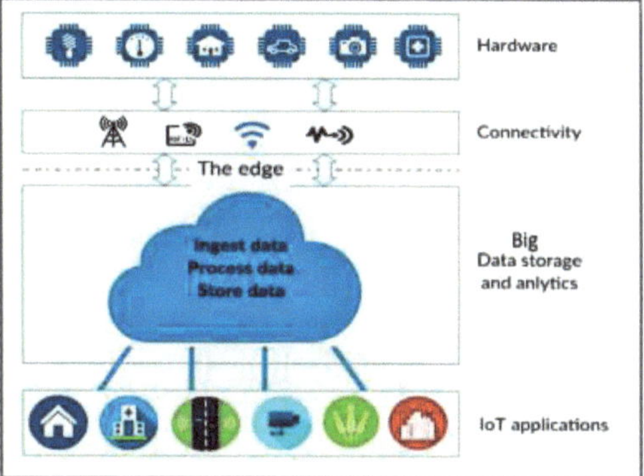

Fig. (1). Internet of Things- Architecture.

Fig. (2). The 5 V's of IoT generated Big Data.

The data generated is exponentially ever-increasing. Therefore, in accordance with vertical and horizontal scaling, software and hardware platforms can be employed to manage the IoT-generated big data within a limited time. Since datasets from one source cannot be the only basis of prediction through available information, the data fusion strategy provided better results than the single dataset technique.

Computational infrastructures for IoT big data Analytics: Over the last few years, the analysis of IoT big data has been upgraded in terms of precision, performance, and high memory requirements using DL techniques. Also, cloud, edge, and fog networks are designed [4].

Cloud Computing technology consists of servers and data centres that allow access to the data whenever in need. The main features of this computing are storage, service and applications over the internet. Cloud and Fog networks share similar services in terms of storage, implementation, and networking, but fog is only available for a particular topographical area and clouds do not depend on a specific area. Fog computing has limited bandwidth, issues with privacy, and low latency, like cloud networks.

Both, fog and edge networks are alternative branches of the cloud network that allow data analysis close to the source of created data. But the fog network is conducted near local servers and edge can be executed in smartphones. Edge computing is strategized to alleviate the limitations offered by cloud networks. It minimizes the utilization of energy, reduces network pressure and response time, increases the efficiency of the bandwidth, and provides easy processing of IoT-generated data Fig. (3). It is a remarkable platform utilized for the growth of urban cities.

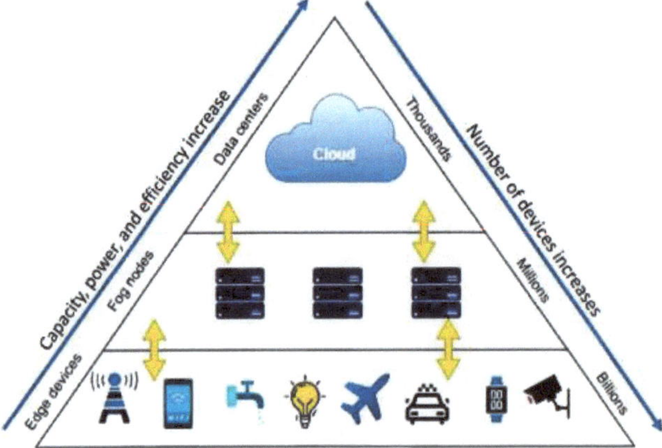

Fig. (3). Fog nodes connected to both Edge devices and cloud network.

Deep Learning

The computer's ability to perform tasks like image recognition and translation of languages requires human intelligence known as artificial intelligence. Over the past few years, artificial intelligence (AI) has become immensely popular due to the ease with which it allows users to complete tasks. AI provides training to computer programs using a specific dataset [5, 6]. Machine Learning (ML) is a subset of artificial intelligence (AI) that allows computer programs to learn the analytical behaviour. ML uses a dataset to train programs so that the programs can help them make correct decisions on their own without the need of being programmed to do so.

In recent years, deep learning (DL) has gained popularity, it is an advanced ML technique [7]. Deep learning models are learning models that have non-linear features and functions that contain a large amount of raw and complex data [8]. Deep learning models perform better than any other ML method [9]. Some practical applications of DL include the application of DL for extracting information from IoT devices [10].

Categories of Deep Learning techniques: Deep learning techniques have been categorised into categories such as supervised learning, unsupervised learning, semi-supervised learning and reinforcement learning as shown in the Fig. (**4**) below.

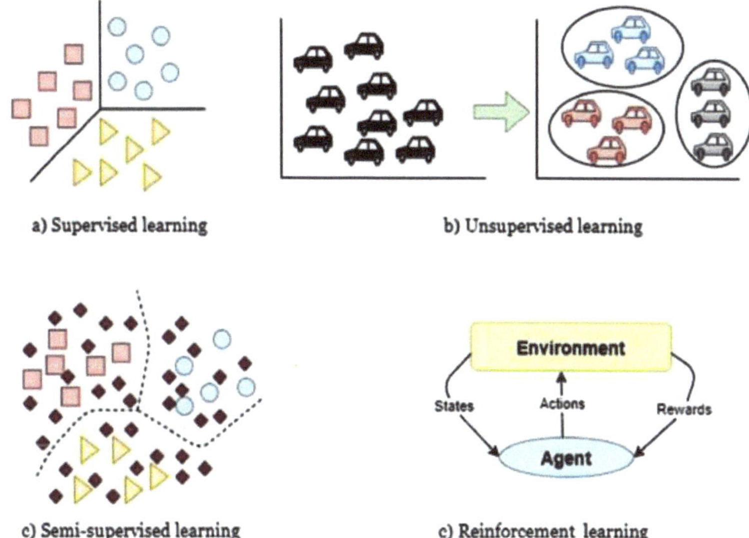

Fig. (4). Different types of learning techniques.

1. Supervised learning

This technique is used to estimate the outcomes for unknown data. In this technique, learning occurs by using the labelled training data that is available. Classification and regression are two widely used applications of supervised learning [11].

2. Unsupervised learning

This technique refers to learning models that use descriptive statistics techniques to understand the patterns that exist in data. The most common application of this technique is to find hidden data structures [12, 13].

3. Semi-supervised learning

This technique involves learning, where the dataset contains few labelled data with a large amount of unlabelled data [14].

4. Reinforcement learning

This technique lies between supervised and unsupervised learning. It allows the agent to learn from the environment thus allowing the agent to act independently [15]. Through this learning, the agent can interact with the environment directly and receive rewards that promote perfect behaviour. One of the most popular reinforcement techniques is Q-learning [16].

Deep Learning Architecture

The deep learning architecture is categorised into three classes by Deng. The three categories are-generative, discriminative and hybrid [17]. Discriminative deep learning architecture uses supervised learning. Generative deep learning uses an unsupervised learning approach. Hybrid deep learning uses both generative and discriminative models. (Fig. **5**) shows the deep learning techniques, their architecture and the different learning types.

Deep Learning Models and Algorithms

Deep learning models can be divided into different types based on the training required. There are two types of basic models; one is the supervised model that is trained using samples of a given dataset whereas the unsupervised models learn through data that is entered and do not have an outcome to learn from the Classical Neural Network. Convolutional Neural Network and Recurrent Neural Network are examples of a supervised model while the Denoising AutoEncoders is an example of an unsupervised model [18].

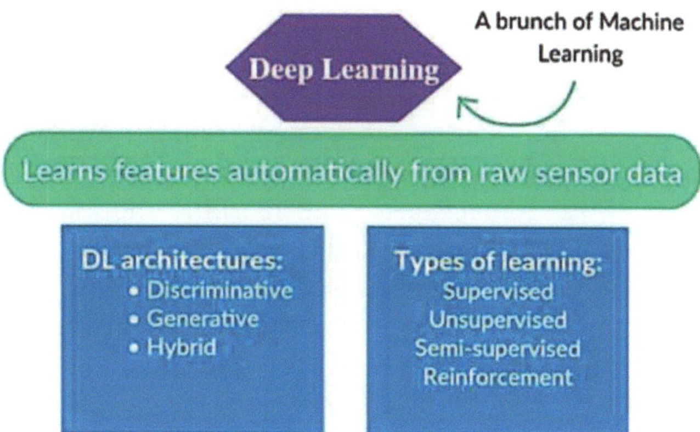

Fig. (5). Deep learning definitions, different architecture, and types of learning models.

Classical Neural Network: This model is a discriminative deep learning architecture type. There are three layers of this model, the input and output layer and the hidden layer. This model can adapt to the basic binary patterns through a series of inputs, simulating the learning patterns of a human brain. This model should be used when a tabular dataset is formatted.

Convolutional Neural Network (CNN): This model is a variation of classical artificial neural networks. This model can handle large amounts of complex data. It was built for image data and it helps in image classification. This model is mostly used when there is complexity in calculating the output of a dataset [19].

Recurrent Neural Networks (RNN): These networks are used to help in the prediction of sequences. Long short-term memory (LSTM) is a popular RNN algorithm. LSTM is a supervised deep learning algorithm that has various applications such as accident prediction, energy management and human activity recognition [20]. Some of the main applications are- pattern recognition, text categorisation and speech recognition.

Denoising AutoEncoders: They work automatically. They encode the input data and then perform an activation function followed by decoding of the data for output. This is mostly used when a recommendation system is to be built. It is also used for face recognition and energy consumption [21].

Non-Intrusive Load Monitoring (NILM): This is an algorithm that is used to infer the appliance level energy consumption from aggregate measurements of voltage and/or current to help monitor electricity consumption effectively. It helps in a better understanding of energy consumption and better demand response [22].

Applications of Deep Learning

Deep learning has various applications in smart cities. Deep learning can be used in many sectors such as the health, energy and transportation systems of smart cities. As summarised in the Table (**1**), researchers like Luo *et al.* [23] and Vazquez Canteli *et al.* [24] have used deep learning models and techniques to come up with innovative alternatives and solutions for the energy demands of smart cities. Baba *et al.* [24] developed a sensor network that can be used for the detection of at-risk areas and violence in smart cities. Reddy and Mehta *et al.* [25] have developed a smart traffic system for the better and more effective management of smart cities. Muhammed *et al.* [26] used deep learning to improve the health sectors of smart cities. Madu *et al.* [27] proposed a framework that is used to evaluate the sustainability of using deep learning.

Table 1. Deep learning applications in smart cities.

Literature Reference	Applications	Application Domain
Ludo *et al.* [23]	Developing an energy prediction system for smart cities to increase energy efficiency and track the energy usage patterns.	Energy
Baba *et al.* [24]	Use of a sensor network system for detecting at-risk areas and areas with high rates of violence in smart cities	Security
Reddy and Mehta [28]	Use of a system for better traffic management in cities	Transportation systems
Vazques Canteli *et al* [25]	Development of an integrated system that manages energy efficiency in cities	Energy
Muhammad *et al.* [26]	Use of a healthcare framework that uses deep learning and big data technologies	Health
Madu *et al* [27]	Use of a framework that evaluated urban sustainability using the deep learning models	Management systems of smart cities

Use of Deep Learning in Smart City Application

The motive for creating sustainable smart cities is to intensify the optimum use of resources in short supply and improvise the quality of life by employing the Internet of things (IoT). The emergence of IoT introduces us to a new concept that is based on accessing the database put together through sensors or devices along with the applications of software platforms to retain the data on the cloud or fog servers that can be resolved by various deep learning (DL) techniques [4] Fig. (**6**). Its application includes a smart home with a personalized lifestyle, more convenient, easy monitoring of electrical appliances and devices; smart healthcare facilities with the application of sensors and actuators in patients and their prescribed medicines; smart transportation with effective control of traffic, pollution and security; smart urban governance for proper SC management involving public opinions on government policies in regard to urbanization; smart waste management; automation of industrial machinery with minimum human involvement and automatic regulation of productivity rates of the machines; introduction of innovative online learning methods for smart education [4, 29, 31].

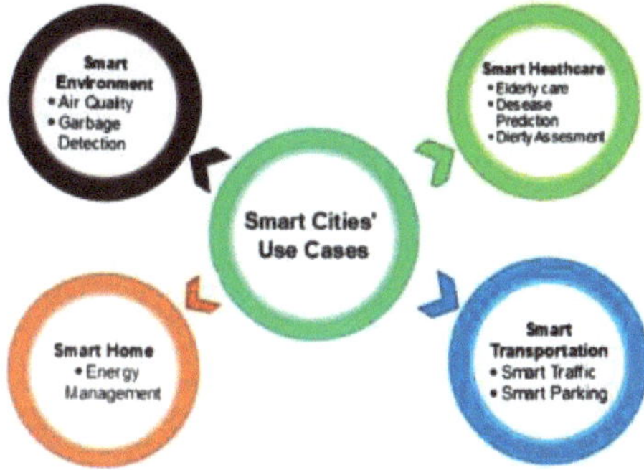

Fig. (6). Applications of IoT and DL in smart cities.

Smart Home

Typically, due to improper implementation of strategies of energy management, a building's energy consumption by different appliances is quite significant. Monitoring of energy usage by appliances in real time has now become easier due to the emergence of new technologies *i.e.* IoT and DL methods. All the smart devices, *viz.* washing machines, lights, air conditioners, television, refrigerators and more at residences are connected *via* the internet that communicate and exchange the gathered information about the current home state with the users. This way, smart homes ameliorate device management and optimize energy utilization.

As mentioned in Table (**2**), Manu *et al.* [30] designed a tri-axial accelerometer based on the LSTM model predicting different activities (walking, jogging, *etc*) by the residents of the home. Home automation systems like Bluetooth and Wi-Fi technology help in controlling the appliances, improving the safety of all the users specifically, for the elderly and disabled. Popa *et al.* [32] proposed a resourceful platform using different models that increase interoperability between sensors and actuators (such as a smart plug, multisensory, door sensor, energy meter and more) used in the environment in real-time, focusing on the reduction of energy consumption or utilisation of energy in the most efficient way and reducing the cost of electrical energy. Siddiqui and Sibal [33] developed a model that finds a balance between the energy efficiency and comfort of the users. For improving efficient energy consumption in smart homes, powerful infrastructures such as recommender systems are used. The model simulated around 80% and 85% accuracy using NILM and TFIDF algorithms, respectively Fig. (**7**). Yan *et al* [34] predicted a hybrid model of a combination between LSTM and the stationary wavelet technique (SWT) for the prediction of energy consumption.

Table 2. IoT Applications.

Case	IoT Application/ Device	Ref	DL Algorithm	Dataset	Computing Infrastructure
Smart Home	Energy Management	Yan *et al.* [34]	LSTM+SWT	*UK DALE*	Cloud Computing
-	-	Siddiqui & Sibal [33]	NILM+DAE+ TFIDF	*REDD*	-
-	Energy Management using sensors and actuators	Popa *et al.* [32]	LSTM+AEs	Authors used their own datasets	-
-	Tri axial Accelerometer	Manu *et al.* [30]	LSTM	*WISDM*	-
Smart Healthcare	Dietary Assessment	Liu *et al.* [36]	CNN	100 datasets	Edge computing
-	Care for Elders	Torti *et al.* [37]	RNN	*Sisfall* dataset	Cloud computing
-	-	Santos *et al.* [38]	CNN	*URFD* dataset	Fog Computing
-	Prediction of disease	Shi *et al.* [40]	CNN	*ImageNet* Dataser	Cloud Computing
-	-	Wang *et al.* [39]	RNN	Cardiology challenge dataset	Cloud computing
Smart Environment	Detection of Garbage	Zhang *et al.* [41]	CNN	A new garbage dataset created by Authors	Edge Computing
-	-	Wang *et al.* [42]	R-CNN	*Coco* dataset	Cloud Computing
-	Quality of Air	Athira *et al.* [43]	GRU	AirNet Dataset	Cloud computing
-	-	Mutis *et al.* [44]	LSTM + CNN	NADA dataset	Edge computing
Smart Transportation	Smart Parking	Bura *et al.* [47]	CNN	*CNRPark & PKlot* dataset	Edge Computing
-	Smart Traffic Management	Liu *et al.* [48]	RNN	*Taxi mobility* dataset	-

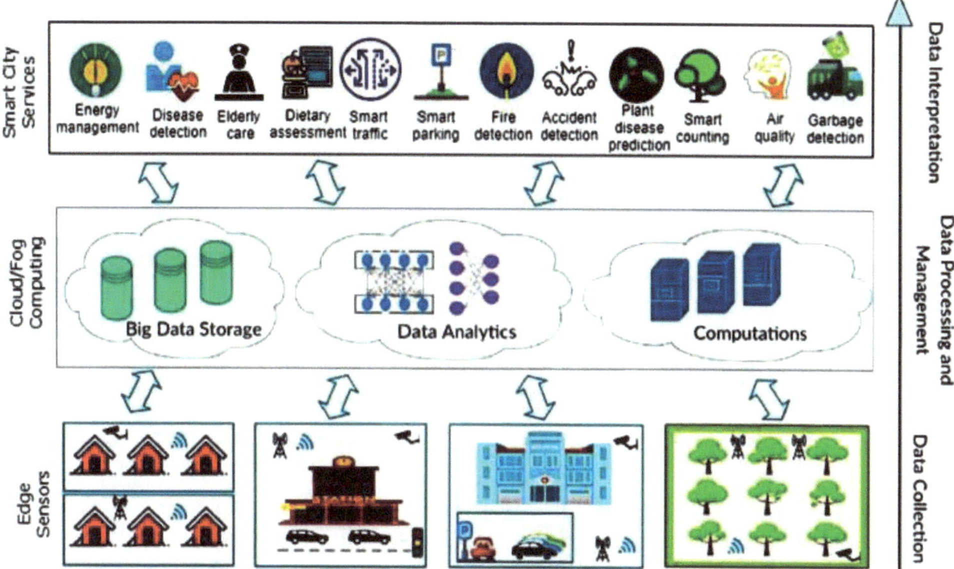

Fig. (7). Smart City Ecosystem.

Smart Healthcare

The IoT devices can help to record different health measurements involving the user's heartbeat, blood sugar levels, and temperature with minimum costs. These are linked to the internet and the data is reported directly to doctors (online). Smart healthcare gives the potential to monitor health and enhances the care of patients. For several healthcare facilities, such as dietary assessment, prediction of diseases and care of elders, a bunch of DL techniques have been proposed.

Liu *et al.* [35] suggest a CNN model using edge computing, an advanced computer-based system for the recognition of food for assessing accurate diet for evaluating the efficacy of weight loss interventions. RNN-embedded software in wireless devices proposed by Torti *et al.* [36] showed 98% accuracy in revealing the user's fall by notifying to a remote system. IoT techniques proposed by Santos *et al.* [37] include a model that uses CNN and fog computing for the detection of human fall and different human activities. The model using CNN has also been reported by Wang *et al.* [38] for the detection of Breast Arterial Calcification (BAC), an effective indication for the identification of coronary heart disease or cardiovascular diseases. Another CNN model was suggested by Shi *et al.* [39] using non-medical images to anticipate invasive diseases in ductal carcinoma patients.

Smart Environment

With the advancement of IoT and the availability of modernized sensors in smart cities since the past few years, the term environment monitoring has turned into a Smart environment monitoring (SEM) system. For the world to achieve sustainable growth and a healthy society, appropriate monitoring of the quality of air, pollution, and garbage management is necessary [4, 40].

A new approach proposed by Zhang *et al.* [41] for the cleanliness of smart cities involved the use of faster R-CNN to define various categories of wastes in the city that were extracted from the cameras of the vehicle on edge servers and later, the total amount of garbage was enumerated from the data transferred to the cloud. Another model using faster R-CNN and ResNet network algorithms was designed by Wang *et al.* [42] with the aim of improvising garbage assessment and management in smart cities for a healthier urban environment. Athira *et al.* [43] presented three DL models for the prediction of the quality of air using the AirNet Dataset. The DL model overcame the problems faced by traditional air quality prediction methods. Mutis *et al.* [44] proposed an automated indoor air quality sensing DL-based technique using visual sensors for occupancy sensing and analysed it using human motion techniques with the aim of improvising the indoor environment.

Smart Transportation

Large metro cities with sizable populations bear tremendous traffic loads that use a substantial amount of time as well as fuel, impairing roads and other infrastructure. Smart transportation involves the use of advanced and optimized devices based on DL models ameliorating the efficiency of transportation, safety and security of vehicles, managing crowd density and movement in the city, and providing innovative solutions for traffic management and smart parking [44 - 46].

Bura *et al.* [47] used an edge computing network and a CNN model providing solutions for smart parking that overcomes struggles of traffic congestion and unavailability of parking space in urban cities. Eventually, the emergence of cost-effective novel technological innovations that have become more adapted to systems such as the detection of license plates, vision-based parking spot detection, and smart-parking meters has replaced the expensive sensors that were deployed traditionally in parking lots. Edge devices in real-time propose an effective solution. The RNN model proposed by Liu *et al.* [48] predicts the mobility of vehicles in any area of the city in a particular prediction period.

Challenges of Deep Learning in Smart Cities

As the need for solutions of various problems has been delegated to technology and data, the reliance on Deep learning and Big data analytics has drastically increased, and with that, the challenges concerning the limitations have also been realized.

The rapid changes that deep learning have introduced in the city operation are a testament to the aforementioned discussions. Deep learning is now involved in the operation, support and maintenance of these smart cities and helps in local transportation, electricity supply, healthcare advancements, connectivity, and various other things [49].

However, even after major advancements in data collection and technologies used by data scientists, it still remains a challenge to effectively integrate suitable technologies and incorporate them within smart city services [50]. Some technological limitations include:

1. Data

Deep learning algorithms, like the human brain, depend heavily on training, and for training, large quantities of data sets are required by them to achieve desired results. Terabytes of data need to be provided by researchers and multiple parameters need to be defined for a model to run effectively. With more parameters, more data is needed for the training of the algorithm. The availability of such a huge corpus of data remains a challenge for any deep-learning algorithm

2. Overfitting in Neural Networks

The training of a model may differ from what input a model might get in unseen real-time data and because of a deficiency of training data pertaining to that situation, there might be an error in the deep learning model. Models that are typically trained for maximizing performance on training datasets usually suffer from this problem when unseen data is fed into the model.

3. Hyperparameter Optimization

Before any learning model is trained, there are certain parameters that need to be defined, these are called hyperparameters. Any changes to these parameters cause large changes in the performance of the model. The inability to modify hyperparameters in relevance to the model can impact the implementation of the model.

4. Hardware

Dealing with such large amounts of data and processing requires industry-grade hardware systems that can take the load of processing the data. These components are expensive and also consume a lot of energy. There is also an added cost of scaling down of this technology in industries to fit it within drones, robots and mobile devices.

5. Lack of Flexibility and Multitasking

Trained models of deep learning can achieve impressive efficiency and accuracy but are rarely modular to fit different domains of application. They are highly focused models that only work on specific applications.

The limitations and challenges don't only pertain to the deficit in specialists in the field or the technology, there are several other factors that affect the use of deep learning in smart cities [51].

With the demand to incorporate the new technologies with the existing services and departments, it is assumed that the initial investment towards these technologies is very expensive, but it is less understood that the implementation of such technologies will increase the efficiency and the output.

As these technologies will be implemented in real-time situations, it is required to collect historic data and also real-time data for these algorithms to work. It remains a difficult task to develop frameworks that utilize both big data and fast data analytics while being lightweight ML algorithms for resource-constrained devices ensuring security and privacy [52].

Future Trends in Smart Cities using Deep Learning

Deep learning models are based on transferring learning to solve problems. This type of learning requires few resources and is less time-consuming. There are various advantages linked with the use of deep learning in smart cities. Some of the advantages are:

1. Better service performance- Due to the deep learning methods which accelerate learning, a new task does not have to be started from scratch and previous knowledge can be used to complete the task faster.

2. Lesser time and efforts are required as the data is already available from various sources.

3. Multi-tasking helps to save time and efforts.

4. Smart cities use data analytics for the efficiency of several applications such as smart packing and elderly care applications.

Deep learning models find various applications and in the future, they will be used commonly in smart cities. The training model used in deep learning provides correct results when familiar data and models are used in both the training as well as testing of the data. Transfer learning is a model in which the training is transferred from one to another platform. In the future, researchers should focus on integrating technologies into smart city applications. This aids in better interaction between the user and the devices. In the future, technologies and devices would be more user-friendly and wearable. The integration of speech recognition technology in smart devices is another area of research. Some of the future applications are as follows:

1. Use of Mobile Data, 5g And 6g Along with Iot Analytics for Better Connectivity

Mobile devices are used as data collection platforms. Mobiles contain embedded communications sensors and detectors [53]. The data that is collected is processed by deep learning approaches and can be used to design solutions for smart cities. With the growing use of mobile devices, now 5G wireless networks that are scalable and have flexible platforms are being set-up to minimise the cost associated and also the power that is required. The new network system provides high rates of data transport with high reliability [54]. It surpasses the 4G network speed by 100x [55]. Using the new radio access technologies, 5 G network was developed. Using this wireless network in combination with software can help develop a smart city and create newer opportunities for IoT [56]. Research on new 6G networks can help to ease the growing demands due to the fast-growing mobile data traffic [57]. 6G technology can further help to reduce costs and help in efficient energy use.

2. Blockchain for Secure Networks

Blockchain technology is gaining popularity in the recent few years and helps in the implementation of security strategies. There are various other applications of a blockchain system. Blockchains use decentralised architectures and help to build a secure environment for IoT applications [58]. Blockchain technology is also used to manage processes between service providers and users [59].

3. Dependable IoT Analytics

Smart cities require systems that can detect malicious attacks and are dependable and scalable. Using deep learning approaches, many of the weaknesses of IoT applications in smart cities can be identified and solved to avoid system failures. IoT architecture needs to be expanded so that it can support the growing demands of smart city applications [60]. One of the most important IoT applications is to enhance the interaction between users and smart devices that play an important role in the smart city.

4. Privacy in Smart Cities

A recurring challenge faced by citizens of smart cities is the privacy issue. In smart cities, a large amount of data is collected and analysed so citizens often feel unsafe while sharing their data for the fear its misuse by companies or the government. There are various techniques by which the privacy of smart city citizens can be safeguarded. Some of these techniques are data distribution, data modification, data mining algorithms and privacy preservation [61]. Healthcare records and medical data are the most sensitive data and should be safeguarded [62]. More advanced techniques should be developed for specific applications. Laws and regulations also need to be enforced to protect the privacy of citizens [63].

5. Using Deep Learning from Knowledge Fusion

Smart cities collect large amounts of data that can often be interconnected together for better results. For example, bad weather can lead to traffic congestion which may lead to excess fuel consumption which in turn could lead to more air pollution which causes cardiovascular diseases. Smart cities use Cyber-Physical - Social systems and the data that is collected from cyber, physical and social environment contains different characteristics. This data can be correlated together to generate data that gives better results. The knowledge fusion technology requires techniques that can process such diverse data thus deep learning techniques are good for knowledge fusion technology [64].

6. Using Deep Learning for Distributed Intelligence

In smart cities, data is distributed by data centres to smaller units such as sensor nodes and gateways of wireless sensor networks. For this, computing devices are not powerful enough in comparison with servers in data centres. Thus, using deep learning, lightweight models can be designed. In smart cities, transfer learning can also help in the development of distributed intelligence systems [65].

CONCLUSION

Deep Learning and Big Data analytics are one of the most prominent advancements in that have created insights that could never have been achieved manually. With the emergence of smart cities and the integration of learning algorithms within these cities, the progress such smart cities make with the use of data and technologies is discussed. As said by the English poet John Dryden "He who would search for pearls must dive below." If we wish to search for solutions to problems, we must dive deeper than the surface data.

REFERENCES

[1]   C. Iwendi, P.K.R. Maddikunta, T.R. Gadekallu, K. Lakshmanna, A.K. Bashir, and M.J. Piran, "A metaheuristic optimization approach for energy efficiency in the IoT networks", *Softw. Pract. Exper.,* p. 1, 2020.

[2]   G.T. Reddy, M.P.K. Reddy, K. Lakshmanna, R. Kaluri, D.S. Rajput, G. Srivastava, and T. Baker, "Analysis of dimensionality reduction techniques on big data", *IEEE Access,* vol. 8, pp. 54776-54788, 2020.
[http://dx.doi.org/10.1109/ACCESS.2020.2980942]

[3]   M. Numan, F. Subhan, W.Z. Khan, S. Hakak, S. Haider, G.T. Reddy, A. Jolfaei, and M. Alazab, "A systematic review on clone node detection in static wireless sensor networks", *IEEE Access,* vol. 8, pp. 65450-65461, 2020.
[http://dx.doi.org/10.1109/ACCESS.2020.2983091]

[4]   S.B. Atitallah, M. Driss, W. Boulila, and H.B. Ghézala, "Leveraging Deep Learning and IoT big data analytics to support the smart cities development: Review and future directions", *Comput. Sci. Rev.,* vol. 38, p. 100303, 2020.
[http://dx.doi.org/10.1016/j.cosrev.2020.100303]

[5]   J. Qiu, Q. Wu, G. Ding, Y. Xu, and S. Feng, "A survey of machine learning for big data processing", *EURASIP J. Adv. Signal Process.,* vol. 2016, no. 1, p. 67, 2016.
[http://dx.doi.org/10.1186/s13634-016-0355-x]

[6]   R. Mitchell, J. Michalski, and T. Carbonell, "An artificial intelligence approach", Available from: https://link.springer.com/content/pdf/10.1007/978-3-662-12405-5. pdf

[7]   Y. LeCun, Y. Bengio, and G. Hinton, "Deep learning", *Nature,* vol. 521, no. 7553, pp. 436-444, 2015.
[http://dx.doi.org/10.1038/nature14539] [PMID: 26017442]

[8]   Xue-Wen Chen, and Xiaotong Lin, "Big data deep learning: Challenges and perspectives", *IEEE Access,* vol. 2, pp. 514-525, 2014. Available at: https://ieeexplore.ieee.org/abstract/document/6817512/
[http://dx.doi.org/10.1109/ACCESS.2014.2325029]

[9]   R. Shokri, and V. Shmatikov, "Privacy-preserving deep learning", *Proceedings of the 22nd ACM SIGSAC Conference on Computer and Communications Security,* 2015, pp. 1310-1321.

[10]   H. Li, K. Ota, and M. Dong, "Learning IoT in edge: Deep learning for the internet of things with edge computing", *IEEE Netw.,* vol. 32, no. 1, pp. 96-101, 2018.
[http://dx.doi.org/10.1109/MNET.2018.1700202]

[11]   E. Brynjolfsson, and A. Mcafee, "The business of artificial intelligence", *Harvard Bus. Rev.,* 2017pp. 1-20. Available at: https://hbr.org/cover-story/2017/07/the-businessof-artificial-

[12]   D. James, "Unsupervised Learning", In: *Springer Texts in Statistics* Springer, 2013, pp. 373-418.
[http://dx.doi.org/10.1007/978-1-4614-7138-7_10]

[13]   T. Hastie, and R. Tibshirani, "Unsupervised learning", In: *Elements Stat. Learn.* Springer, 2009, pp. 485-585.https://link.springer.com/content/pdf/10

[14]   D.P. Kingma, D.J. Rezende, S. Mohamed, and M. Welling, "Semi-supervised learning with deep generative models", In: *Advances in Neural Information Processing Systems*, 2014, pp. 3581-3589.

[15]   H. van Hasselt, A. Guez, and D. Silver, Deep reinforcement learning with double q-learning. 2015 Available at: www.aaai.org

[16]   H. van Hasselt, A. Guez, and D. Silver, "Deep reinforcement learning with double q-learning", *Thirtieth AAAI Conference on Artificial Intelligence,* vol. 30, 2016, p. 1.

[17]   L. Deng, "A tutorial survey of architectures, algorithms, and applications for deep learning", *APSIPA Trans. Signal. Inf. Process.,* vol. 3, no. 1, p. 3, 2014.
[http://dx.doi.org/10.1017/atsip.2013.9]

[18]   G. James, D. Witten, T. Hastie, and R. Tibshirani, "Unsupervised Learning", In: *In: An Introduction to Statistical Learning.* vol. 103. Springer: New York, NY, 2013, pp. 373-418.
[http://dx.doi.org/10.1007/978-1-4614-7138-7_10]

[19]   J. Gu, Z. Wang, J. Kuen, L. Ma, A. Shahroudy, B. Shuai, T. Liu, X. Wang, G. Wang, J. Cai, and T. Chen, "Recent advances in convolutional neural networks", *Pattern Recognit.,* vol. 77, pp. 354-377, 2018. Available at: https://www.sciencedirect.com/science/article/pii/S0031320317304120
[http://dx.doi.org/10.1016/j.patcog.2017.10.013]

[20]   Olah. "Understanding LSTM networks". 2015. https://colah.github.io/posts/2015-08-Understandig-LSTMs/

[21]   H.I. Suk, S.W. Lee, and D. Shen, "Latent feature representation with stacked auto-encoder for AD/MCI diagnosis", *Brain Struct. Funct.,* vol. 220, no. 2, pp. 841-859, 2015.
[http://dx.doi.org/10.1007/s00429-013-0687-3] [PMID: 24363140]

[22]   J. Kelly, and W. Knottenbelt, "Neural nilm: Deep neural networks applied to energy disaggregation", Proceedings of the 2nd ACM International Conference on Embedded Systems for Energy-efficient Built Environments, pp. 55-64, 2015.
[http://dx.doi.org/10.1145/2821650.2821672]

[23]   H. Luo, H. Cai, H. Yu, Y. Sun, Z. Bi, and L. Jiang, "A short-term energy prediction system based on edge computing for smart city", *Future Gener. Comput. Syst.,* vol. 101, pp. 444-457, 2019.
[http://dx.doi.org/10.1016/j.future.2019.06.030]

[24]   J.R. Vázquez-Canteli, S. Ulyanin, J. Kämpf, and Z. Nagy, "Fusing TensorFlow with building energy simulation for intelligent energy management in smart cities", *Sustain Cities Soc.,* vol. 45, pp. 243-257, 2019.
[http://dx.doi.org/10.1016/j.scs.2018.11.021]

[25]   D.V.S. Reddy, and R.V.K. Mehta, "Smart traffic management system for smart cities using reinforcement learning algorithm", *Int. J. Recent Technol. Eng.,* vol. 7, no. 6, pp. 12-15, 2019.

[26]   T. Muhammed, R. Mehmood, A. Albeshri, and I. Katib, "Ube Health: A personalized ubiquitous cloud and edge-enabled networked healthcare system for smart cities", *IEEE Access,* vol. 6, pp. 32258-32285, 2018.
[http://dx.doi.org/10.1109/ACCESS.2018.2846609]

[27]   C.N. Madu, C. Kuei, and P. Lee, "Urban sustainability management: A deep learning perspective", *Sustain Cities Soc.,* vol. 30, pp. 1-17, 2017.
[http://dx.doi.org/10.1016/j.scs.2016.12.012]

[28]   M. Baba, V. Gui, C. Cernazanu, and D. Pescaru, "A sensor network approach for violence detection in smart cities using deep learning", *Sensors,* vol. 19, no. 7, p. 1676, 2019.
[http://dx.doi.org/10.3390/s19071676] [PMID: 30965646]

[29]   E. Al Nuaimi, H. Al Neyadi, N. Mohamed, and J. Al-Jaroodi, "Applications of big data to smart cities", *J. Internet Serv. Appl.,* vol. 6, no. 1, p. 25, 2015.
[http://dx.doi.org/10.1186/s13174-015-0041-5]

[30]   R. Manu, "Smart Home Automation using IoT and Deep Learning", *IRJET,* 2019.

[31]   S. Bhattacharya, S. Somayaji, T. Gadekallu, M. Alazab, and P. Maddikunta, "A review on deep learning for future smart cities", *Internet Technol. Lett.,* 2020.

[32]   D. Popa, F. Pop, C. Serbanescu, and A. Castiglione, "Deep learning model for home automation and energy reduction in a smart home environment platform", *Neural Comput. Appl.,* vol. 31, no. 5, pp. 1317-1337, 2019.
[http://dx.doi.org/10.1007/s00521-018-3724-6]

[33]   S. Abdul, and S. Ananya, "Energy disaggregation in smart home appliances: A deep learning approach", *Energy,* 2002.

[34]   K. Yan, W. Li, Z. Ji, M. Qi, and Y. Du, "A hybrid LSTM neural network for energy consumption forecasting of individual households", *IEEE Access,* vol. 7, pp. 157633-157642, 2019.
[http://dx.doi.org/10.1109/ACCESS.2019.2949065]

[35]   C. Liu, Y. Cao, Y. Luo, G. Chen, V. Vokkarane, M. Yunsheng, S. Chen, and P. Hou, "A new deep learning-based food recognition system for dietary assessment on an edge computing service infrastructure", *IEEE Trans. Serv. Comput.,* vol. 11, no. 2, pp. 249-261, 2018.
[http://dx.doi.org/10.1109/TSC.2017.2662008]

[36]   E. Torti, A. Fontanella, M. Musci, N. Blago, D. Pau, F. Leporati, and M. Piastra, "Embedded real-time fall detection with deep learning on wearable devices", *21st Euromicro Conference on Digital System Design (DSD),* 2018, pp. 405-412.
[http://dx.doi.org/10.1109/DSD.2018.00075]

[37]   G. Santos, P. Endo, K. Monteiro, E. Rocha, I. Silva, T. Lynn, and T. Lynn, "Accelerometer-based human fall detection using convolutional neural networks", *Sensors,* vol. 19, no. 7, p. 1644, 2019.
[http://dx.doi.org/10.3390/s19071644] [PMID: 30959877]

[38]   J. Wang, H. Ding, F.A. Bidgoli, B. Zhou, C. Iribarren, S. Molloi, and P. Baldi, "Detecting cardiovascular disease from mammograms with deep learning", *IEEE Trans. Med. Imaging,* vol. 36, no. 5, pp. 1172-1181, 2017.
[http://dx.doi.org/10.1109/TMI.2017.2655486] [PMID: 28113340]

[39]   B. Shi, L. Grimm, and M. Mazurowski, "Prediction of occult invasive disease in ductal carcinoma in situ using deep learning features", *J. Am. Coll. Radio,* 2018.
[http://dx.doi.org/10.1016/j.jacr.2017.11.036]

[40]   S.L. Ullo, and G.R. Sinha, "Advances in smart environment monitoring systems using IoT and sensors", *Sensors,* vol. 20, no. 11, p. 3113, 2020.
[http://dx.doi.org/10.3390/s20113113] [PMID: 32486411]

[41]   P. Zhang, Q. Zhao, J. Gao, W. Li, and J. Lu, "Urban Street cleanliness assessment using mobile edge computing and deep learning", *IEEE Access,* vol. 7, pp. 63550-63563, 2019.
[http://dx.doi.org/10.1109/ACCESS.2019.2914270]

[42]   X. Wang, Y. Han, V.C.M. Leung, D. Niyato, X. Yan, and X. Chen, "Convergence of edge computing and deep learning: A comprehensive survey", *IEEE Communications Surveys & Tutorials,* vol. 22, no. 2, pp. 869-904, 2020.
[http://dx.doi.org/10.1109/COMST.2020.2970550]

[43]   P. Athira, "Deep AirNet: Applying recurrent networks for air quality prediction", *Procedia Comput. Sci.,* 2018.

[44]   I. Mutis, A. Ambekar, and V. Joshi, "Real-time space occupancy sensing and human motion analysis using deep learning for indoor air quality control", *Autom. Constr.,* p. 116, 2020.
[http://dx.doi.org/10.1016/j.autcon.2020.103237]

[45]   S. Khan, S. Nazir, I. García-Magariño, and A. Hussain, "Deep learning-based urban big data fusion in smart cities: Towards traffic monitoring and flow-preserving fusion", *Comput. Electr. Eng.,* vol. 89, p. 106906, 2021.
[http://dx.doi.org/10.1016/j.compeleceng.2020.106906]

[46]   M. Zichichi, S. Ferretti, and G. D'Angelo, "A distributed ledger based infrastructure for smart transportation system and social good", *2020 IEEE 17Th Annual Consumer Communications & Networking Conference.,* 2020, Las Vegas, NV, USA.
[http://dx.doi.org/10.1109/CCNC46108.2020.9045640]

[47]   H. Bura, N. Lin, and N. Kumar, "An edge based smart parking solution using camera networks and deep learning", *2018 IEEE International Conference on Cognitive Computing, ICCC,* 2018, pp. 17-24 San Francisco, CA, USA.
[http://dx.doi.org/10.1109/ICCC.2018.00010]

[48]   W. Liu, "Applying deep recurrent neural network to predict vehicle mobility", *2018 IEEE Vehicular Networking Conference,* 2018, Taipei, Taiwan.
[http://dx.doi.org/10.1109/VNC.2018.8628362]

[49]   T. Kurc, S. Bakas, X. Ren, A. Bagari, A. Momeni, Y. Huang, L. Zhang, A. Kumar, M. Thibault, Q. Qi, Q. Wang, A. Kori, O. Gevaert, Y. Zhang, D. Shen, M. Khened, X. Ding, G. Krishnamurthi, J. Kalpathy-Cramer, J. Davis, T. Zhao, R. Gupta, J. Saltz, and K. Farahani, "Segmentation and classification in digital pathology for glioma research: Challenges and deep learning approaches", *Front. Neurosci.,* vol. 14, p. 27, 2020.
[http://dx.doi.org/10.3389/fnins.2020.00027] [PMID: 32153349]

[50]   P. Angelov, and A. Sperduti, "Challenges in deep learning", 2016.

[51]   A. Arpteg, B. Brinne, L. Crnkovic-Friis, and J. Bosch, "Software engineering challenges of deep learning", *2018 44th Euromicro Conference on Software Engineering and Advanced Applications (SEAA),* 2018, pp. 50-59 Prague, Czech Republic.
[http://dx.doi.org/10.1109/SEAA.2018.00018]

[52]   J. Hestness, N. Ardalani, and G. Diamos, "Beyond human-level accuracy: Computational challenges in deep learning", *Proceedings of the 24th Symposium on Principles and Practice of Parallel Programming,* 2019, pp. 1-14.
[http://dx.doi.org/10.1145/3293883.3295710]

[53]   P. Sundsøy, J. Bjelland, B-A. Reme, A.M. Iqbal, and E. Jahani, "Deep learning applied to mobile phone data for individual income classification", *Proceedings of the 2016 International Conference on Artificial Intelligence: Technologies and Applications,* 2016. Available at: https://www.atlantis-press.com/proceedings/icaita-16/25849475
[http://dx.doi.org/10.2991/icaita-16.2016.24]

[54]   I.U. Din, H. Asmat, and M. Guizani, "A review of information centric network-based internet of things: Communication architectures, design issues, and research opportunities", *Multimedia Tools Appl.,* vol. 78, no. 21, pp. 30241-30256, 2019.
[http://dx.doi.org/10.1007/s11042-018-6943-z]

[55]   D. Minoli, and B. Occhiogrosso, "Practical aspects for the integration of 5g networks and IoT applications in smart cities environments", *Wirel. Commun. Mob. Comput.,* vol. 2019, pp. 1-30, 2019.
[http://dx.doi.org/10.1155/2019/5710834]

[56]   S.R. S, T. Dragičević, P. Siano, and S.R.S. Prabaharan, "Future generation 5g wireless networks for smart grid: A comprehensive review", *Energies,* vol. 12, no. 11, p. 2140, 2019.
[http://dx.doi.org/10.3390/en12112140]

[57]   M. Agiwal, A. Roy, and N. Saxena, "Next generation 5g wireless networks: A comprehensive survey", *IEEE Commun. Surv. Tutor.,* vol. 18, no. 3, pp. 1617-1655, 2016. Available from: https://ieeexplore.ieee.org/abstract/document/7414384/
[http://dx.doi.org/10.1109/COMST.2016.2532458]

[58]   T.M. Fernández-Caramés, and P. Fraga-Lamas, "A review on the use of blockchain for the internet of things", *IEEE Access,* vol. 6, pp. 32979-33001, 2018. Available from: https://ieeexplore.ieee.org/abstract/document/8370027/
[http://dx.doi.org/10.1109/ACCESS.2018.2842685]

[59]   M. Ali, M. Vecchio, and M. Pincheira, "Tutorials, applications of blockchains in the internet of things: A comprehensive survey", *IEEE Commun. Surv. Tutor.,* pp. 1676-1717, 2018. Available from: https://ieeexplore.ieee.org/abstract/document/8580364/

[60]   A. Chakraborty, M. Jindal, and S. Gupta, Post-COVID-19 view of indian economy with emphasis on service sector: A regression implementation. *Pervasive Healthcare.* Springer: Cham, 2022, pp. 295-323.
[http://dx.doi.org/10.1007/978-3-030-77746-3_19]

[61]   M. Jindal, and A. Kazim, "11 systematic review and deliberation of various multi-criteria decision-making techniques", *Multi-Criteria Decision Modelling,* pp. 189-204, 2021.

[62]   A. Chakraborty, M. Jindal, M.R. Khosravi, P. Singh, A. Shankar, and M. Diwakar, "A secure iot-based cloud platform selection using entropy distance approach and fuzzy set theory", *Wirel. Commun. Mob. Comput.,* vol. 2021, pp. 1-11, 2021.
[http://dx.doi.org/10.1155/2021/6697467]

[63]   A. Kazim, M. Jindal, R. Sharma, R. Choudhary, V. Kumar Sharma, and E. Bajal, "Big data analytics and artificial intelligence in business and marketing: Cloud security and encryption influencing business", *Proceedings of the International Conference on Innovative Computing & Communication (ICICC) 2021,* 2021.
[http://dx.doi.org/10.2139/ssrn.3884455]

[64]   F. Al-Turjman, S.P. Yadav, M. Kumar, V. Yadav, and T. Stephan, *Transforming management with AI.Big-Data, and IoT* Springer, 2022.

[65]   S. P. Yadav, B. S. Bhati, D. P. Mahato, and S. Kumar, *Federated learning for IoT applications* Springer, 2022.
[http://dx.doi.org/10.1007/978-3-030-85559-8]

CHAPTER 6

IoT Enabled Energy Optimization Through an Intelligent Home Automation

N. Chitra Kiran[1,*], J. Viswanatha Rao[2], Sagaya Aurelia[3], M. G. Skanda[4] and M. Lakshminarayana[5]

[1] *Department of Electronics and Communication Engineering, Alliance University, Bengaluru, Karnataka, India*

[2] *VNR Vignana Jyothi Institute of Engineering and Technology, Hyderabad, India*

[3] *Department of Computer Science, CHRIST University, Bengaluru, Karnataka, India*

[4] *Department of Industrial & Production Engineering, JSS S&T University, (SJCE) Mysore, India*

[5] *Department of Medical Electronics Engineering, M S Ramaiah Institute Of Technology, Bengaluru, Karnataka, India*

Abstract: The benefit of IoT devices is that they allow for automation; nevertheless, billions of connected devices connected with one another waste a substantial amount of energy. IoT systems will have difficulty in wide adoption if the energy requirements are not adequately managed. This study proposes a solution for IoT devices to regulate their energy consumption. Both hardware and software aspects are taken into consideration. Using a mobile computer or smartphone with Internet connectivity to interact with actual scenarios has grown more prevalent as technology has advanced over the years. An intelligent home automation system based on android applications has been developed to save electricity and human energy. This study aims to create comprehensive Energy optimization through intelligent home automation utilizing widely available mobile applications and Wi-Fi technologies. The devices are turned on and off using Wi-Fi. Intelligent home, in the area of electronics, automation is the most purposely misused term. Numerous technological revolutions have occurred as a result of this demand for automation. These were more essential than any other technologies due to their ease of use. These can be used in place of household current switches, resulting in sparks and, in rare instances, such as fires. A unique energy optimization system was developed to control household appliances while taking advantage of Wi-Fi benefits.

Keywords: Automation, IoT, Optimization, Wi-Fi.

---

[*] **Corresponding author N. Chitra Kiran:** Department of Electronics and Communication Engineering, Alliance University, Bengaluru, Karnataka, India; E-mail: chitrakiran555@gmail.com

1. INTRODUCTION

Because of the world's rapid population growth, power producers have had difficulty projecting electricity consumption. There will be a shortage of energy in a few years according to scientists. Energy generation is a costly option, taking a lot of time and money, but on the other side, energy consumption can be minimized by applying some preventive measures [1]. The last few decades have seen a plethora of research on energy consumption prediction and energy forecasting is the first step in optimizing energy use. As a result of our recent energy consumption, we must make a prognosis for the following hour, or month; as devices need the same amount of energy continually, using the concept of energy optimization in smart homes would ensure that the appliances are receiving the exact amount of electricity they require. Humidity, illumination, humidity, air velocity, and pollution levels are just a few factors that influence the optimization process [2].

The swarm-like collaboration of IoT devices is required for the successful deployment of IoT services as well as the development of renewable energy implementations. The primary purpose of IoT nodes is to gather information about the physical world. A battery-powered detector, a controller, and a communication network make up the hardware of an IoT device. The purpose of a sensor is to collect data from its surroundings. Data can include flow velocity, temps, pressure, physical motions, distances, weight, and so on. The data is then processed on the device before being sent through the communication network to other servers [3]. The essential components of the IoT environment are represented in Fig. (**1**).

Sensors are Internet of Things (IoT) devices that gather, process, and transfer data to its intended location. As a result, sensors are the IoT system's power hogs. The devices' limited battery life is a significant roadblock to full-fledged IoT usage. Large volumes of data can only be collected and processed at a higher cost of power usage. According to the study, the governing technology regulating IoT devices uses about 81 percent of an embedded system's total energy consumption. Unreliable software has been demonstrated to drive energy-efficient hardware inefficiently, which results in larger power consumption. Furthermore, the gadgets are unaware of a feedback mechanism that might notify consumers of an algorithm's power use [4].

In smart houses, a wide range of IoT applications can be explored. An intelligent home attempts to provide certain services which support the consumer's satisfaction and enjoyment, as opposed to a traditional home, which is a combination of simple housing and furniture to provide a place to live. As a result of IoT-related battery difficulties and the rapid increase in power requirements, many studies on alternative energy have lately been conducted. This form of novel energy generation, on the other hand, demands a long-term, large-scale investigation, making it a highly uncertain, forward-looking endeavor. To address these difficulties, autonomous and efficient network processing is required and a method for decreasing excessive energy consumption by precisely regulating IoT based on user usage patterns [5]. To address these concerns, IoT users' usage data must be studied, and an intelligent manager as a platform to monitor and manage this analyzed data is necessary. The term "intelligent supervisor" refers to a manager who provides services such as network technology to reduce energy usage, as well as services that create a customized environment for the user in line with the objective of a smart home. IoT platforms currently offer intelligent services; nonetheless, the great majority of these services process huge volumes of data and perform mathematical operations faster and more precisely than a human. By analyzing and assessing user data, a smart home intelligent manager maintains groupings of devices and provides user-customized services [6]. As a result, smart houses can foresee and plan for a variety of situations and scenarios. These forecasts and preparations allow IoT applications to be regulated and managed depending on the data received, reducing network utilization and energy losses. The purpose of this research is to employ a user-friendly, low-cost design that is also simple to install to control household appliances in a smart home. This technology makes the system unique in that it can be accessed from anywhere with an internet connection. The use of Arduino programs to offer the user with a remote control of multiple lights, fans, and appliances in their home, as well as data storage on the cloud, is presented. They will be able to operate on their own thanks to sensors. Sensors will allow them to be controlled autonomously [7].

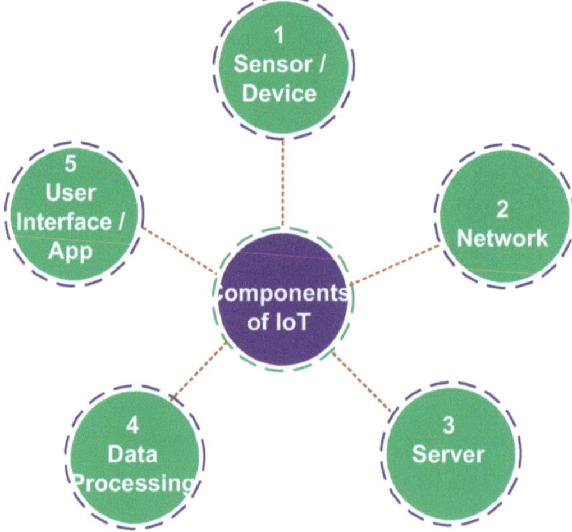

Fig. (1). IoT System Elements.

2. BACKGROUND AND MOTIVATION

Concerns about global warming and local air pollution, a scarcity of water for thermal power generation, and the finite nature of fossil energy resources highlight the critical need for efficient power utilization and the use of renewable energy sources. According to many studies, a non-fossil energy system is practically difficult to realize without efficient energy use and/or reductions in energy consumption, as well as a high level of renewable energy integration, both at the national and provincial levels.

Energy supply, which includes upstream refining processes, energy conversion processes, which include the supply and distribution of energy carriers, and energy demand, which includes energy consumption in buildings, transportation, and industry, are the three major components of the energy supply chain. These three elements, as well as their constituents, are depicted in Fig. (**2**). The goal of this article is to show how the Internet of Things (IoT) can assist with various aspects of the energy supply chain. This project's goal is to show how the Internet of Things can help with energy efficiency, demand reduction, and greater renewable energy use.

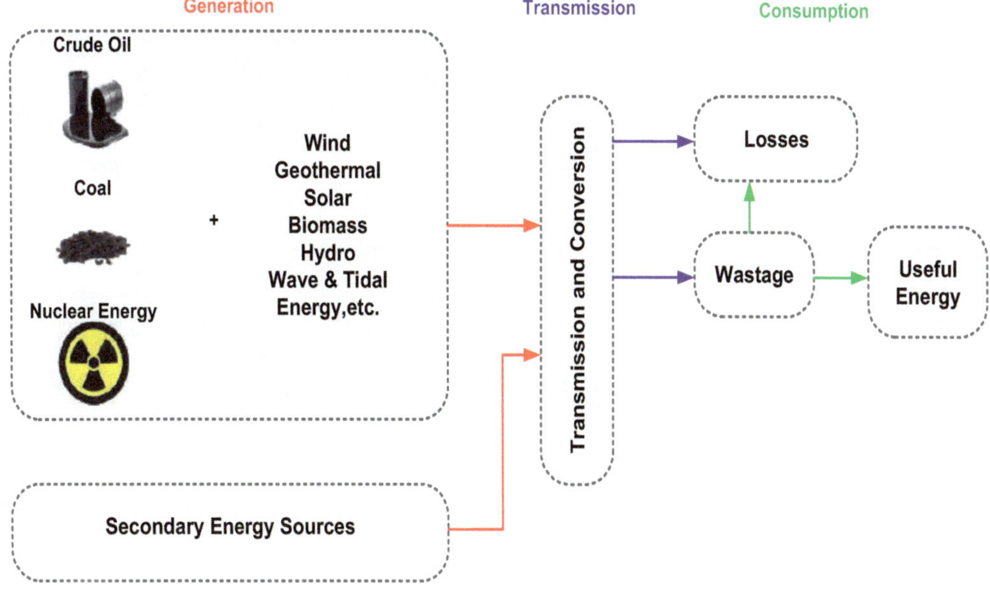

Fig. (2). The supply chain of Energy management.

3. LITERATURE REVIEW

- As a result of this research, an energy management system for the Internet of Things and devices such as hardware and software are both taken into consideration. This is due to the modeling of energy use during sensing, processing, and communication. There has been a proposal for a multi-agent system to simulate IoT devices and their energy consumption. Multi-agent systems are optimized by using a genetic algorithm. MATLAB environment and other simulation tools are used to test the system. The multi-agent system's independent intelligence resulted in a considerable increase in energy consumption [8].
- In this study, several newly proposed optimization algorithms exceeded the benchmark examples in terms of accuracy, although they have yet to be applied to the optimization of energy. An in-depth analysis of energy-saving and scheduling solutions was undertaken in this study. Heat transfer, visual and thermal, and clean air comfort have all been well studied. It was also interesting to see how smart houses use cloud and cloud technologies approaches [9, 10].
- This work collects data from appliances using IoT-enabled embedded systems to address the approaching power issue. The data that has been collected for analysis is stored on a cloud server. Through the Internet, the microcontroller talks with the cloud server [11, 12]. The user is presented with a dashboard that visually depicts the status of all appliances using graphs and charts. This visualization can be used to examine each device's power usage, alerting the user to any power waste and other relevant information. The dashboard also has features that allow the user to control the devices remotely with a single button press.
- This study presents a smart HEMS architecture that addresses both energy use and generation [13, 14]. The home server collects and analyses energy consumption and generation data to estimate energy consumption and regulates the home energy use schedule to save money on energy. The remote energy management server collects energy data from a variety of home servers, compares it, and generates relevant statistical analysis data [15].
- In the pursuit of smarter environments in our homes and across the domains of medical care, transportation, energy grids, and industrial automation, IoT devices, such as smartphones and wearables, have already transformed many aspects of our daily lives by enabling ubiquitous machine-to-machine, machine to human, and even human-to-human communication [16]. This article examines the current state of energy management solutions for mobile and IoT devices, to improve performance and quality of service while working within the devices' various resource limits [17].

4. PROPOSED INTELLIGENT AUTOMATION SYSTEM

To control a wide range of devices, this system is meant to be of low cost and scalable. Wi-Fi, is a wireless technology that uses a radiofrequency to transport data. Wi-Fi's data transmission speeds are between 1 and 2 megabits per second. Wi-Fi utilizes the 2.4 GHz Band radio to deliver data. It makes use of the frequency division multiplexing technology. The range of a Wi-Fi technology is between 40 and 300 feet. The automation of the project is controlled using an Arduino UNO. The Arduino UNO's Wi-Fi module will receive the data transmitted from the PC *via* Wi-Fi. The Arduino UNO reads data and finds the best way to control the electrical devices connected *via* Relays.

Fig. (**3**) displays the proposed system's general schematic diagram. The load and the four-channel relay are both powered. The Arduino is connected to the load through a relay. To connect the mobile application to the appliance, the Wi-Fi module is connected to the Arduino. The regulator connects the Arduino to the transformer.

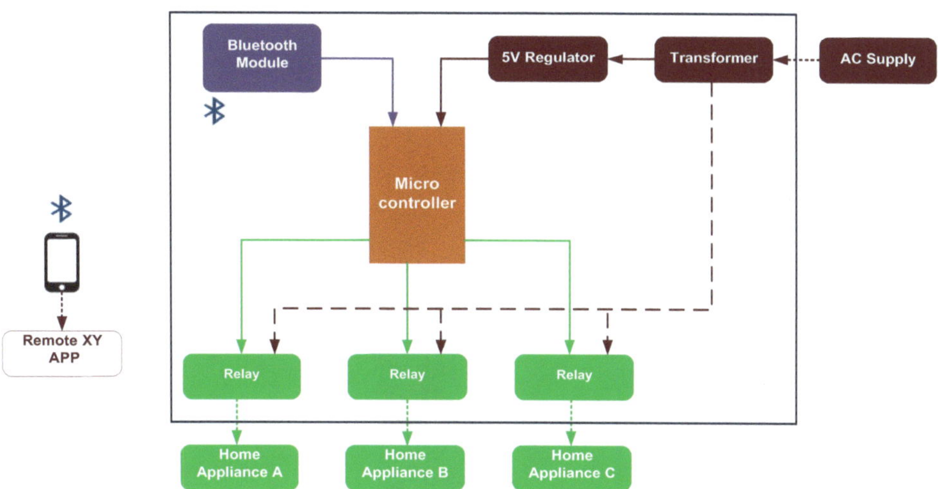

Fig. (3). Intelligent Home Automation System with Bluetooth Interface.

5. SIMULATION OF AN INTELLIGENT AUTOMATION SYSTEM USING CISCO PACKET TRACER

Cisco Packet Tracer's role is to help us understand networking principles through hands-on experience while also gaining Cisco-specific skills. Surprisingly, this program supports a wide range of networking devices in addition to Cisco hardware.

We created and simulated a whole home automation system using the Cisco packet tracer by connecting various gadgets to a Wi-Fi system. We have a cell phone with which we can control all appliances by interacting with them in a few situations. The following are some examples of conditions:

● If the window is open, switch off the fan.

● If the window is closed, switch it to ON.

● We can open/close the window remotely using our mobile device, and if the window is open, the fan is turned off, and *vice versa*.

The Condition and status of appliances used for the simulation in Cisco Packet Tracer can be viewed in Fig. (4), mentioning the status of all the appliances, including their current status like open, close, on, off, *etc*.

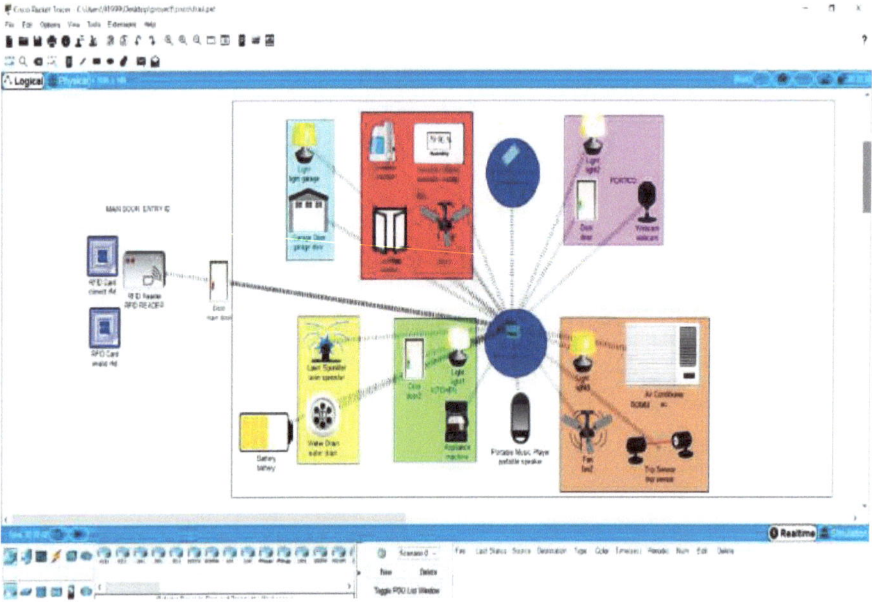

Fig. (4). Simulation of the proposed system with Cisco Packet Tracer.

5.1. Description of Software

After connections are given, the remote XY software is used to implement the software part of the system. Remote XY is used to completely monitor both the load and appliances and set up conditions for automation of home appliances.

Algorithm

Step 1: Configure the connection between the Wi-Fi module and Arduino.

Step 2: Pin Tx and Rx to interface the Wi-Fi module.

Step 3: initialize the output pin to zero.

A0 – Load 1

A1 – Load 2

A2 – Load 3

Step 4: Connect the Wi-Fi with the username and password specified.

Step 5: Control the appliance through the mobile application Remote XY.

An Overview of Code Generation Using Remote XY

RemoteXY is a simple tool for creating and using a mobile graphical user interface for controller boards that can be controlled from a smartphone or tablet.

The system includes the following components: Editor of mobile graphical interfaces for controller boards, which may be found at remotexy.com.

RemoteXY is a mobile app that lets us connect to the controller and control it through a graphical interface.

RemoteXY enables the user to create any graphical management interface by combining control, display, and decorating elements. Using the online editor, you may create a graphical interface for any work by arranging the items on the screen as shown in Fig. (5).

You get the source code for the microcontroller that implements your interface when you finish developing the graphical interface. The source code establishes a framework for your program's interaction with the controls and display. As a result, you may easily incorporate the control system into the purpose for which the gadget is being developed.

The microcontroller device can be managed using the user interface of the smartphone used. The mobile application Remote XY was used to manage the devices.

Smartphone0

Physical   Config   Devices   Programming   Attributes

IoT Server - Device Conditions

	Actions		Enabled	Name	Condition	Actions
Edit	Remove		Yes	fan	window On is true	Set fan1 Status to Low
Edit	Remove		Yes	fan1	window On is false	Set fan1 Status to High
Edit	Remove		Yes	camera	door Lock is Unlock	Set webcam On to true
Edit	Remove		Yes	webcam	door Lock is Lock	Set webcam On to false
Edit	Remove		Yes	humidity	humidity monitor Humidity >= 40 %	Set humidifier Status to false
Edit	Remove		Yes	light2	door Lock is Unlock	Set light2 Status to On
Edit	Remove		Yes	Light2	door Lock is Lock	Set light2 Status to Dim
Edit	Remove		Yes	Humidity	humidity monitor Humidity <= 40 %	Set humidifier Status to true
Edit	Remove		Yes	machine	battery Available power < 30 %	Set machine On to false
Edit	Remove		Yes	ac	ac On is true	Set fan2 Status to Off
Edit	Remove		Yes	acc	ac On is false	Set fan2 Status to High
Edit	Remove		Yes	light1	door2 Lock is Unlock	Set light1 Status to On
Edit	Remove		Yes	light1off	door2 Lock is Lock	Set light1 Status to Off
Edit	Remove		Yes	water save	lawn sprinkler Status is true	Set water drain Status to true
Edit	Remove		Yes	water save1	lawn sprinkler Status is false	Set water drain Status to false
Edit	Remove		Yes	garage light	garage door On is true	Set light garage Status to On
Edit	Remove		Yes	garge light	garage door On is false	Set light garage Status to Off
Edit	Remove		Yes	main door	RFID READER Status is Valid	Set main door Lock to Unlock
Edit	Remove		Yes	door main	RFID READER Status is Invalid	Set main door Lock to Lock
Edit	Remove		Yes	LIGHT3	trip sensor On is true	Set light3 Status to On
Edit	Remove		Yes	light3	trip sensor On is false	Set light3 Status to Off

Fig. (5). Conditions and status of appliance.

With only one mobile application, a huge number of devices with various graphical administration interfaces can be managed. Because the device's interface description is stored on the microcontroller board, Fig. (**6**) shows the flow diagram of the RemoteXY application interface with the Arduino board. RemoteXY app receives the Arduino board sk**etc**h through the GUI and that is transmitted through Wi-fi.

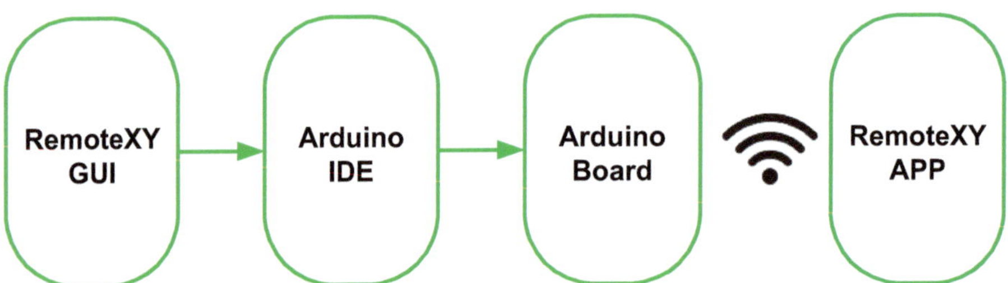

Fig. (6). Arduino Interfacing with Wi-Fi Module.

Fig. (**7**) represents the flowchart of the proposed Energy Management System. The operation process contains two stages. In the first stage, the command is generated from the Remote XY app. After the command is received by the system, the status of the relay is verified by the system. If the command is not received, the system will wait for the command. The relay is operated in the second stage and it performs the ON/OFFF operations based on the commands sent from the Remote XY application.

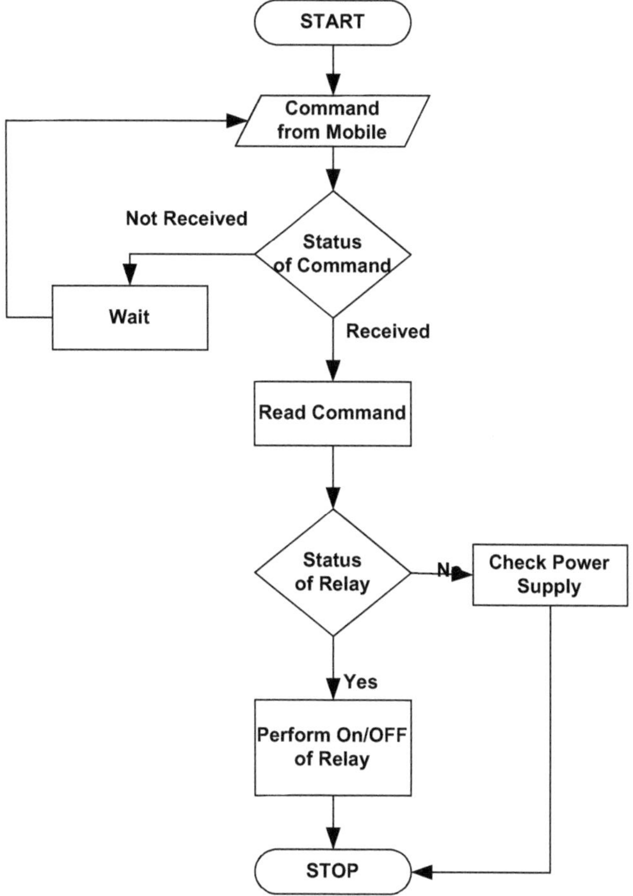

Fig. (7). Flow diagram of the process of Energy Management.

6. HARDWARE IMPLEMENTATION

This wifi-controlled intelligent home automation module is a comprehensive module that combines each appliance with the Wi-Fi control app. In addition to these pre-existing systems, the module offers unique features, such as the ability to use it in both old and modern buildings. The application with the system can control the status as well as the quantity of appliances, and the simulation design illustrates how the appliances perform in real time when we run them in the control area. Fig. (8) depicts the proposed system's general schematic diagram.

The load and the four-channel relay are both given power. The Arduino is connected to the load through a relay. The Arduino is attached to the Wi-Fi module, which allows the mobile app to communicate with the appliance. The Arduino is connected to the transformer *via* the regulator.

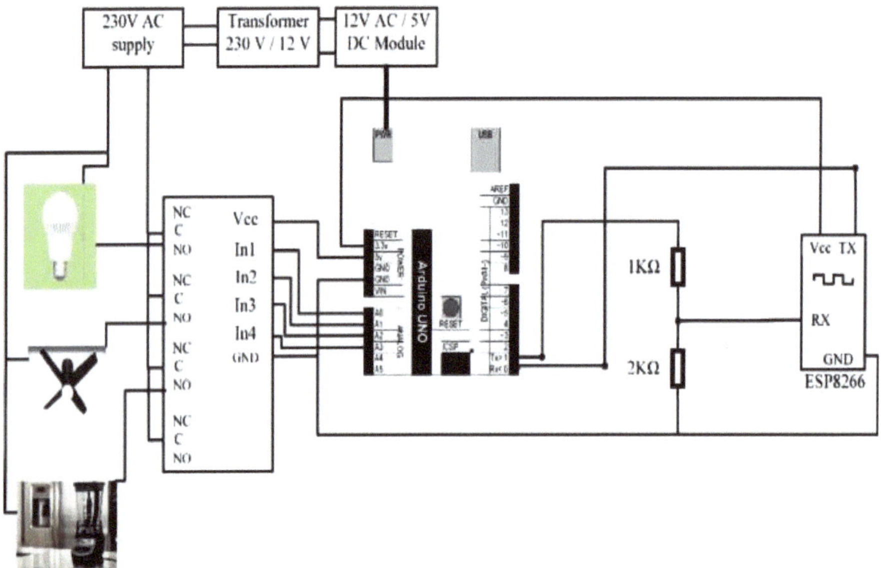

Fig. (8). Schematic Diagram.

6.1. Wi-Fi Module Interface Circuit

The mobile embedded system uses an ESP8266 Wi-Fi module to transport data from an Arduino to a mobile device using the RemoteXY app. The Wi-Fi module requires a voltage of 3.3V. To interface Esp8266 with Arduino, a potential divider circuit is utilized to lower the 5V provided by the Arduino TX pin to 3.3V as shown in Fig. (**9**).

The entire setup is relocated to the field after the software implementation is completed to create a workable prototype. The Arduino and the four-channel relay are isolated from the field to produce a prototype system in the field. The remote XY software can be accessed from any device connected to the same network once the program is turned on. Table **1** shows the Arduino IDE and remote XY settings. After setting up the system, the household appliances can be monitored and managed.

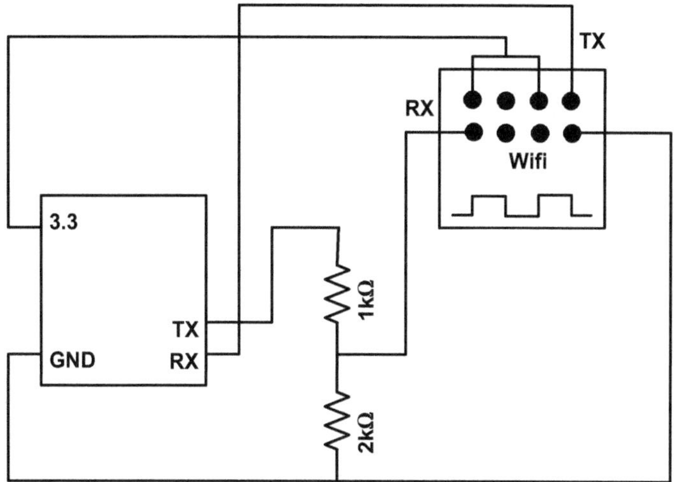

Fig. (9). Arduino Interfacing with Wi-Fi Module.

Table 1. Condition for Switch in remote XY.

Values	Data	Type
0 - OFF (left position) 1 - ON (right position)	Switch position	Unsigned char

The microcontroller receives information from the switch regarding one of two fixed positions: on or off. Unlike the buttons, the switch maintains its location. To alter the state of the switch, adjust the slider or press the required side of the switch.

Settings of the switch allow specifying the different values:

- Variable identity - the name of the switch and the variable in the microcontroller's source code, which allows the variable of C rules to be given a name.
- Set the caption to "ON" by turning on the switch. The default setting is "ON" - which is already included. Any language may be used to ask.
- Set the caption to "OFF" to turn off the switch. "OFF" is the default - it's included. Any language may be used to ask.

PIN linked - You have the option of connecting this switch to a specific controller pin or not connecting it at all. If the button is attached to a pin, further code will be generated to control the microcontroller's output through this switch. Fig. (**10**) shows the screen of the Remote XY app that has the buttons for four loads connected to the Arduino board.

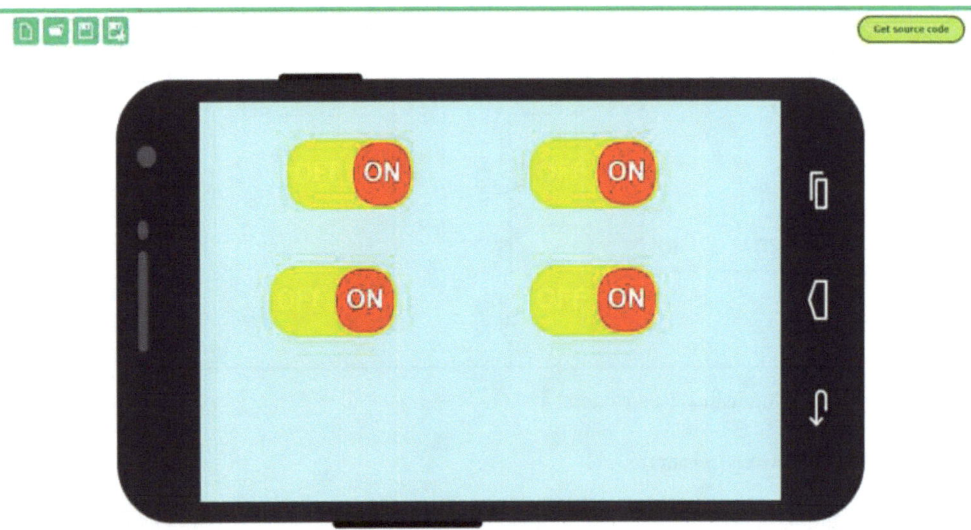

Fig. (10). Remote XY Mobile Application.

The entire arrangement in Fig. (**11**) includes all of the hardware components needed for testing. This system is then tweaked to fit a larger region, such as on-the-ground functional prototype testing. The load is connected to the Arduino *via* the relay. The Mobile application is connected to the appliance *via* a Wi-Fi module. The application we're utilizing is Remote XY. The mobile's switch will allow us to control the appliances that are connected to it. The control of appliances *via* wireless mode will be enabled by the excellent receiver and transmission ends of both the Wi-Fi module and the microcontroller. The Wi-Fi module gets information about the switch state in the phone and sends it to the microcontroller, which then uses the relay circuit to control the appliances.

The hardware prototype contains four different loads that can be controlled through Wi-fi. Fig. (**12a**) shows the number of Loads connected at a particular period. Two 40W incandescent lamps and two 9W LEDs are connected as load. A minimum of a single lamp was turned ON at a period and a maximum of all loads are connected. The experiment was conducted by turning ON and OFF the lamps at different power combinations and the power consumption was measured.

Fig. (11). Working model of Hardware.

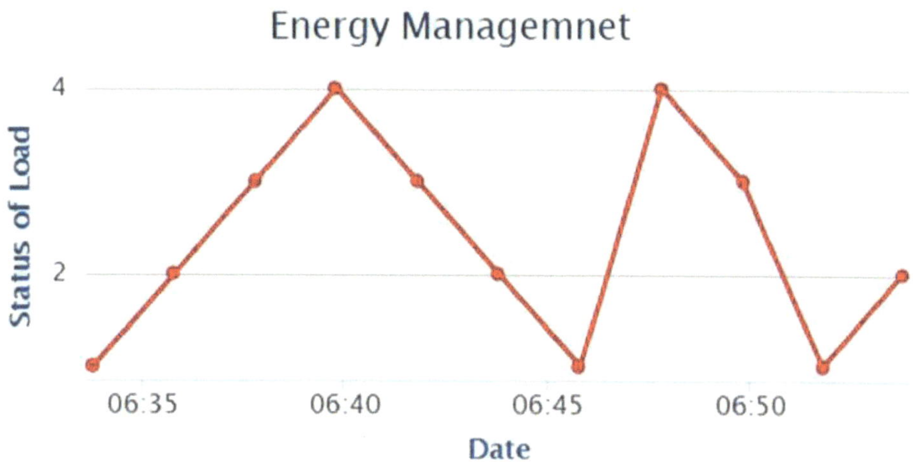

Fig. (12a). Graph for number of Loads connected.

Fig. (**12 b**) shows the power consumption in watts at different load conditions. It is observed that a maximum of 98W is consumed when all lamps are turned ON and a 9 W is consumed when a single lamp is turned ON. By measuring the power consumption at different combinations of loads, the user can optimize the energy consumption for their home.

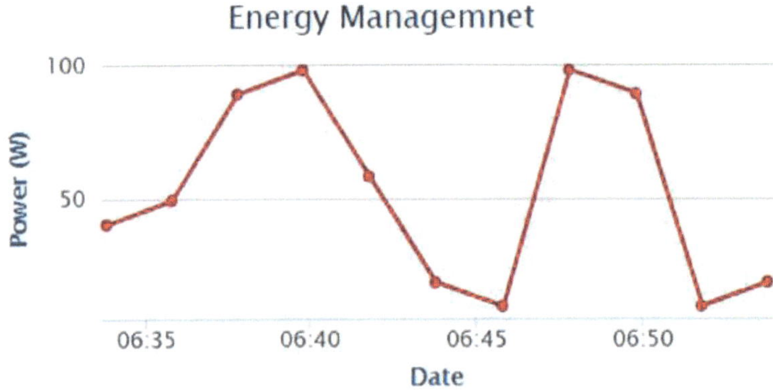

Fig. (12b). Graph of Power consumption at different load conditions.

7. NOVELTY OF THE PROPOSED METHOD

This article will demonstrate how the Internet of Things (IoT) may help the energy supply chain. To demonstrate how the Internet of Things can improve energy efficiency, reduce demand, and increase renewable energy consumption. With the use of Wi-Fi, a novel energy efficiency system was designed to regulate household appliances. The proposed system has been tested by attaching sample appliances to it and controlling them with a wireless mobile device. The Wi-Fi module worked well with Android apps. An inexpensive home automation system was therefore designed, installed, and tested.

CONCLUSION

By connecting sample appliances to the proposed system and successfully controlling the appliances from a wireless mobile device, the suggested system has been experimentally proved to perform well. Android applications were successfully tested with the Wi-Fi module. As a result, a low-cost home automation system was built, installed, and tested successfully. This system's future potential includes making homes increasingly smarter. Sensors such as motion sensors, light sensors, and temperature sensors can be integrated into homes to offer automated device switching based on the conditions. The Internet of Things (IoT) and cloud computing are two of the most popular technologies.

We may now employ them in our automation to create a better tomorrow. We can use Artificial Intelligence (AI) to create a home automation model that will take automation to the next level.

REFERENCES

[1]　H. Jo, and Y.I. Yoon, "Intelligent smart home energy efficiency model using artificial tensor flow engine", *Hum. Cent. Comput. Inf. Sci.,* vol. 8, no. 9, 2018.
[http://dx.doi.org/10.1186/s13673-018-0132-y]

[2]　V. Vakiloroaya, B. Samali, A. Fakhar, and K. Pishghadam, "A review of different strategies for HVAC energy saving", *Energy Convers. Manage.,* vol. 77, pp. 738-754, 2014.
[http://dx.doi.org/10.1016/j.enconman.2013.10.023]

[3]　Y.H. Lin, Z.T. Chou, C.W. Yu, and R.H. Jan, "Optimal and maximized configurable power saving protocols for corona-based wireless sensor networks", *IEEE Trans. Mobile Comput.,* vol. 14, no. 12, pp. 2544-2559, 2015.
[http://dx.doi.org/10.1109/TMC.2015.2404796]

[4]　R. Chow, "The last mile for IoT privacy", *IEEE Secur. Priv.,* vol. 15, no. 6, pp. 73-76, 2017.
[http://dx.doi.org/10.1109/MSP.2017.4251118]

[5]　T. Song, R. Li, B. Mei, J. Yu, X. Xing, and X. Cheng, "A privacy preserving communication protocol for IoT applications in smart homes", *IEEE Internet Things J.,* vol. 4, no. 6, pp. 1844-1852, 2017.
[http://dx.doi.org/10.1109/JIOT.2017.2707489]

[6]　Shanzhi Chen, Hui Xu, Dake Liu, Bo Hu, and Hucheng Wang, "A vision of IoT: Applications, challenges, and opportunities with China perspective", *IEEE Internet Things J.,* vol. 1, no. 4, pp. 349-359, 2014.
[http://dx.doi.org/10.1109/JIOT.2014.2337336]

[7]　C.S. Lee, D.H. Kim, and J.D. Kim, "An energy efficient active RFID protocol to avoid overhearing problem", *IEEE Sens. J.,* vol. 14, no. 1, pp. 15-24, 2014.
[http://dx.doi.org/10.1109/JSEN.2013.2279391]

[8]　V. Namboodiri, and L. Gao, "Energy-aware tag anticollision protocols for RFID systems", *IEEE Transactions on Mobile Computing,* vol. 9, no. 1, pp. 44-59, 2010.
[http://dx.doi.org/10.1109/TMC.2009.96]

[9]　K. Christidis, and M. Devetsikiotis, "Blockchains and smart contracts for the internet of things", *IEEE Access,* vol. 4, pp. 2292-2303, 2016.
[http://dx.doi.org/10.1109/ACCESS.2016.2566339]

[10]　C. Zhu, V.C.M. Leung, L. Shu, and E.C-H. Ngai, "Green internet of things for smart world", *IEEE Access,* vol. 3, pp. 2151-2162, 2015.
[http://dx.doi.org/10.1109/ACCESS.2015.2497312]

[11]　N.H. Motlagh, M. Bagaa, and T. Taleb, "Energy and delay aware task assignment mechanism for UAV-based IoT platform", *IEEE Internet Things J.,* vol. 6, no. 4, pp. 6523-6536, 2019.
[http://dx.doi.org/10.1109/JIOT.2019.2907873]

[12]　E. Rodriguez-Diaz, J.C. Vasquez, and J.M. Guerrero, "Intelligent DC homes in future sustainable energy systems: When efficiency and intelligence work together", *IEEE Consum. Electron. Mag.,* vol. 5, no. 1, pp. 74-80, 2016.
[http://dx.doi.org/10.1109/MCE.2015.2484699]

[13]　V. Ravindran, R. Ponraj, C. Krishnakumar, S. Ragunathan, V. Ramkumar, and K. Swaminathan, "IoT-based smart transformer monitoring system with Raspberry Pi", *2021 Innovations in Power and Advanced Computing Technologies (i-PACT),* 2021, Kuala Lumpur, Malaysia.
[http://dx.doi.org/10.1109/i-PACT52855.2021.9696779]

[14] V. Ravindran, and C. Vennila, "An energy-efficient clustering protocol for iot wireless sensor networks based on cluster supervisor management", *Comptes rendus de l'Académie bulgare des Sciences,* vol. 74, no. 12, 2021.
[http://dx.doi.org/10.7546/CRABS.2021.12.12]

[15] V. Ravindran, and C. Vennila, "Energy consumption in cluster communication using Mcsbch approach in WSN", *J. Intell. Fuzzy Syst. Applications in Engineering and Technology,* vol. 43, no. 12022, pp. 1669-1679, 2022.
[http://dx.doi.org/10.3233/JIFS-212632]

[16] SP Yadav, DP Mahato, and NT Linh, *Distributed artificial intelligence: A modern approach.* CRC Press, 2020.
[http://dx.doi.org/10.1201/9781003038467]

[17] S.P. Yadav, S. Zaidi, A. Mishra, and V. Yadav, "Survey on machine learning in speech emotion recognition and vision systems using a recurrent neural network (RNN)", *Arch. Comput. Methods Eng.,* vol. 29, no. 3, pp. 1753-1770, 2022.
[http://dx.doi.org/10.1007/s11831-021-09647-x]

CHAPTER 7

Garbage Management and Monitoring System Using IOT Applications

A. Kumaraswamy[1,*], Chandra Sekhar Kolli[2], Sagaya Aurelia[3], P. Vasantha Kumar[4] and M. Lakshminarayana[5]

[1] *Sri Venkateswara College of Engineering, Sriperumbudur, Tamilnadu, India*

[2] *Department of Computer Science, Gandhi Institute of Technology and Management, Visakhapatnam, Andhra Pradesh, India*

[3] *Department of Computer Science, CHRIST University, Bengaluru, Karnataka, India*

[4] *School of Excellence in Law, The Tamil Nadu Dr. Ambedkar Law University, Chennai, India*

[5] *Department of Medical Electronics Engineering, M S Ramaiah Institute Of Technology, Bengaluru, Karnataka, India*

Abstract: The main purpose of this application, in addition to boosting the vision of a smart city, is to reduce humankind's effort and resources while simultaneously enhancing the vision. The squashing of the dustbin will occur on a regular schedule. It will be possible to manage waste more efficiently when these sensible garbage bins are implemented on a large scale and replace our previously designed dumpster, as it eliminates the need for waste to be piled up on the roadside in the first place. When managing the trash containers, wireless sensor systems in networks (WSN) in connection with the IoT technologies are used. On the other hand, sensors are used to monitor the container contents in real-time, with results displayed on the website, and the sensed contents are then evaluated to determine the optimal container distribution. This allows for the processing of a variety of waste types depending on the needs of the customer. As a result of installing ultrasonic sensors in each bin, garbage levels are continuously checked. As a result of this notification, the bin will be cleared.

Keywords: Internet Protocol, Sensible Garbage Bin, Ultrasonic Sensors.

---

* **Corresponding author A. Kumaraswamy:** Sri Venkateswara College of Engineering, Sriperumbudur, Tamilnadu, India; E-mail: kumaraswamy@svce.ac.in

1. INTRODUCTION

As cities continue to grow, waste collection agencies are overworked and unable to maintain themselves. Many objects, from cars to metal and machinery, end up at improperly managed and unsupervised dump sites, where they spread diseases and increase pollution [1]. When it comes to managing garbage after its generation, the majority of these solutions have proven effective. The issue of keeping cities clean is becoming increasingly critical as smart cities develop. Garbage production is out of control, and manual labor is required to remove that, but it is time-consuming.

As the world's population grows, so does the amount of waste produced. This has resulted in several potentially dangerous situations. Due to the massive amount of garbage accumulating on wide expanses of land, hazardous landfills are formed. Toxic fumes from the decaying trash fill the air, polluting the local ecosystem. Waste dumped in water bodies pollutes the oceans and seas that connect them, affecting the quality of drinking water and the life of aquatic animals. Because of this, harmful gases are released into the air, which harm the entire ecosystem [2]. As a result, waste management has become a major concern in the modern world. A lot of things can be modified and prevented if the waste created is appropriately handled at the source level. Fig. (**1**) displays the process flow diagram of the Smart waste Management System.

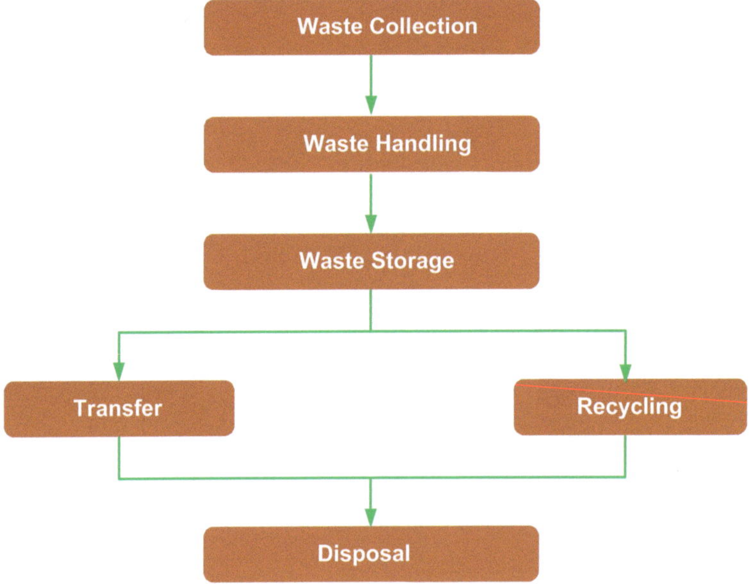

Fig. (1). Process flow diagram of Smart waste management system.

The newest report from the World Bank predicts that global waste would increase by 70 percent over present levels by 2050 unless urgent action is taken see Fig. (**2**), What a Waste 2.0: A Global Assessment of Proper Waste Management to 2050). 3.4 billion tons of waste is predicted to be generated annually in the next 30 years, which is increased from 2.01 billion tonnes in 2016. This is a result of increased urbanization and population growth. Only 16 percent of the world's population lives in high-income countries, yet they generate 34 percent of the world's garbage. A quarter (23%) of worldwide trash generation is generated in East Asia and the Pacific region. Moreover, by 2050, the amount of garbage generated in Sub-Saharan Africa is expected to triple, while the amount of garbage generated in South Asia is anticipated to nearly double.

Fig. (2). From now until 2050, a global scenario of waste management-Picture Source-World Bank (2018)

The percentage mentioned in Table **1** is as per the World Bank report in 2018. Municipal solid trash is divided into five distinct categories:

Table 1. Solid Trash Occupancy level based on its 5 distinct categories.

Category	Percentage
Food / Biodegradable wastes	43%
Paper Wastes	18%
Plastic Trashes	11%
Bottles, Cans	7%
Metal trashes	5%

- Glass, bottles, cans, paper, metals, and certain plastics are examples of recyclable materials.
- Tetra packages and waste plastic materials such as toys and waste garments are examples of composite wastes.
- Food and kitchen scraps and green craps are all biodegradable wastes (Leaves agricultural wastes *etc.*,) and Papers (which can also be composted),
- Sand, pebbles, building, and improper disposal are examples of inert waste.
- E-wastes, pharmaceuticals, chemicals, paints, batteries, household hazardous garbage, and toxic waste.

India, like any other developing country, is currently dealing with some serious problems in managing municipal solid wastes. Throughout the country, open waste dumping is common. This is due to the incorrect perception that it is the simplest and cheapest form of disposal. In addition, there is a lack of desire and resources to enhance current disposal processes. Deposition of waste along roadsides, riverbanks, and marginal lands, and then 'hoping' for it to disappear, is both foolish and dangerous. Chemical and biological contaminants in the garbage will inevitably poison the surrounding natural environment and make their way back to humans, affecting health, quality of life, and working activities.

Fig. (3) depicts an annual bar chart of regional trash creation worldwide, which demonstrates that waste mismanagement is increasing in East Asian and Pacific countries. The statistical numbers in the bar chart are taken from a World Bank report. The World Bank has spent over $4.7 billion on over 340 waste management systems in different parts of the world since 2000. It is crucial to assist governments in making critical financing, policy, and planning decisions for solid waste management. The points below were among the options:

- The most in-need countries, especially those with the fastest developing economies, should be funded to implement waste management systems that reduce trash production.

- Comprehensive waste reduction and recycling programs are helping major garbage-producing countries limit their use of plastics and marine litter.
- Civic education, biological management, and coordinated food waste management solutions all contribute to the reduction of food waste in the food industry.

Fig. (3). Annual Bar Chart of Regional Waste generation in million Tones.

As a result, unrestricted dumping costs society in the long term. Table **2** describes the Waste Management Taxonomy of various hardware and general requirements and their functionalities.

Because of this, a real-time Garbage management system is crucial for monitoring and reducing trash accumulation. Using ultrasonic sensors, a container's trash level can be monitored. Wi-Fi transmits the Transmission Control Protocol with Internet Protocol to the website *via* Arduino UNO that receives the data. There is a website that displays to you how much waste is in the containers. Depending on whether the containers are full or not, you can take action by sending a text message to a garbage truck.

Table 2. Waste management Taxonomy.

Waste Management Taxonomy		
Criteria	**Hardware Required**	**Functionalities**
Based on IoT Technology	RFIDs Sensors Wireless Sensor Networks (WSN) GPS, GSM, Arduino and other controllers	All functions are based on user requirements on social context and experimental data.
General Requirement	Garbage Bins and Vehicles for Transporting Bio and Bio-degradable wastes	Collecting waste from Bins based on the location and type of waste.

2. LITERATURE SURVEY

Utilizing a smart system for managing waste, a system is designed to reduce resources such as human efforts, time, and cost. Smart bins, smart control, and monitoring systems, and garbage vehicles make up the three subsystems of the waste management system. Both portions of the research were carried out separately [3 - 5]. We need to design a system that gets and tracks garbages in different locations. Part two focuses on how to use this method in a specific city. To improve the system, it can be linked to GPS to locate the bin and notify a message to a nearby garbage vehicle to clear it, or it can be connected to the internet of things so that bins can be monitored and emptied from anywhere.

As a result of our research, we have been able to compile a complete list of Internet of Things-enabled waste management models. We are particularly interested in the deployment of sensible devices as a major enabler technology in old waste management practices [6 - 9]. It's important to know the strengths and shortcomings of different models so that you can better understand them. Because of its findings, this survey lays the groundwork for the development of innovative waste management methods.

This study on waste management and smart waste management system provides increased advantages to society since it deals with different sensors, which are used to detect the sort of garbage and categorize it, while an actuator alerts the management to collect it [10 - 12]. It will be a cheaper method when compared to the current garbage management procedure and also improve the cleanliness of the community.

This waste collection management solution uses an IoT prototype with sensors to impart intelligence to waste bins. Massive datasets can be read and collected, as well as sent through the Internet. Using advanced algorithms to examine such data, garbage collection mechanisms can be dynamically managed [13 - 15]. Many simulations are run to determine the advantages of this system over a standard system. To recreate the scenario, information from Pune (a city in India) is used, demonstrating the opportunities for various parties to develop and promote the growth of the Smart Waste Management strategy.

This study looks at how to collect and decompose garbage in such a way that the waste's benefits are maximized while the waste itself is efficiently reduced. This research looks at waste segregation on two levels: the first is at the individual household level, and the second is at the societal level [16]. Here the author deals with composting biodegradable waste and KNN, a deep learning algorithm, is used to generate a warning message for several combinations of multiple sensor data, such as the quantity of biological and non-biodegradable material and the proportion of harmful gas.

To categorize digestible and indigestible waste, the proposed method uses a CNN-Convolutional Neural Network, a common deep learning algorithm. Also included in the concept is a constructional design for a smart garbage that can make use of a microprocessor and a variety of different sensors. IoT and Bluetooth connectivity are used for data surveilling in the suggested technique [17 - 20]. The Internet of Things (IoT) offers remote control of real-time data, while Bluetooth allows for short-range data monitoring *via* an Android app. As a way to gauge the effectiveness of the model, the accuracy of waste label categorization, sensor data analysis, and utility scale of the system are all listed and evaluated [21 - 24].

In this study, the future of Compost Mushroom in agricultural management will be investigated, with a focus on its use. Compost Mushroom was largely employed in agriculture as a mushroom medium, animal feed, plant compost, fertilizer, and other purposes, according to previous studies. The broader usage of Compost Mushroom, that too in the 2nd cultivation, is discussed in this study. The Compost Mushroom was also utilized in the generation of renewable energy such as methane fuel, biofuel, and bioethanol.

A total of 200 computer programmers responded to the survey. The strongest predictor was 'collection and recycling,' followed by consciousness and regulations according to a multiple regression study. This highlights the significance of effective e-waste collection and recycling, as well as educating the people about the risk of e-waste and enforcing the e-waste policy. The policy implication is that policymakers in the software sector can use the developed model to design e-waste development strategies.

The entire system is presented as proposed module 1 and proposed module 2 in this article discussed in sections 3.1 and 3.2.

3. PROPOSED SYSTEM

In the proposed module 1, an Arduino Uno board with a developed Sensible trash bin was used and its alert notifications were sent as a text message by GSM, similarly, in module 2, some external features were added and notifications were monitored *via* web page created exclusively for this purpose.

3.1. Proposed Module-1

Three ultrasonic sensors were attached to the trash bin for measuring the distance between the particles inside *i.e.*, wastes. However, it is not cheap in terms of cost and requires more power. There's no need to litter the city with many containers that aren't coordinated. Only one surface-level sensor instead of three makes it more inexpensive and gets the same results.

When compared to the current system, it uses advanced technologies. This is accomplished with the help of a GSM modem and a microcontroller, as well as an ultrasonic sensor. This is done by using ultrasonic sensors that determine how far away the garbage is from being deposited on top of the bin. By utilizing the GSM modem, we could be able to send a text asking the consumer or the one who uses that bin to empty the trash once it is full. Using this system will be extremely convenient for the user as shown in Fig. (**2**).

In this case, the application will be java programmed. There's a loud alert that sounds when the bin is full and has to be emptied. There are also three different stages of fullness symbolized by LED lights. Similarly, our Chennai Municipal Waste Management System may use this application to inform the garbage collectors of the exact time to empty a particular bin.

The ultrasonic sensor block diagram is shown in Fig. (**4**). In Ultrasonic Sensing, time is measured by sending and receiving an ultrasonic signal. An ultrasonic wave travels a certain distance before being reflected due to a change in impedance. The time-off light interval is the distance between the two signals.

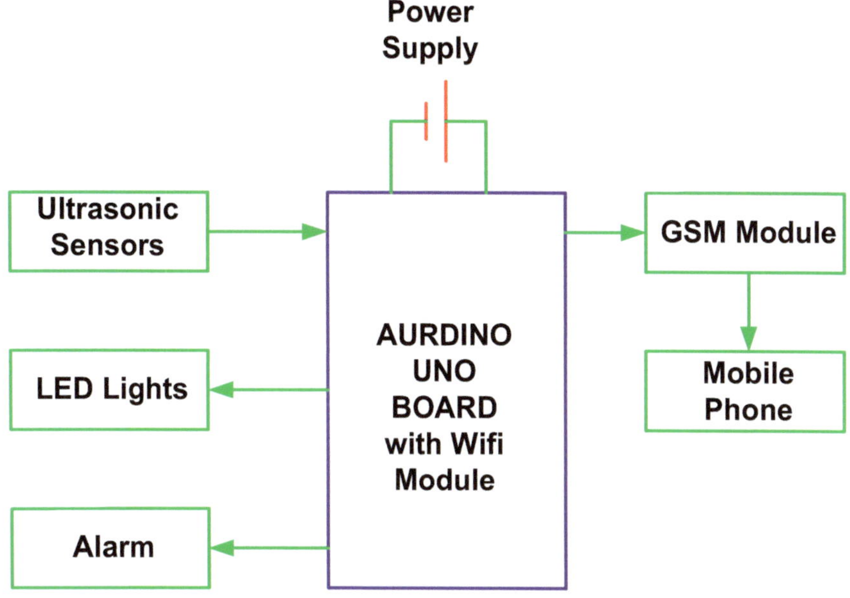

Fig. (4). Block Diagram of Proposed Model-1.

In the first module of this research, we send messages using a GSM modem including the GSM/GPRS modem, along with USB and RS-232 (Serial Port) for connecting to other devices. Three LEDs indicate the 2 different levels of the garbage height in the bin, with the highest level being the tallest. To ensure that no additional waste is disposed of in the bin, a built-in alarm blasts three times. In this way, we can control the overflowing bins. Once this has been done, the user receives a notification that the dustbin must be discarded. This message is sent over the GSM modem. In Fig. **(5)**, you can see the results of the system implementation prototype as a screenshot.

3.2. Proposed Module-2

The proposed architecture of a waste management system is divided into three parts:

- Sensible dumpsters,
- Management and control systems
- Transport System

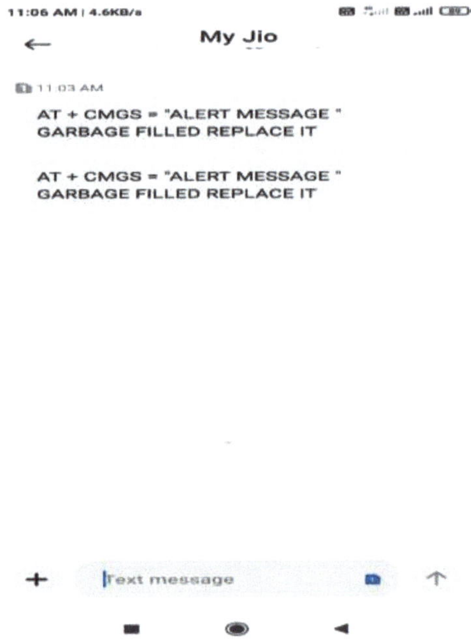

Fig. (5). Screenshot of Message received from GSM module.

The system architecture is depicted in Fig. (**6**).

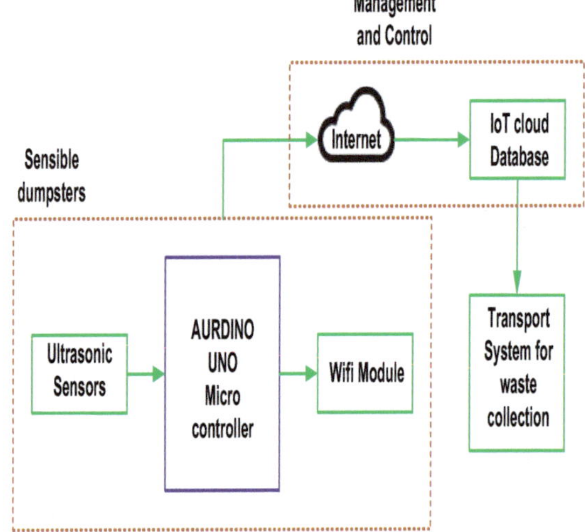

Fig. (6). Proposed Module-2 Block Diagram.

3.2.1. Sensible Dumpsters

In this construction process, we use two bins, one for collecting degradable wastes and the other bin for non-degradable wastes, each of which contains an Ultrasonic sensor, an Arduino-Uno controller, and a WI-FI module as shown in Fig. (7).

3.2.2. Sensor Usage

Using sound waves, the Ultrasonic Sensor detects the distance between current items in containers. An ultrasonic sensor is used to detect distance by sending sound waves at a constant time and then waiting for the range to be determined.

Distance, D = SpeedofSound*Time taken2 (1)

Based on equation (1), the level of the bin is evaluated. These sensors will be at the top of the dustbins.

3.2.3. Wi-Fi Module

The Wi-Fi is a set of self SOC with an integrated IP protocol for transferring detected data to a web page. Every other Wi-Fi package contains an AT Command firmware that may be used to set the Wi-Fi mode to the user, proxy server, or client and access point. The Internet protocol is employed to communicate data from the bin to the monitoring and control system *fff* the Wi-Fi module.

3.2.4. Arduino-Uno Controller

It is an open-source controller based on simple hardware that functions similarly to a computer and is used to connect and control sensors using Arduino software.

3.2.5. Management and Control System

It displays the dustbin status in real-time, and the sensor information is saved in a server to be displayed in a graph and used to support the container distribution choice. If the bin is full, the proposed framework sends a message with the bin status and location to the garbage truck.

3.2.6. Transport System

In every city, there will be few vehicles in use exclusively for garbage collection. With that transport system, they will collect degradable and non-degradable waste in every locality. As per the proposed model, when the bin gets filled with whatever wastes, the system will send an alert message to the vehicle operator's navigation system.

Fig. (7). IoT architecture With Ultrasonic Sensor.

3.2.7. Webpage of Garbage Management System

To determine the level of waste in each bucket in this application, ultrasonic sensors are used to read the data. The levels are divided into degradable and non-degradable waste bins as in Fig. **(8)** a webpage is created for the garbage management system, based on SQL.

Fig. (8). Webpage of Garbage Management System.

The flow describes the sensed output at the equipment (Dustbin) and is programmed in such a way that status will be sent to the vehicle truck carrying garbage's through the various components. (Fig. **9**) shows the screenshot of the status of the Bin sent to the truck which includes the address of the Bin location. So, it is easy for the vehicle driver to collect the garbage and optimize the route to collect the garbage at various locations. Also, through the Wi-fi module, the same will be displayed on the webpage created exclusively for monitoring management as depicted in Fig. (**5**).

Fig. (9). Screenshot of Alert given to the Vehicle.

When the bin is occupied with full waste or trash, a message is sent to the vehicle to empty the bin; the Wi-Fi module is used to send data to the web page through the Transmission Control Protocol with the Internet Protocol data kept in a server or database for future analysis to manage container distribution in appropriate areas as well a text message will be sent from the GSM as shown in Fig. (**9**). The flowchart in Fig. (**10**) describes the flow of the proposed module 2.

4. NOVELTY OF THIS PROPOSED WORK

Module 1 and 2 findings and screenshots were examined according to the planned flow, and this prototype is limited to a single trashcan. This application's major goal is to decrease human labour and resources while promoting the vision of a smart city. The trashcan will be smashed on a regular basis. It will be easier to handle waste when these practical rubbish bins replace our previously built dumpster, as they reduce the requirement for wastes to be stacked up on the roadside.

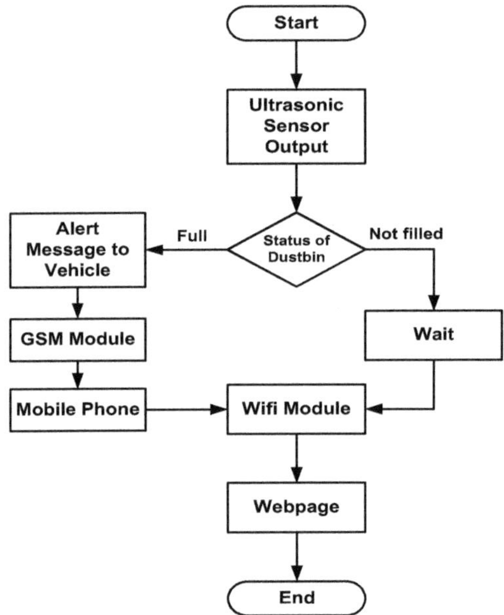

Fig. (10). Flow chart of Proposed Module 2.

CONCLUSION

The results and screenshots of Module-1 and module 2 were analyzed as per the proposed flow and more importantly, this prototype's implementation is confined to a single dustbin. Using IoT principles and creating a database for each bin that can be managed to employ SQL technology, as well as providing a login webpage to ensure approved entry, several bins, each with a unique ID, can be integrated. The waste management system is one of the most significant systems, as it aids in environmental cleanliness and avoids problems in clean-up activities in cities where many are attempting to implement the smart city concept and deliver more effective services. Garbage management can be improved by installing tracking technology in garbage trucks to identify the optimum and the shortest path for trash trucks.

REFERENCES

[1]　T. Olivares, F. Royo, and A.M. Ortiz, "An experimental test bed for smart cities applications", *The Proceedings of the 11th ACM International Symposium on Mobility Management and Wireless Access,* 2013, pp. 115-118.
[http://dx.doi.org/10.1145/2508222.2508243]

[2]　T. Sánchez López, D.C. Ranasinghe, M. Harrison, and D. McFarlane, "Adding sense to the internet of

things", *Pers. Ubiquitous Comput.,* vol. 16, no. 3, pp. 291-308, 2012.
[http://dx.doi.org/10.1007/s00779-011-0399-8]

[3]   I. Hong, S. Park, B. Lee, J. Lee, D. Jeong, and S. Park, "IoT-based smart garbage system for efficient food waste management", *Sci. World J.,* vol. 2014, pp. 1-13, 2014.
[http://dx.doi.org/10.1155/2014/646953] [PMID: 25258730]

[4]   A. Medvedev, P. Fedchenkov, A. Zaslavsky, and S. Khoruzhnikov, "Waste Management as an IoT-Enabled Service in Smart Cities", In: "Internet of things, smart spaces, and next generation networks and systems", In: *lecture notes in computer science,* S. Balandin, S. Andreev, Y. Koucheryavy, S. Khoruzhnikov, Eds., vol. 92274. Springer: Cham, 2015.
[http://dx.doi.org/10.1007/978-3-319-23126-6_10]

[5]   T. Gomes, N. Brito, J. Mendes, J. Cabral, and A. Tavares, "WECO: A wireless platform for monitoring recycling point spots", *IEEE 16th Mediterranean Electrotechnical Conference (MELECON),* 2012, pp. 468-472 Yasmine Hammamet, Tunisia.
[http://dx.doi.org/10.1109/MELCON.2012.6196474]

[6]   A. Medvedev, P. Fedchenkov, A. Zaslavsky, T. Anagnostopoulos, and S. Khoruzhnikov, "Waste management as an IoT enabled service in Smart Cities", In: "Internet of things, smart spaces, and next generation networks and systems", In: *lecture notes in computer science,* S. Balandin, S. Andreev, Y. Koucheryavy, S. Khoruzhnikov, Eds., vol. 92274. Springer: Cham, 2015.
[http://dx.doi.org/10.1007/978-3-319-23126-6_10]

[7]   F. McLeod, G. Erdogan, T. Cherrett, T. Bektas, N. Davies, D. Shingleton, C. Speed, J. Dickinson, and S. Norgate, "Improving collection efficiency through remote monitoring of charity assets", *Waste Manag.,* vol. 34, no. 2, pp. 273-280, 2014.
[http://dx.doi.org/10.1016/j.wasman.2013.11.006] [PMID: 24332998]

[8]   P. Muthukumaran, and S.B. Sarkar, "Solid waste disposal and water distribution system using the mobile adhoc network", *IEEE International Conference on Emerging Trends in Communication, Control, Signal Processing & Computing Applications (C2SPCA),* 2013, pp. 1-4 Bangalore, India.
[http://dx.doi.org/10.1109/C2SPCA.2013.6749351]

[9]   T. Anagnostopoulos, and A. Zaslavsky, "Robust waste collection exploiting cost efficiency of IoT potentiality in smart cities", *IEEE 1st International Conference on Recent Advances in Internet of Things (RIoT),* 2015, pp. 1-6 Singapore.
[http://dx.doi.org/10.1109/RIOT.2015.7104901]

[10]   F.C. Delicato, P.F. Pires, T. Batista, E. Cavalcante, B. Costa, and T. Barros, "Towards an IoT ecosystem", *The proceedings of the 1st ACM international workshop on software engineering for systems-of-systems,* 2013, pp. 25-28.
[http://dx.doi.org/10.1145/2489850.2489855]

[11]   D. Wahidur Rahman, "Intelligent waste management system using deep learning with IoT", *J. King Saud University - Computer and Information Sciences,* 2020.
[http://dx.doi.org/10.3390/s17050977]

[12]   A. Rovetta, F. Xiumin, F. Vicentini, Z. Minghua, A. Giusti, and H. Qichang, "Early detection and evaluation of waste through sensorized containers for a collection monitoring application", *Waste Manag.,* vol. 29, no. 12, pp. 2939-2949, 2009.
[http://dx.doi.org/10.1016/j.wasman.2009.08.016] [PMID: 19783420]

[13]   T. Anagnostopoulos, A. Zaslavsky, K. Kolomvatsos, A. Medvedev, P. Amirian, J. Morley, and S. Hadjieftymiades, "Challenges and opportunities of waste management in iot-enabled smart cities: A Survey", *IEEE Trans. Sustain. Comput.,* vol. 2, no. 3, pp. 275-289, 2017.
[http://dx.doi.org/10.1109/TSUSC.2017.2691049]

[14]   S. Jagtap, A. Gandhi, R. Bochare, A. Patil, and A. Shitole, "Waste management improvement in cities using IoT", *2020 International Conference on Power Electronics & IoT Applications in Renewable Energy and its Control (PARC),* 2020, pp. 382-385 Mathura, India.

[http://dx.doi.org/10.1109/PARC49193.2020.236631]

[15] G.K. Shyam, S.S. Manvi, and P. Bharti, "Smart waste management using Internet-of-Things (IoT)", *2017 2nd International Conference on Computing and Communications Technologies.*, 2017, pp. 199-203.

[16] W. Chen, Y. Wang, P. Huang, Y. Huang, and M. Tsai, "A smart iot system for waste management", *2018 1st International Cognitive Cities Conference (IC3)*, 2018, pp. 202-203.
[http://dx.doi.org/10.1109/IC3.2018.00-24]

[17] K.N. Fallavi, V.R. Kumar, and B.M. Chaithra, "Smart waste management using internet of things: A survey", *2017 International Conference on I-SMAC (IoT in Social, Mobile, Analytics and Cloud) (I-SMAC)*, 2017, pp. 60-64 Palladam, India.
[http://dx.doi.org/10.1109/I-SMAC.2017.8058247]

[18] S.V. Kumar, T.S. Kumaran, A.K. Kumar, and M. Mathapati, "Smart garbage monitoring and clearance system using internet of things", *IEEE International Conference on Smart Technologies and Management for Computing, Communication, Controls, Energy and Materials (ICSTM)*, 2017, pp. 184-189 Chennai, India.
[http://dx.doi.org/10.1109/ICSTM.2017.8089148]

[19] A. Khan, and A. Khachane, "Survey on iot in waste management system", *2nd International Conference on I-SMAC (IoT in Social, Mobile, Analytics and Cloud)*, 2018, pp. 27-29.
[http://dx.doi.org/10.1109/I-SMAC.2018.8653767]

[20] V. Ravindran, R. Ponraj, C. Krishnakumar, S. Ragunathan, V. Ramkumar, and K. Swaminathan, "IoT-based smart transformer monitoring system with Raspberry Pi", *Innovations in Power and Advanced Computing Technologies (i-PACT)*, pp. 1-7, 2021.
[http://dx.doi.org/10.1109/i-PACT52855.2021.9696779]

[21] V. Ravindran, and C. Vennila, "An energy-efficient clustering protocol for Iot wireless sensor networks based on cluster supervisor management", *Comptes rendus de l'Académie bulgare des Sciences,* vol. 74, no. 12, 2021.
[http://dx.doi.org/10.7546/CRABS.2021.12.12]

[22] V. Ravindran, and C. Vennila, "Energy consumption in cluster communication using Mcsbch approach in WSN", *Journal of Intelligent & Fuzzy Systems: Applications in Engineering and Technology,* pp. 1-11, 2022.
[http://dx.doi.org/10.3233/JIFS-212632]

[23] SP Yadav, DP Mahato, and NT Linh, *Distributed artificial intelligence: A modern approach.* CRC Press, 2020.
[http://dx.doi.org/10.1201/9781003038467]

[24] S.P. Yadav, S. Zaidi, A. Mishra, and V. Yadav, "Survey on machine learning in speech emotion recognition and vision systems using a recurrent neural network (RNN)", *Arch. Comput. Methods Eng.,* vol. 29, no. 3, pp. 1753-1770, 2022.
[http://dx.doi.org/10.1007/s11831-021-09647-x]

CHAPTER 8

Power Generation Prediction in Solar PV system by Machine Learning Approach

Rajesh Kumar Patnaik[1,*], **Chandra Sekhar Kolli**[2], **N. Mohan**[3], **S. Kirubakaran**[4] and **Ranjan Walia**[5]

[1] *Department of Electrical and Electronics Engineering, GMR Institute of Technology, Rajam, Andhra Pradesh- 532127, India*

[2] *Department of Computer Science, Gandhi Institute of Technology and Management, Visakhapatnam, Andhra Pradesh, India*

[3] *Department of EEE, JSS Science and Technology University Mysuru, Karnataka-570006, India*

[4] *Department of ECE, KPR Institute of Engineering and Technology, Coimbatore, Tamil Nadu- 641407, India*

[5] *Department of Electrical Engineering, Model Institute of Engineering and Technology, Jammu, Jammu & Kashmir - 181122, India*

Abstract: Solar energy is becoming more and more incorporated into the global power grid. As a result, enhancing the accuracy of solar energy projections is crucial for effective power grid planning, control, and operations. A fast, accurate and advanced estimation method is desperately needed to prevent PV's detrimental consequences on electricity and energy networks. For the optimum integration of solar technology into existing power systems, which benefits both grids and station operators, accurate prediction of solar production is crucial. The purpose of this research is to test the effectiveness of the machine learning model for projecting PV solar output. Using ANN in this research, weather parameters with the Power Generation for the next day appear to have been predicted. The evaluation findings suggest that the models' accuracy is sufficient to be employed with existing works and their approaches. Machine learning was shown to be capable of accurately predicting power while removing the difficulties associated with predicted solar irradiance data in this study.

Keywords: ANN, Machine Learning, PV System, Power System, Solar.

---

* **Corresponding author Rajesh Kumar Patnaik:** Department of Electrical and Electronics Engineering, GMR Institute of Technology, Rajam, Andhra Pradesh- 532127, India; E-mail: rajeshkumar.p@gmrit.edu.in

Satya Prakash Yadav, Sansar Singh Chauhan, Sanjeev Kumar Pippal and Victor Hugo C. de Albuquerque (Eds.)

1. INTRODUCTION

A lot of countries have done a lot of work in the power sector in recent years. Deep learning has opened up new possibilities and posed new obstacles in the field of power load forecasting [1]. The fundamental job of the power system is to supply users with a safe and dependable source of electricity [2]. As a result, energy forecasting is crucial for the power industry. Accurate power load forecasting is critical for saving energy, decreasing power generation costs, and boosting social and economic benefits. Energy load forecasting has grown increasingly important in the power system as power reform and marketization have progressed. The accuracy of power demand forecasting must also be improved for the power system's steady and efficient functioning. It is impossible to regenerate non-renewable energy sources including coal, oil, and gas in a short period as their consumption rate much exceed their regeneration rate. Consider fossil fuels, which not only have finite reserves and will eventually run out but whose price also rises daily [3, 4].

Renewable energy development has advanced largely as a result of the limited reserves of fossil fuels. Photovoltaic (PV) cells are the most common means of harnessing solar energy for electricity generation. Solar energy has a variety of advantages, along with its resistance to illustrative circumstances such as growing oil prices, its clean environment, and the minimization of imports and reliance on external resources. While solar cells are commonly recognized as a potential source of future energy production, their low return on investment and huge upfront costs limit their broad use. One cause for this is that the supply is unreliable due to the variable character of the weather [5, 6]. Remember that the amount of solar energy available each day has a significant impact on the amount of power produced by the system when sizing a photovoltaic system. As a result, the quantity of electricity created is governed by solar irradiance on a specific day, which is influenced by a range of geographical locations, periods, and weather systems. Solar output is the quantity of radiation from the sun inside the solar spectral region [7].

2. RELATED WORKS

- The most significant factor in determining the size of a solar power producing system is the daily mean solar irradiation. To estimate how much power will be generated by solar panels, consider the average sun irradiation in the area. This information may be used to estimate the size of the system as well as calculate ROI and system load. The mean solar irradiation Wh/m 2 has been predicted using a variety of regression algorithms and solar irradiance factors. This research compares forecasting using artificial neural networks (ANN) with traditional regression approaches. Additionally, we demonstrate that including azimuth and zenith parameters in the model results in significant performance improvements [2 - 4].

- The industry, according to this framework, should establish a standard for itself. Furthermore, by modeling future cloud positions using satellite-based data, short-term forecasting of solar PV energy output has been improved. Finally, the model's accuracy varies depending on the meteorological conditions of the forecasting area. As a result, training a model on a single site is likely to yield better results than training it on multiple sites at once. Similarly, because climatic conditions change annually, a model that is trained on a single meteorological season rather than many may perform better [8 - 11].

- The most important findings are that both machine learning and classical time series techniques have been routinely employed to forecast load demand. Similarly, for the price of power, a wide range of time series and ML approaches were used. The article also gives an overview of the methods employed in the competition for the forecasting of wind and solar electricity. In comparison to loading demands and power costs, the number of validated prediction models for turbines and solar PV modules' generated power is minimal. The application of ML approaches has been sporadic, whereas classical time series have been heavily relied upon. The algorithms Random Forest and Support Vector Machine are used for solar PV panels [12 - 14]

- Before estimating the power of a solar PV system, it is necessary to forecast sun irradiation. The aerosol index is used as input data for a neural network-based intelligent model. Based on daily weather classification, the artificial neural network applies the Nonlinear Auto-Regressive for Exogenous Input data technique to predict the upcoming day's 4-hour solar radiation outputs. Previously, models used temperature, moisture, prevailing winds, and wind speed data to calculate an exact prediction for PV power generation 4 hours in the future. The suggested PV forecasting model's projected outcomes are assessed using statistical measures like the Mean Square Error technique [15 - 17].

- An investigation into estimating the output power of solar photovoltaic (PV) plants using fuzzy logic and artificial neural networks is presented in this research. It is possible to make reasonable forecasts about the output of solar plants using fuzzy logic and high-performance computer processors. When used for forecasting, the ANN technique combines machine learning with pattern recognition to produce accurate results. It is the primary goal of the research reported in this paper to undertake solar PV plant production forecasting, which will be important for effective load management and for investigating the dependability of the electrical power distribution system [18 - 20].

3. ISSUES IN ARTIFICIAL NEURAL TRAINING

While training any ANN with predictable data or information, the following challenges will arise.

- Weights' Initial Values
- The Rate of Learning
- Oversampling or Overfitting
- Scaling of the input

3.1. Weights Initial Value

Starting with the right weights is crucial. If the weights are set too close to zero, the network will converge to a linear model. Starting weights are usually selected at a random distance from zero. Excessively large values usually provide unsatisfactory outcomes because the model is under-fitted. Early weights close to zero, as well as + and - values, are generally preferred.

3.2. Rate of Learning

Eventually, the answer will be chosen with how rapidly the back-learning propagation procedure develops. A large learning rate may lead to poor results, whereas a lower learning rate renders learning extremely difficult. It is common for non-advanced methods to begin with a strong learning rate and then eventually decrease till a precise decreasing gain inaccuracy is attained in a tolerable length of calculation time. This technique is not considered progressive.

3.3. Oversampling or Overfitting

Applying a penalizing term to the minimization issue, as explained in the Lasso, is a typical cure for overfitting. R () + J () is normally chosen as the function to reduce *via* back-propagation, where;

$$J(\theta)=\sum_{km}\beta 2mk+\sum_{j}\sum_{nm}\alpha 2nm, j \tag{1}$$

And 0 is the factor that synchronizes the magnitude of the penalization. The weights will shrink toward zero if the amount is large. The procedure described above is known as weight decay.

3.4. Scaling of the Input

The scaling of the input has the potential to transform the scaling of the performance gradient weights, and thus the overall output results. As a result, standardizing all input data is normal to practice. Normally, the data is centered (zero mean) with a one-standard-deviation standard deviation.

4. IMPORTANT ELEMENTS IN ARTIFICIAL NEURAL NETWORK (ANN) FOR PV

Deep learning is a subset of machine learning. It resembles a brain implanted in a gadget that is programmed to perform specific duties. ANN is a mathematical system that converts inputs to another type of output based on a defined transfer function. In layman's terms, ANN is a set of predetermined processes that relate a system's patterns, transfer function, and data. This can also be represented as the activity of neurons in the human brain. Initially, there is a distinction between a conventional present system and an ANN. It is a typically defined system that will receive data in a similar format, process the data according to the programming flow, and generate an output. It cannot conclude on its own when the data provided is insufficient. ANN, on the other hand, does not function in the way that a conventional system would. It functions similarly to a human brain, making decisions or manipulating inputs based on the system's circumstances. We introduce several intermediate phases in the ANN or machine learning algorithm to make the computational process more advanced.

The variance in the neural network's computational flow is determined by the data computation flow. There are several versions.

4.1. Feed-forward ANN Network

The values are obtained externally and then pushed forward to the following levels for manipulation and decision-making. The processed output data will not be reused in the following cycle. It will reduce the system's processing time and energy consumption. However, the manipulation must be precise and accurate in its transfer function. This results in an error-free output.

4.2. Feed-backward ANN Network

A feedback path exists between the Primary and Solution Layers in this backward type. Due to the utilization of feedback, we must incorporate memory into the network pattern. This form of neural schema is utilized for error checking, resulting in more precise output solution details. However, the downside is that the feedback processing time, a function utilized for error checking in the feedback path, and the network's power consumption are increased. As a result, to obtain a more precise answer, we must make concessions to the aforementioned shortcomings.

The Following Algorithm 1 Depicts the Simplified Operation of an ANN

Step 1: The supplied data is given weighting values.

The values of X1, X2,...., and Xn are depicted in the preceding diagram.

Step 2: Each intermediate layer receives the data associated with its corresponding input layer.

Step 3: All adjustments are performed on the intermediate layer.

Algorithm 2: Proposed Functionality of PV Prediction System

Step 1: Start the Sensor data export from a microcontroller.

Step 2: Deploying the sensor materials as per the requirement.

Step 3: As the manipulated data is to be received from various sensing elements. We have to allocate a unique Identity Number to each sensor.

Step 4: Verification of Id number with their passwords given.

Step 5: Declare the Local Variables for Temperature, Humidity, Soil Moisture, Rainfall estimation, Pressure, Time, i=40.

// Temperature = Temp, Voltage= Volt, Current= C, Time = T

Step 6: In Cloud Servers, the data is displayed inside the Dashboards and Worksheets.

Step 7: ANN is used to split the data according to the proportion supplied as testing and training data.

Step 8: If training values equal testing values, the equivalent parameters should be approximated. Make the value visible.

Also, go to step 7

Step 9: For T -1 to check

If Voltage is less than or equal to 50% then "Load is OFF"

Else "Load is ON".

Go to Steps 5 & 6

Step 10: End the program

Models of Prediction

In this section, we'll go over the exact processes that were taken for various models and forecasts.

Machine Learning Algorithm 3

Step1: Filter data depending on availability for each forecast horizon.

Step 2: Delete observations made at night;

Step 3: Divide the dataset into training and a test set;

Step 4: Define a factor set (*e.g.*, $K = (1,...,10)$ for ANN;

Step 5: use fold I as the validation set for each parameter p in the parameter set;

Step 6: Define a parameter set (*e.g.*, $K = (1,..., 10)$ for ANN;

Step 7: Define optional data that should be pre-processed;

Step 8: Assemble the model on the remaining $K - 1$ fold; End

Step 9: By predicting values for the validation set.

Step 10: End

Algorithm 3 depicts the machine learning algorithm that was used for each area and model. These parameters are divided into hourly increments and range from 15 minutes to 5 hours. Because each site has its own set of requirements, each is trained separately. It also helps to compare how different models perform in different climates. Below is a more detailed explanation of each model.

The weather parameters gathered from Google Datasheets were then used as input for processing. These data are divided into two categories: training data (60%) and test data (40%). Using a Feed-forward Artificial Neural Network to forecast the weather parameters with the Power Generation for the next day's report. Finally, we check the apparent and actual parameter values from the designed system. The correctness and performance of a proposed system are verified using the Mean Square function given as:

$$MSE = \sqrt{\frac{1}{n} \sum y1 - y2} \qquad (2)$$

Here, n gives the number of data recorded, y1 and y2 show predicted and estimated values. For the detailed impact of environmental parameters on the earth's atmosphere, we make a separate data comparison. This illustration provides a high-level overview of the photovoltaic details of the proposed system. Additionally, we can observe that the projected values will be closer to the true values when compared to the real values.

5. PROPOSED METHODOLOGY

The Solar PV Power Generation prediction model using an Artificial Neural network is explained in this paper. This model predicts the temperature and the power generated by the solar panels at a given date based on the previous weather data. The block diagram Power Generation Prediction in Solar PV systems by Machine Learning Approach is depicted in Fig. (**1**). This model consists of a Sensor Unit, an Arduino Uno board, and a Data management unit. The current temperature, Voltage, and current sensors are utilized to measure the Power Generation Prediction in the Solar PV system. The outputs of these Sensing units were given to the Arduino Uno board. The output of the Arduino board is displayed in Thingspeak through the internet.

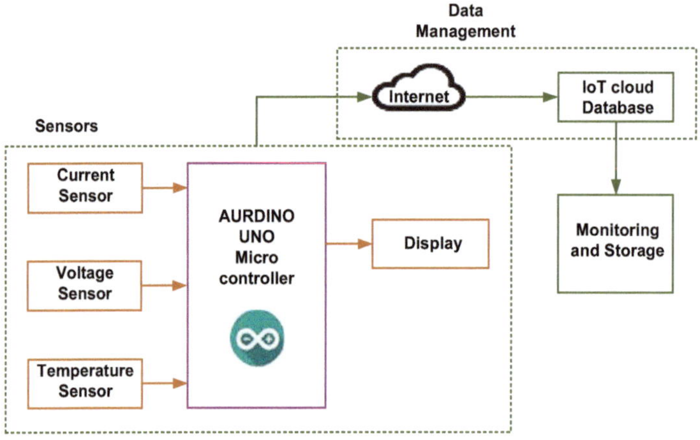

Fig. (1). Block Diagram of the Proposed System.

5.1. Current Sensing Unit

The current Sensing Unit reduces high-voltage currents to a safe level, allowing a standard ammeter to safely detect the actual electrical current flowing in an AC and DC transmission line given in Fig. (**2**).

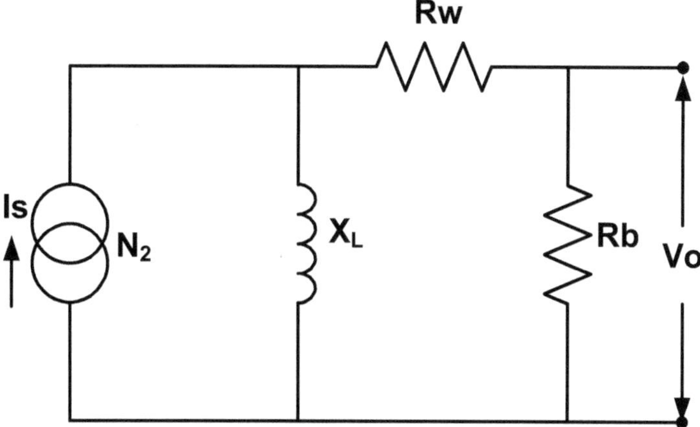

Fig. (2). Current sensing unit.

5.2. Voltage Sensing Unit

The Voltage Sensor is essentially a Voltage Divider made of two resistors with resistances of 30K and 7.5K, resulting in a 5 to 1 voltage divider. (Fig. **3**) depicts the Voltage Sensor Module's schematic with a 25V input voltage limit.

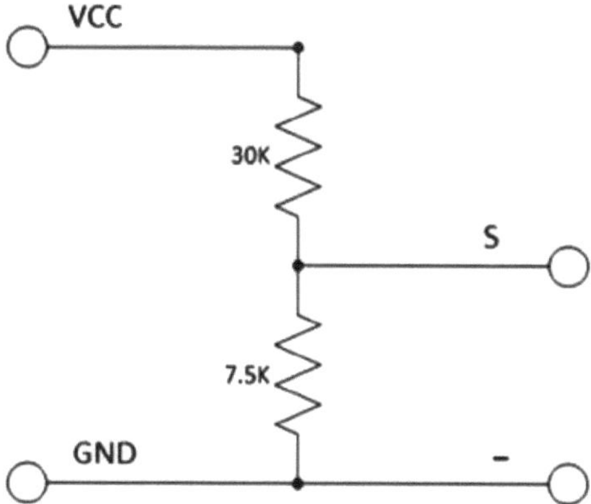

Fig. (3). Voltage Sensor Schematic.

5.3. The PV Generation Prediction Process and Implementation with Sensor Outputs

The weather data is manipulated by the microcontroller and then stored in the cloud. The data is displayed on the MQTT dashboard platform. (Fig. **4**) gives the Output Data flow Path Prediction Process. The MQTT dashboard is a graphical user interface that displays the ambient temperature, voltage value, and current value. To train and test these data, a feed-forward ANN with the specifications listed in Table **1** is utilized. If a match is identified, the system forecasts the weather and displays the results *via* any wireless devices or online apps. Following that, it will be returned to the stage of training and testing. The microcontroller may collect Sensor data and send it to the prediction process and then to web applications. The status of the controller is displayed in the MQTT dashboard. The graphical user interface (GUI) assists farmers and non-technical users in making decisions.

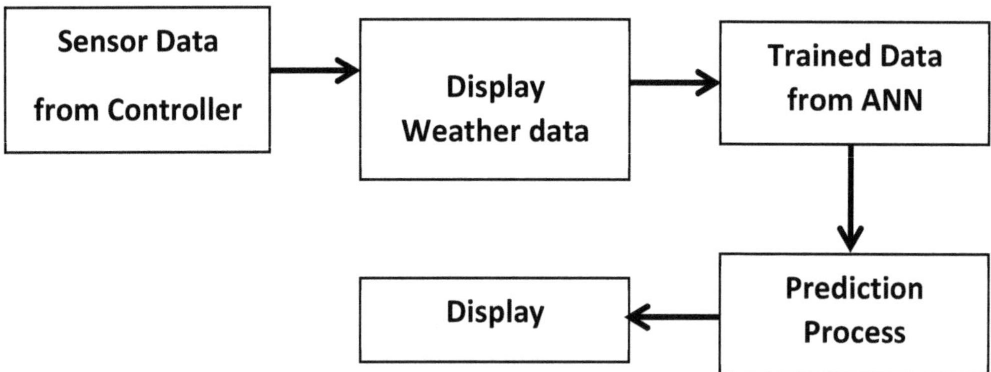

Fig. (4). Output Data flow Path Prediction Process.

Table 1. Fundamental requisites of our Artificial Neural Network model.

Specification	Methodology
Neural Network model	Multi-Layered Perceptron (MLP)
Number of intermediate Layers	12
The function of Intermediate layers used for Activation	Sigmoid/Logistic functions
The function of the Solution layer used for Activation	Fully Linear type

The actual connection diagram of various sensors with the controller is depicted in Fig. (**5**). Our proposed system is illustrated in Algorithm 1. It forecasts weather data for the next day and activates the PV generation prediction System.

Fig. (5). Various Sensor connections with the Controller.

As a further benefit, the proposed methodology checks the temperature around the deployed circumstances, temperature and voltage value, and atmospheric pressure, as in Fig. (**6**). The proposed system configuration, as well as the components used, such as controllers and sensors, have been described. On the connection board, there is also a schematic representation of a circuit for the sensing detectors and consoles.

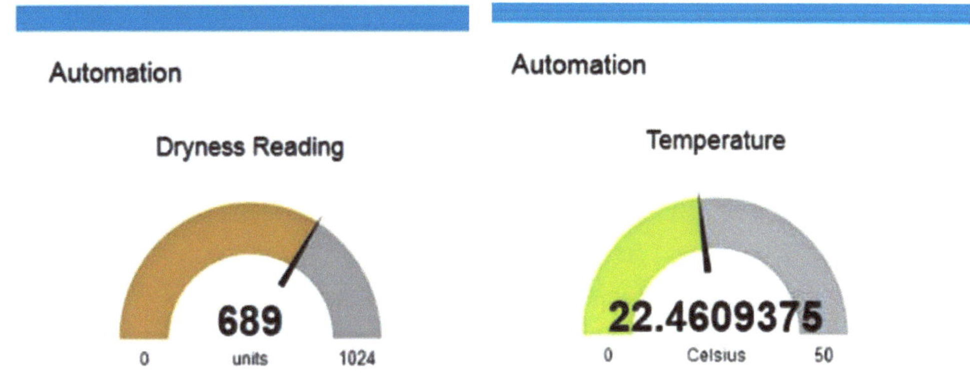

Fig. (6). The output of the sensor values.

6. VARIABILITY IN DATA

There is a lot of fluctuation in the output of a single PV panel, as demonstrated in Fig. (**7**) (cloudy days) and (Fig. **8**) (sunny days), as well as errors in the overall cloud cover prediction. Even though the two forecasts appear to be very close, the actual energy production may be quite different, showing the inherent uncertainty in the input data. Local flaws in the input data mix with the forecasting approach to cause significant systemic errors.

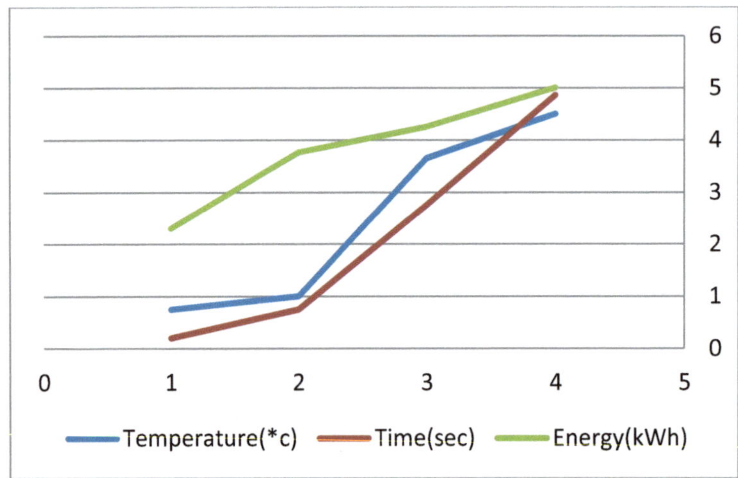

Fig. (7). Variations on a cloudy day.

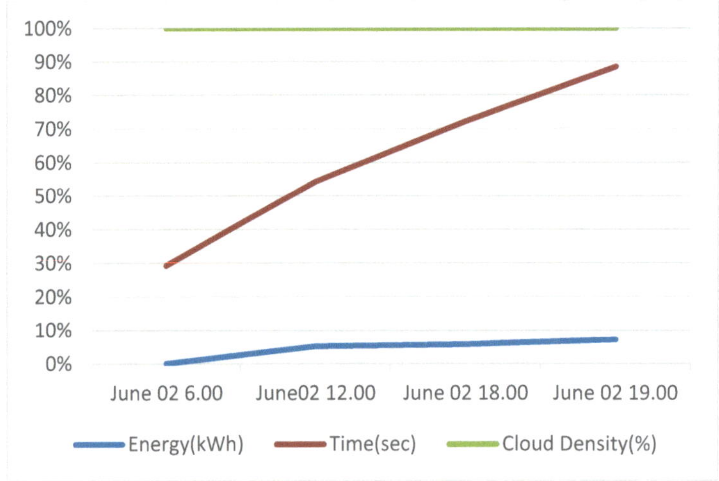

Fig. (8). Variations on a sunny day.

Even though the two forecasts appear to be very close, the actual energy production may be quite different, showing the inherent uncertainty in the input data. Local flaws in the input data mix with the forecasting approach to cause significant global errors.

6.1. Data Processing

Overall, the dataset has been relatively clean. As a result, the majority of data processing is involved with accurately sorting the data. The datasets were filtered by computing a lead time for when real-time data became available. The dataset was sorted for this lead time to guarantee that no dataset contained inaccessible information. When the data was properly sorted, a data row was created that had the corresponding weather data in various locations as well as lagged variables. It is vital to understand that when a prediction is made on any time horizon, it is referring to forecasting the energy output of a 15-minute interval within that time horizon, not the energy output of the next time step. As a result, a one-hour projection refers to the energy output of 15 minutes in that hour rather than the energy output of the following hour.

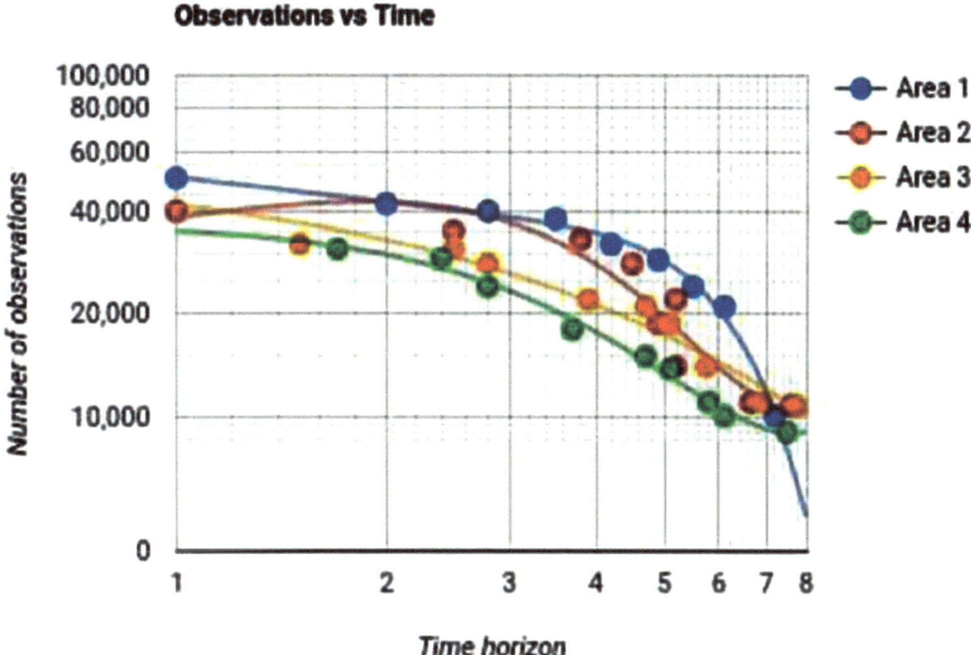

Fig. 9. Fitting models at various locations.

The data from the previous night had to be destroyed as well, which was a mandatory data deletion obligation. Because energy output throughout the night is more easily forecasted, performance measurements would be boosted, providing an incorrect picture of the models' performance. Furthermore, including midnight data forces the model to choose between fitting daytime data well and fitting nighttime data well, the latter of which is useless. Because sundown in Sweden varies by season, any observation with clear sky radiation of greater than 8- 15 W/M2 was considered daytime.

7. RESULTS

7.1. Temperature Values

For making this IoT-based system to be cost-effective, a microcontroller has been used. Also, the power consumption of the smart system is less. (Fig. **10**) represents the Comparison of Recorded and Estimated temperatures.

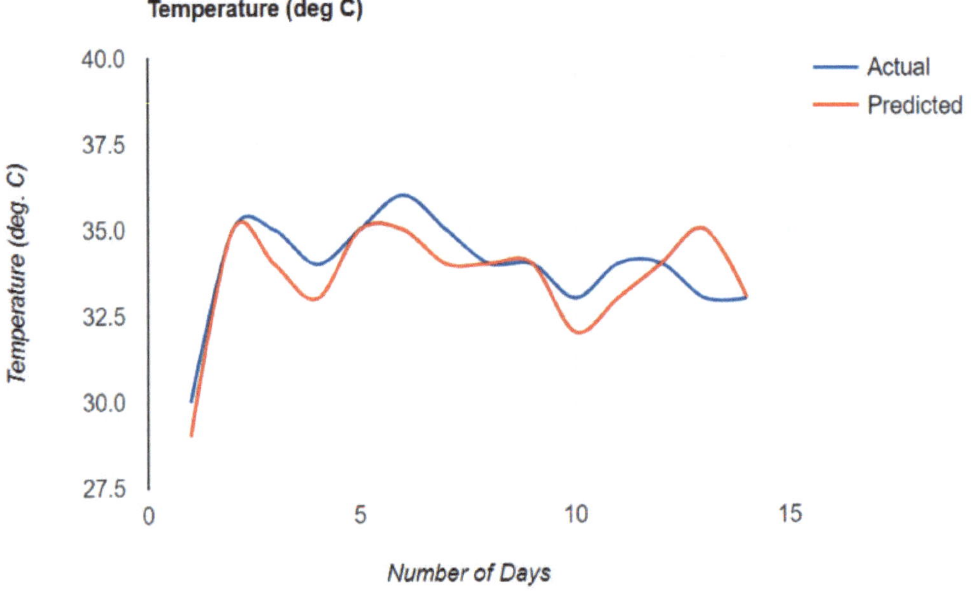

Fig. (10). Recorded *Vs* Estimated Temperature.

7.2. Power Generated Values

In the solar system, the efficiency of the implemented system will be decided on the number of kWh observed from the light sources. From (Fig. **11**), we may see that efficiency stability reaches when it attains 50% of our observed time. *i.e*, from the 10-time units, it is stable on reaching a value in the range of 6 kWh to 8 kWh.

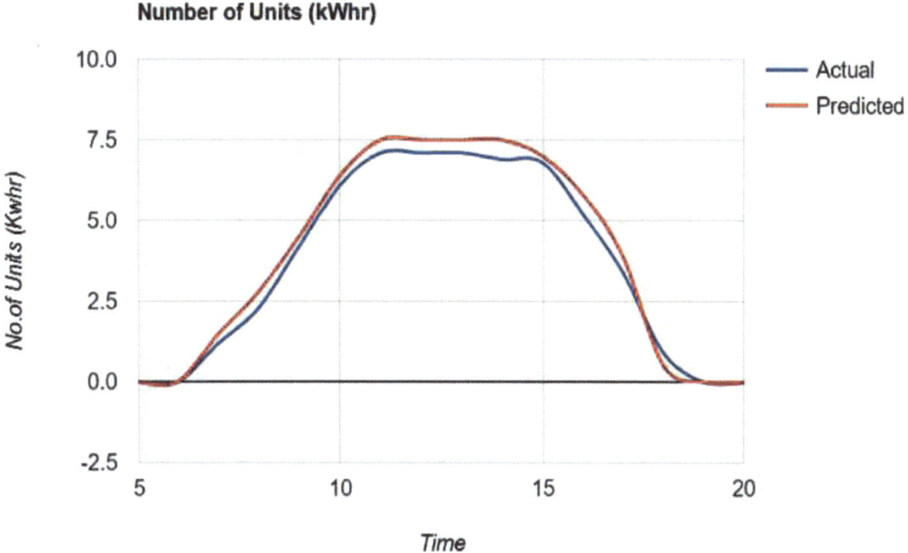

Fig. (11). Actual and Predicted data concerning time.

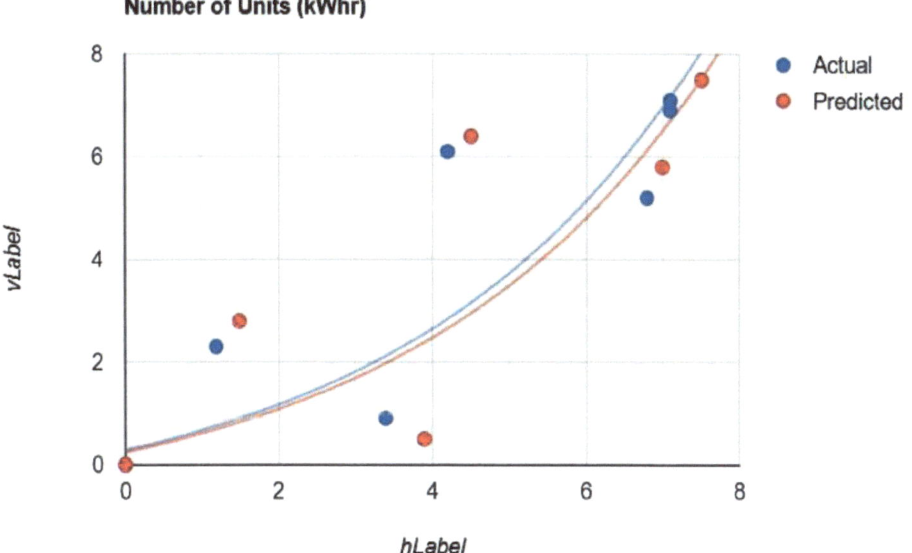

Fig. (12). Actual and Predicted data estimation.

Sample variables were taken for the comparison of predicted and actual data, as represented in Fig. (**12**).

In Fig. (**13**), temperature and energy generated are linear depending on temperature. As the temperature increases, the solar panel may undergo physical changes in its composition. Hence, we may take note of temperature and units stored. As temperature increases from 20 degrees, the units attain a maximum value between 2kWhr to 7kWhr.

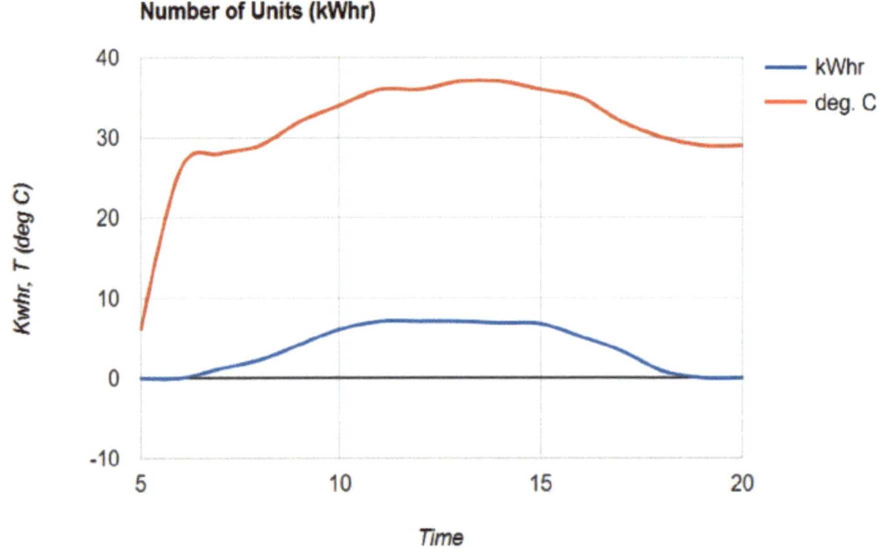

Fig. (13). Graph indicating KWhr (Power) and °C (temperature) variations concerning the time.

Generally, all solar systems based on the panel temperature play a vital role in the life of the panel board used. As days increase, the system temperature also increases. We can observe from (Fig. **14**) that the temperature starts to increase from 30 degree to 40 degree. After some tempt compensation method, the temperature starts to decline from 38 degree as the days are increased.

From (Fig. **15**) above, the kWhr units observed from the light source are increasing from 2 kWh to 7kWhr. Also, as the energy from the atmosphere is stable it will result in instability in the observation of units.

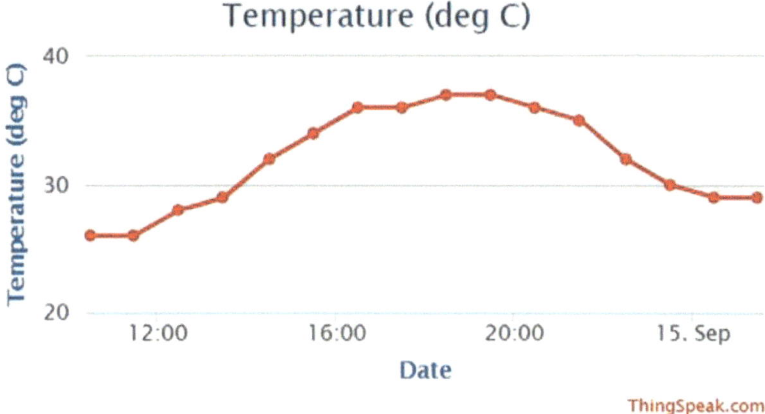

Fig. (14). Temperature Variations on different days.

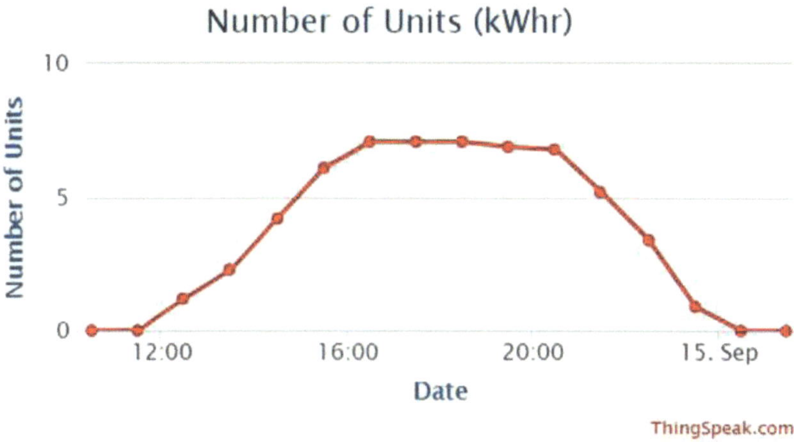

Fig. (15). Date wise predictions.

8. THE OUTCOME OF THIS METHODOLOGY

- In terms of methodology, there are several factors to consider for optimizing the results. One option to consider is implementing distinct models for distinct seasons. By dividing the year into winter and summer seasons and then training the models independently, the outcomes are likely to improve. To tie this to the previously noted performance measurement issues and the fact that models perform better when trained on more particular periods, one could attempt to model exclusively during peak hours. In this case, the model would not have to make a trade-off between modifying the parameters to perform well on morning and night data as well as data collected during the mid-day hours.

- The disadvantage of utilizing a single model for an entire year is that the model will be trained on data that will fluctuate owing to changing weather conditions. This forces the model to become more generalized throughout the year. If the model is trained for only the winter months, it may focus only on these aspects without needing to make a trade-off between fitting the summer and winter data properly. On the other hand, having separate models for different climates would necessitate model changes regularly, which could be cumbersome in an operating situation.

CONCLUSION

As a result, the proposed system is entitled to an average accuracy of greater than 85% for all meteorological parameters discovered utilizing our proposed system, the purpose of this project was to create and deploy an improved smart meteorological data system. The installation method for this system has been thoroughly developed and designed to be as user-friendly as possible. The findings of these investigations indicate that these machine learning models are capable of forecasting weather variables relevant to solar generating with a degree of consistency comparable to that of conventional methods. Forecasts for a given area were also made utilizing historical data from nearby places; additionally, it was demonstrated that this method is more effective than concentrating just on the area where weather forecasting is conducted. The proposed method is capable of determining actual weather factors in the surroundings, such as overcast days and sunny days, about the temperature obtained *via* the dashboard. As a result of this data, which will be merged with data from weather stations, this prediction system will improve even further. As a result, the proposed framework is less expensive than more traditional methods of doing tasks.

REFERENCES

[1]   S. Yadav, D.P. Mahato, and N. Linh, *Distributed Artificial Intelligence: A Modern Approach* CRC Press, 2020.
[http://dx.doi.org/10.13140/RG.2.2.19776.69128]

[2]   A. Kumar, M. Rizwan, and U. Nangia, "Artificial neural network-based model for short term solar radiation forecasting considering aerosol index", *2018 2nd IEEE International Conference on Power Electronics, Intelligent Control, and Energy Systems (ICPEICES),* 2018, pp. 212-217 Delhi, India.
[http://dx.doi.org/10.1109/ICPEICES.2018.8897290]

[3]   M.K. Park, J.M. Lee, W.H. Kang, J.M. Choi, and K.H. Lee, "Predictive model for PV power generation using RNN (LSTM)", *J. Mech. Sci. Technol.,* vol. 35, no. 2, pp. 795-803, 2021.
[http://dx.doi.org/10.1007/s12206-021-0140-0]

[4]   S. Bourhnane, M.R. Abid, R. Lghoul, K. Zine-Dine, N. Elkamoun, and D. Benhaddou, "Machine learning for energy consumption prediction and scheduling in smart buildings", *SN Applied Sciences,* vol. 2, no. 2, p. 297, 2020.
[http://dx.doi.org/10.1007/s42452-020-2024-9]

[5]   M.J. Sanjari, H.B. Gooi, and N.K.C. Nair, "Power generation forecast of hybrid PV–wind system", *IEEE Trans. Sustain. Energy,* vol. 11, no. 2, pp. 703-712, 2020.
[http://dx.doi.org/10.1109/TSTE.2019.2903900]

[6]   Y.K. Wu, Y.C. Wu, J.S. Hong, L.H. Phan, and Q.D. Phan, "Probabilistic forecast of wind power generation with data processing and numerical weather predictions", *IEEE Trans. Ind. Appl.,* vol. 57, no. 1, pp. 36-45, 2021.
[http://dx.doi.org/10.1109/TIA.2020.3037264]

[7]   T. Hiyama, and K. Kitabayashi, "Neural network based estimation of maximum power generation from PV module using environmental information", *IEEE Trans. Energ. Convers.,* vol. 12, no. 3, pp. 241-247, 1997.
[http://dx.doi.org/10.1109/60.629709]

[8]   Z.W. Zheng, Y.Y. Chen, M.M. Huo, and B. Zhao, "An overview: The development of prediction technology of wind and photovoltaic power generation", *Energy Procedia,* vol. 12, pp. 601-608, 2011.
[http://dx.doi.org/10.1016/j.egypro.2011.10.081]

[9]   I.K. Nti, M. Teimeh, O. Nyarko-Boateng, and A.F. Adekoya, "Electricity load forecasting: A systematic review", *J. Electr. Syst. Inf. Technol,* vol. 7, no. 1, p. 13, 2020.
[http://dx.doi.org/10.1186/s43067-020-00021-8]

[10]   V. Veeramsetty, and R. Deshmukh, "Electric power load forecasting on a 33/11 kV substation using artificial neural networks", *SN Applied Sciences,* vol. 2, no. 5, p. 855, 2020.
[http://dx.doi.org/10.1007/s42452-020-2601-y]

[11]   S. Malakar, S. Goswami, B. Ganguli, A. Chakrabarti, S.S. Roy, K. Boopathi, and A.G. Rangaraj, "Designing a long short-term network for short-term forecasting of global horizontal irradiance", *SN Applied Sciences,* vol. 3, no. 4, p. 477, 2021.
[http://dx.doi.org/10.1007/s42452-021-04421-x]

[12]   R. Anaadumba, Q. Liu, B.D. Marah, F.M. Nakoty, X. Liu, and Y. Zhang, "A renewable energy forecasting and control approach to secured edge-level efficiency in a distributed micro-grid", *Cybersecurity,* vol. 4, no. 1, p. 1, 2021.
[http://dx.doi.org/10.1186/s42400-020-00065-3]

[13]   D. Su, E. Batzelis, and B. Pal, "Machine learning algorithms in forecasting of photovoltaic power generation", *2019 International Conference on Smart Energy Systems and Technologies (SEST),* 2019, pp. 1-6 Porto, Portugal.
[http://dx.doi.org/10.1109/SEST.2019.8849106]

[14]   R. Vijay, and R. Ponraj, "Dynamic performance enhancement of modified sepic converter", *2021 2nd International Conference for Emerging Technology (INCET),* 2021, pp. 1-5 Belagavi, India.
[http://dx.doi.org/10.1109/INCET51464.2021.9456403]

[15]   S. Alketbi, A.B. Nassif, M.A. Eddin, I. Shahin, and A. Elnagar, "Predicting the power of a combined cycle power plant using machine learning methods", *2020 International Conference on Communications, Computing, Cybersecurity, and Informatics (CCCI),* 2020, pp. 1-5 Sharjah, United Arab Emirates.
[http://dx.doi.org/10.1109/CCCI49893.2020.9256742]

[16]   S.N. Nnamchi, O.A. Nnamchi, and J.D. Busingye, "Modeling, simulation, and prediction of global energy indices: A differential approach", *Front. Energy,* vol. 16, pp. 375-392, 2021.
[http://dx.doi.org/10.1007/s11708-021-0723-6]

[17]   V. Ravindran, "Simulated design and implementation of solar based water pumping system", *2021 2nd International Conference for Emerging Technology (INCET)*, 2021, pp. 1-5 Belagavi, India.
[http://dx.doi.org/10.1109/INCET51464.2021.9456131]

[18]   D. Mukherjee, S. Chakraborty, P.K. Guchhait, and J. Bhunia, "Machine learning-based solar power generation forecasting with and without MPPT controller", *2020 IEEE 1st International Conference for Convergence in Engineering (ICCE)*, 2020, pp. 44-48 Kolkata, India.
[http://dx.doi.org/10.1109/ICCE50343.2020.9290685]

[19]   G.M. Khan, J. Ali, and S.A. Mahmud, "Wind power forecasting : An application of machine learning in renewable energy", *2014 International Joint Conference on Neural Networks (IJCNN)*, 2014, pp. 1130-1137 Beijing, China.
[http://dx.doi.org/10.1109/IJCNN.2014.6889771]

[20]   A. Khalyasmaa, "Prediction of solar power generation based on random forest regressor model", *2019 International Multi-Conference on Engineering, Computer and Information Sciences (SIBIRCON)*, 2019.
[http://dx.doi.org/10.1109/SIBIRCON48586.2019.8958063]

An Efficient Framework and Implementation of a Weather Prediction System

Smitha Shekar[1,*], G. Harish[1], K. N. Asha[1] and K. P. Asha Rani[1]

[1] *Department of Computer Science & Engineering, Dr. Ambedkar Institute of Technology, Mallathahalli, Bangalore, Karnataka - 560056, India*

Abstract: The majority of today's weather forecasting studies have been focused on complex physical models. These models are usually run on hundreds of nodes in a High-Performance Computing system, which consumes a lot more power. Despite the employment of these costly and complex tools, projections are frequently incorrect due to inaccurate beginning conditions, measurements or a lack of understanding of atmospheric dynamics. Furthermore, solving complex models like this often takes a long time. The Internet of Things has helped any field that deals with technology. Using an IoT device, a prototype based on a machine learning approach is proposed in this study with an efficient framework, and implementation of an automated weather prediction system based on Artificial Neural Network algorithms was designed and developed. This system includes a technologically advanced irrigation system for our convenience. Using ANN in this research, the weather for the next day appears to have been predicted. The evaluation findings suggest that the model's accuracy is sufficient for existing works and their approaches.

Keywords: ANN, Forecasting, IoT, Weather Prediction.

1. INTRODUCTION

All around the world, weather patterns change rapidly and continuously. People's lives are greatly affected by the weather. Weather monitoring enables data analysis and forecasting to provide important weather information. Predicting the weather is challenging since there are so many variables that affect weather changes. From the viewpoints of system architecture and information processing, existing weather monitoring and prediction systems can be characterized by taking into account system operations and processing technologies. Every aspect of our lives, from agriculture and business to travel and the daily commute, is inf-

---

[*] **Corresponding author Smitha Shekar:** Department of Computer Science & Engineering, Dr. Ambedkar Institute of Technology, Mallathahalli, Bangalore, Karnataka - 560056, India; E-mail: smithashekarb.cs@drait.edu.in

Satya Prakash Yadav, Sansar Singh Chauhan, Sanjeev Kumar Pippal and Victor Hugo C. de Albuquerque (Eds.)

luenced by weather forecasts to a large extent. Climate change and its implications are affecting the entire planet, thus accurate weather forecasting is essential for smooth travel and safe operations [1].

Weather service is among the most challenging tasks in a country. Smart technology and web- development technologies are just used to implement the system in real time. Most of the solutions are interoperable with third-party IoT platforms such as ThinkSpeak, firebase, and others. We have, regrettably, conjured up our Graphical-based methodology and a Telemetry dashboard, which are both seamless to use and intuitive [2].

Every situation calls for accurate forecasting. As a result, the model parameters of the weather forecasting model must be handled differently. There is a connection between statistical approaches and data that does not follow a linear pattern, and on the other hand, is related to artificial intelligence methods. Neuro-fuzzy logic and neural networks are among the artificial intelligence learning paradigms. One of these is neural networks. The application of ANN improves weather forecasting accuracy. A lot of variables are included in the daily weather data, such as the temperature, humidity and rainfall amounts, cloud distance and size, wind speed and direction. Although all of these elements are nonlinear, combining them is necessary to determine the temperature, rainfall, humidity, and weather status for the following day. A complicated model is required for such applications, one of which is capable of producing results based on the patterns created from training data provided to the model. Selecting the input data and parameters for a weather forecasting ANN model is critical [3]. The input data must come from a specific location where the model is trained and evaluated to produce reliable results. It's also important to note that the volume of input data that goes into the model helps it perform better by generating outcomes that are very comparable to anticipated and actual output data. Because of any noise in the data, it must be cleaned up. All of the parameters are expressed in different units, and leveling simplifies the linkage of input to output parameters. Training and testing samples should be divided in appropriate proportions to allow for a precise estimate, verification, and validation of the findings. For reliable results, the neural network model must be well-structured. Nonlinear data can be more accurately predicted with the help of a multi-layer ANN. Any given neural network layer will have its activation function, which is dependent on the situation [4].

Due to their computational complexity, these models are too expensive to run. A different type of model is the data mining model, which is based on probabilities and/or similarity patterns, rather than historical data. Each category of prediction is similarly handled by the model, and the model is expected to have the modest level of accuracy. Modeled output may be required for daily weather forecasts as well as weekly or monthly weather plans. Hence, forecasting relies heavily on precision to obtain the greatest results out of the various models [5].

2. RELATED WORKS

- Many primary sectors, such as agriculture, rely on the weather for production. This rapid climate change makes traditional weather prediction methods less accurate and more time-consuming. Improved and dependable weather forecasting technologies are needed to solve these challenges. Economic and social conditions are affected by these forecasts. The major goal of this project is to create a weather forecasting system that can be used in remote places. Meteorological conditions are predicted using data analytics and machine learning methods such as random forest classification (RFC). We provide a reduced, accessible weather forecasting model [6 - 8].
- When it comes down to it, the weather is made up of many variables including rainfall and wind speed. For researchers, the environmental weather forecast is a challenging task that has attracted a lot of attention in recent years. There are a broad variety of weather figure methods that may be used to study the current weather or the weather through time by using accessible meteorological data. Determining meteorological characteristics with precision is becoming increasingly difficult due to their dynamic context [9 - 13]. To predict air characteristics, different machine learning algorithms are linked together in a network. Various applications based on Numerical Weather Prediction outputs are also examined.
- Within 24 hours, forecast models for wind farm production are presented in this work. Feed-forward neural networks are being used to provide accurate wind power predictions. Furthermore, the ideal architecture for each forecasting model is determined through sensitivity analysis by altering the main parameters of the artificial neural network. Based on the data gained, numerical weather prediction models are compared to actual weather conditions [14 - 16].
- The very first attempt to predict the weather quantitatively has required a greater workforce than the previous attempts have done. Since powerful computers and improved modeling tools were developed, weather prediction has returned to the early models. Then, in Weather Prediction, the simple-basic equations are used as forecast equations. As meteorological variables vary over time, equations can be used in our research to generate new values of those variables in the future for prediction. Short-range weather data from a particular station is used to determine the weather conditions in one particular area [17]. The results gained suggest that it is capable of predicting the weather conditions more correctly and precisely than any other method now available.

- Using a variety of sensors, we propose to build a weather forecasting system based on Arduino. On this page, we'll show how a portable weather monitoring and rain forecasting device can be used to keep track of the weather. Meteorology is a branch of meteorology that measures temperature changes over time and characterizes the troposphere. Climate, on the other hand, refers to a long-term average. Automatic weather monitoring is now possible and even useful thanks to technological advancements. As well as weather aficionados, this method will also be useful to businesses and individuals whose employment is dependent on weather conditions. Examples of how it can be used in agriculture include monitoring weather conditions and sending alerts if they become unfavorable to the planted crops [18]. This approach can be used to help athletes who participate in sports that are highly dependent on the weather.

- A lot of computational power is needed to do traditional weather forecasting, which uses physical principles. Weather forecasting is now possible because of modern advances in machine learning, which have allowed us to experiment with new methods. These capabilities, advantages, and disadvantages of neural networks as they relate to weather prediction will be discussed in this essay. As a way to demonstrate that weather forecasting can be done on a budget, the researchers used open-source machine learning libraries, freely available data, and two off-the-shelf PCs for all of their tests [19].

- Because of the non-linearity of weather forecasting data, different deep learning architectures have been developed. Using Neural Network Architectures, Spatial and Temporal Scales, as well as Datasets and Benchmarks, this study evaluates the state-of-the-art research of deep-learning-based weather forecasting in terms of their design. As a final step, it summarizes its findings while emphasizing model generalization and accuracy, i.e., whether or not the model is suited for a local or regional area, as well as whether or not it can be utilized for short-term or long-term forecasts? It also identifies independent and dependent factors in weather forecasting in each study and evaluates algorithms used to train the dataset in terms of their time efficiency [20 - 22].

3. PROPOSED SYSTEM

(Figs. **1** & **2**) depict the envisioned smart weather forecast system. Atmosphere heat and water content calculating components (DHT22), soil moisture sensors (YL69), climatologic pressure sensors (BMP180), and rain intrusion sensors (FC37) were the devices employed. We organize meteorological attributes like humidity in the air, the moisture level in the soil (SM), barometric pressure, and actual rainfall information from these sensors respectively.

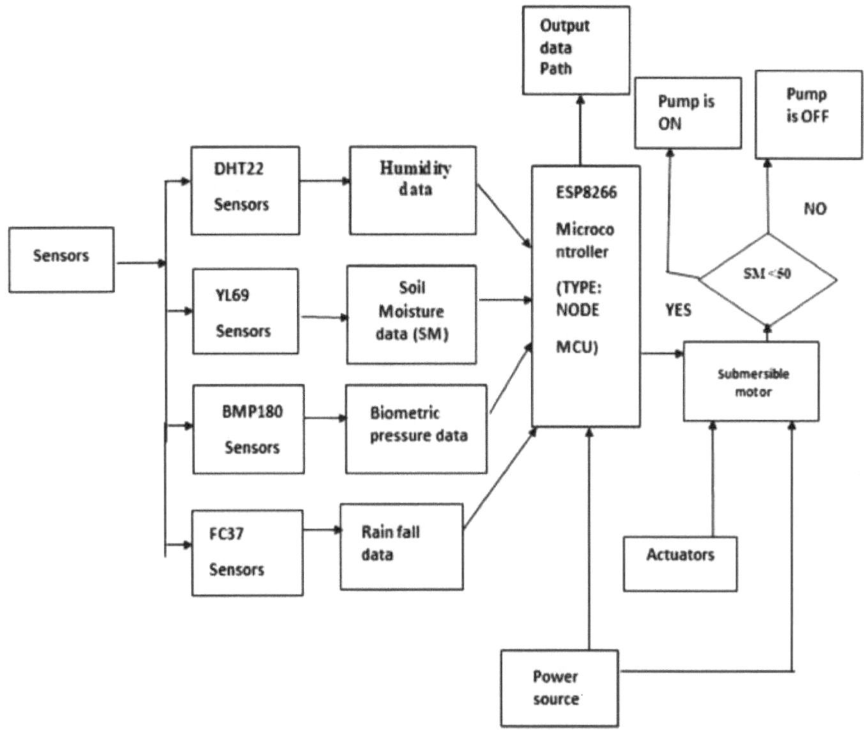

Fig. (1). Proposed smart weather system.

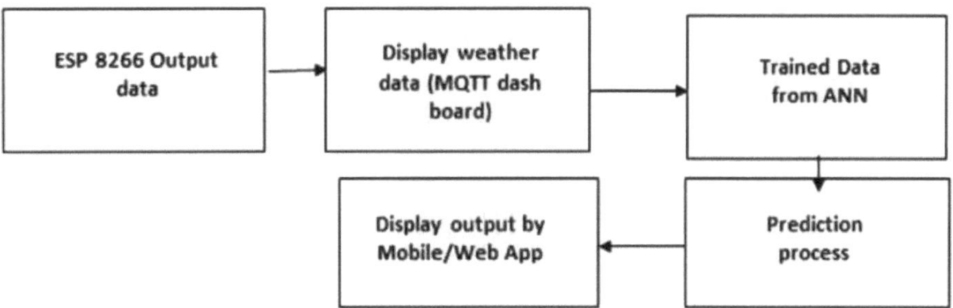

Fig. (2). Output data path.

3.1. System Architecture

The microcontroller manipulates the weather data, which is then stored in the cloud. The MQTT dashboard platform displays the data (Sheet in the Google database). The MQTT dashboard is a Graphical User Interface that showcases atmospheric temperature, humidity in the air, and pump performance. A feed-forward ANN with the specifications stated in Table **1** is used to train and test these data. If a match is found, the system will forecast the weather situation and showcases the results through any wireless devices or web applications. After that, it will be returned to the stage of training purpose and testing purpose. The SM information can be gathered by the microcontroller and sent to the submersible pump. This pump is connected to the relay/Actuators. The pump's status is conveyed in the MQTT dashboard. The GUI helps farmers and non-technical individuals to make a decision. The pump will turn ON if the Moisture in the earth value is less than the reference value (50%). The following Algorithm 1 illustrates our proposed system. It anticipates weather data for the forthcoming day and stimulates the Smart Weather System (SWS). An additional advantage, the proposed methodology checks the temperature around the deployed circumstances, the moisture value of soil, and atmospheric pressure. The projected system configuration and also the components used such as controllers, sensors have been explained. Also, there is a circuit diagram for the sensing detectors and consoles on the connection board.

3.1.1. Node-MCU

At present, Node-MCU is a chip integrated with wireless connectivity to the embedded-based circuit connected to it. The programming model is USB-based with Arduino IDE. It is a 30 pin IC with 9 pins that will be digital, I pin for Analog. As there is wireless connectivity, we can send and receive inputs, and give outputs in an integrated Wifi block. Due to the 2.4 GHz Wi-Fi capacities, it is an equivalent wireless communication protocol. It also has two built-in sensors for humidity- capacitive type and a thermistor for temperature [23, 24].

3.1.2. DHT22 Humidity Sensors

Generally, a humidity sensor starts to work with a change in electrical capacity. A thin strip of Metal oxide exists between the two electrodes. The oxide changes with the atmospheric humidity. It may also contain an NTC (thermistor) on the backside of its chip. It is for detecting humidity changes or resistances variations between the two electrodes.

3.1.3. BMP Sensors

It is a pressure sensing module of the piezo-electrical type. Usually, it is made of a silicon material. This is because of changes in resistance when there is any pressure applied from the outside world. The BMP180 measures both pressure and temperature.

3.1.4. Rain Intrusion Sensors (FC37)

This sensor has two individual boards: one is a collector board and another one is an electronic board. It works based on water droplets collected in the collector board. When the board is **wet,** the output voltage decreases. On other hand, when it is dry, the output increases.

3.2. Artificial Neural Network (ANN) and Components

Deep learning is an auxiliary sector of machine learning. It imitates the human brain deployed in a device that is instructed on specified functions. ANN is a mathematical system that manipulates the inputs on a defined transfer function into another form of output. In simple words, ANN is a bunch of predefined steps that relate a system's patterns, transfer function, and data are given. We can also depict this as a working of neurons in the human brain.

Initially, there is a difference between a normal predefined system and ANN. A normally defined system will get a similar format of the input, process the data as per the programming flow, and produces an output. It cannot make a decision on its own when the data given is not feasible. On the other hand, ANN does not work in the manner stated for a normal system. It works like a human brain, takes a decision, or manipulates the inputs according to the system's circumstances. In ANN or machine learning algorithm, we introduce some intermediate stages for executing the computational process in a sophisticated manner.

3.2.1. Variations in ANN

In the neural network, the data computation flow will decide the variation in their computational flow. The variations are:

1. Feed-forward ANN network

2. Feedback ANN network

- **Feed-forward ANN Network:** In this ANN type, the values are received externally and then moved in the forward direction to the following layers for the manipulation and decision stages.

Here the processed output data will not be used again for the next cycle. It will decrease the processing time and energy consumption of the system designed. But we need to have a precise and accurate transfer function for the manipulation. This gives an Error-Free Output.

- **Feed Backward ANN Network:** In this backward type, a feedback path is available between the Primary and Solution Layer. As the feedback is used, we have to use memory in the network pattern.

This type of neural schema is used for the error checking process where the output solution details are more accurate. But the disadvantages are the feedback processing time, a function used for error checking cycle in the feedback path, and power consumption of the network implemented. Hence, for getting a more accurate solution, we have to compromise the stated disadvantages.

3.2.2. ANN Methodology and its Background

With the development of neural and machine learning, ANN starts from the root of neutral networks. It has three layers in its structure:

1. Primary layer

2. Intermediate layer

3. Solution layer

- **Primary layer**: It acts as a node that gets input data from external systems. This will be provided to the system model to learn about data to be processed. Also, the count of data to be processed will tell about the count of Informative variables used. We can know the concept of the implemented system.

The points used to get the raw data are inactive which implies that the point will not modify the data format. If the processed data received is to be handled by more than one intermediate layer, it will be duplicated here itself.

- **Intermediate layer:** It is a secondary layer that computes the data from the previous input layer and a final decision will be made based on the function defined.

Here the values are given showing transformation based on an implemented system. Depending on this transformation, a decision for satisfying the fitness condition of the system is made.

- **Solution layer:** This layer takes the final decision made on the previous layer. If the implemented system is binary type, the output node shows 1 but for multiple typed–class systems, we have more than one output.

For the understanding we may go through the simple diagram (Fig. **3**) given below:

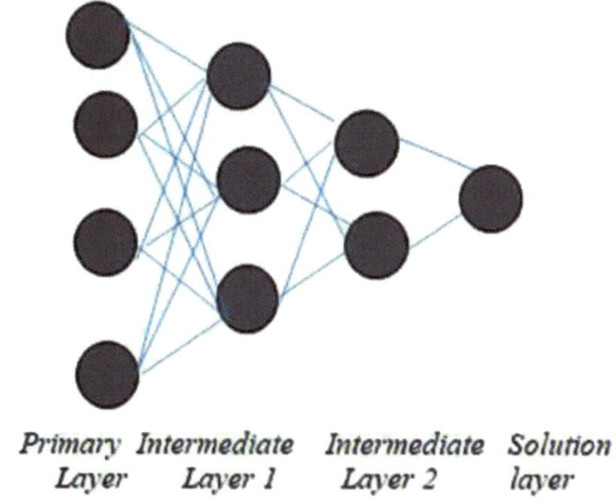

Fig. (3). Simple ANN Structure.

3.2.3. Analytical Eorking of ANN

(Fig. **4**) shows the working of the ANN model. The simplified working of ANN is shown below:

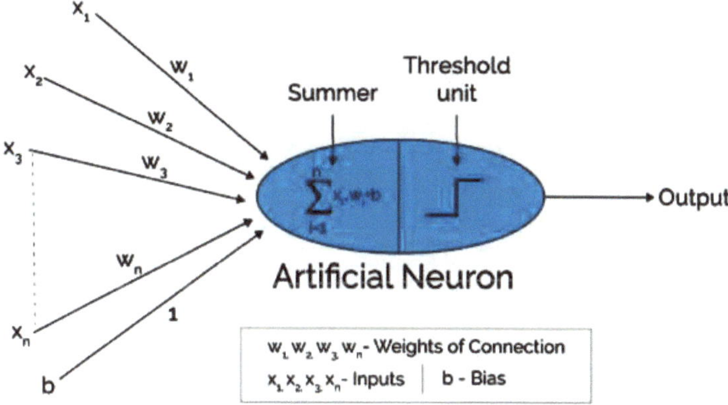

Fig. (4). Analytical working of ANN Model (Source Generalized Model in Data Science.com).

Algorithm 1

Step 1: Input data are given with some weightage values. In the above diagram X_1, X_2,…., X_n are given

Step 2: Each intermediate layer gets its corresponding input data's

Step 3: All the manipulation is performed on the intermediate layer

3.2.4. Types of Manipulation in Intermediate Layers

In the hidden layer, the input data are processed and a feasible decision is taken, and the corresponding output for the same is displayed in the output layer. There are two types of computational types:

1. Based on the weightage

2. Based on the transfer function given

First, a weightage value is given to every input value. The corresponding weightage is multiplied with every input data. The final output is a summation of all multiplied values. Second, for this type, a transfer function is defined for each input type. Hidden layers will observe the corresponding input data and gives output on the function defined separately for each type of input data. The process flow stated above is the Forward propagation model. If the output given is error-free, the process will be stopped. If it is not, the process will be started from the output to the weightage value backward. It is given as a backward propagation model.

4. DATA PROCUREMENT AND ANALYSIS

We computed information from the sensing path every 60 minutes, including temperature, humidity, soil moisture, and atmospheric pressure. As a result, for each weather parameter, we collect 50 data points every day. We took the highest value of the 50 data for each day. In Fig. (**5**), the maximum values of each weather parameter are plotted against the date. We can deduce the following details from the graph.

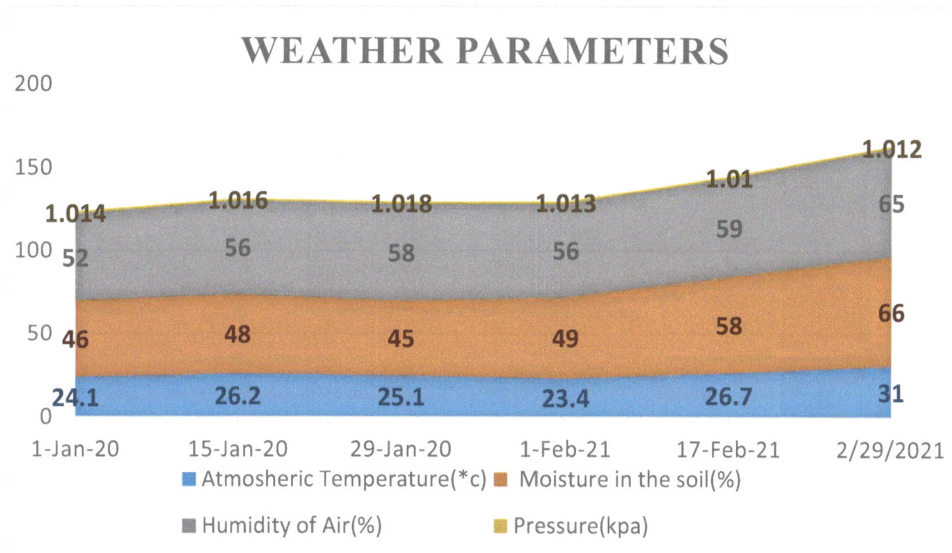

Fig. (5). Parameters manipulated using Smart weather Prediction System.

a. Temperature reached the maximum value as 31 and the minimum value as 23 for the period.
b. Humidity in the air range lies between 52 and 65%.
c. Moisture content of the soil (SM) ranges is 49 to 65%.
d. Atmospheric pressure has a maximum and minimum value of 1.015 and 1.013, respectively.

Algorithm 2: Proposed Functionality of Smart Weather Prediction System

Step 1: Start the ESP node type 8266 microcontroller.

Step 2: Deploying the sensor materials as per the requirement.

Step 3: As the manipulated data is to be received from various sensing elements. We have to allocate a unique Identity Number to each sensor.

Step 4: Verification of Id number with their passwords given.

Step 5: Declare the Local Variables for Temperature, Humidity, Soil Moisture, Rainfall estimation, Pressure, Time, i=50

// Temperature = Temp, Humidity = Hum, Soil Moisture = SM, Rainfall estimation = RE, Pressure = P, Time = Tim

Step 6: Showcasing the values in Dashboard and Sheets in Google Cloud.

Step 7: Separating the data's as per the ratio given as training and tested values using ANN.

Step 8: If trn = tst, then estimate the corresponding parameter value. Display the value.

Also, go to step 7

// Trainig data = t_{rn}, Test data = t_{st}

Step 9: For Tim -1 to check

If SM is less than or equal to 50%, then "submersible pump is ON"

Else "submersible pump is OFF".

Go to Step 5 & 6

Step 10: End program

The weather parameters collected from the Google Datasheets were then used as data for processing purposes. These data are split into subdivisions such as Trained data (60%) and Test data (40%). Feed-forward ANN is used to forecast the weather parameters for the next day's weather report using Artificial Neural Network (ANN).

Finally, we check the values of apparent and actual parameters from the designed system. The correctness and performance of the proposed system are verified using the Mean Square function given as:

$$\text{MSE} = \sqrt{\frac{1}{n} \sum y1 - y2} \tag{1}$$

Here, n is the number of data recorded, y1 and y2 show predicted and estimated values. For the detailed impact of environmental parameters on the earth's atmosphere, we make a separate data comparison from (Figs. **10 – 14**).

This representation outlined information based on weather details on the smart irrigation system stated here. Additionally, we can observe that the comparison between the projected values and real values shows high similarity. This makes the proposed system entitled with an average accuracy value of **95.27%** for all the meteorological parameters which we found using our proposed system.

5. HARDWARE IMPLEMENTATION AND SENSOR OUTPUTS

The system is deployed in the area having rapid changes in the climate for 2 months: January and February which are usually cold months. There was no rainfall throughout that period. The following parameters which impact human survival are temperature, humidity in air, barometric pressure, and moisture present in the soil, which we examine. The following (Figs. **6** & **7**) depict the experimental setup. The MQTT dashboard which is shown in Fig. (**7**) has been implemented for monitoring weather parameters. The state of the submersible pump can be monitored using a threshold value. Using the pump, we can also implement the smart irrigation method.

Table **1** represents the fundamental requisites of our Artificial Neural Network model with its specifications and features. The real-time implementation of the proposed work can be viewed in Fig. (**7**). The output of the temperature sensor is depicted in Fig. (**8**). The complete setup of the sensing circuit using a temperature sensor LM35 and a soil moisture sensor is shown in Fig. (**6**) and its output values are displayed in Fig. (**9**).

Fig. (6). Sensing circuit using Temperature sensor LM35 and Soil Moisture Sensor.

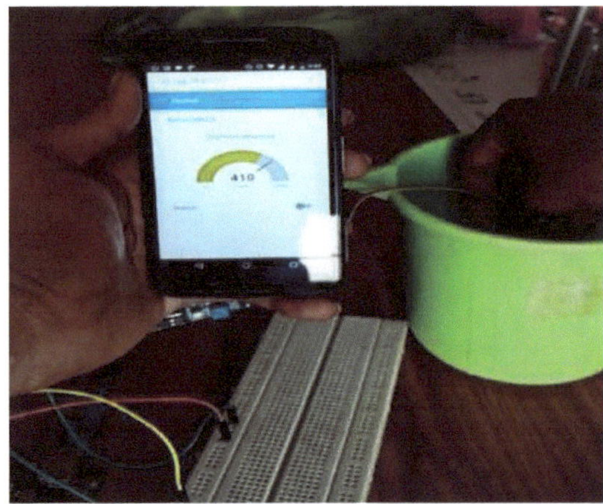

Fig. (7). Moisture sensor placement and implementation.

Table 1. Fundamental requisites of our Artificial Neural Network model.

Specification	Methodology
Neural Network model	Multi-Layered Perceptron**(MLP)**
Number of intermediate Layers	12
The function of **Intermediate layers** used for Activation	Sigmoid/Logistic functions
The function of the **Solution layer used for** Activation	Fully Linear type

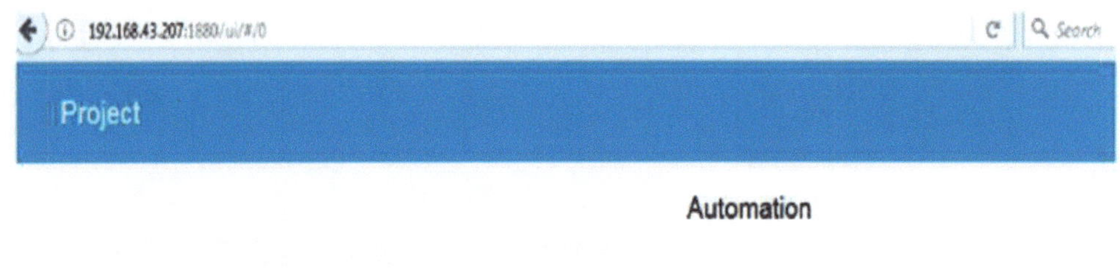

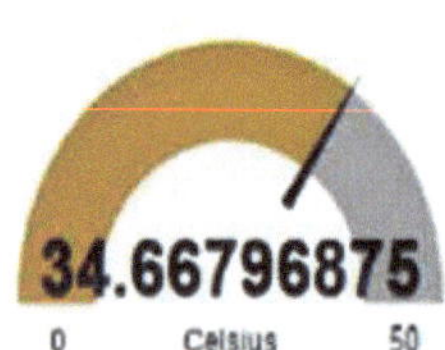

Fig. (8). Temperature Sensor Output.

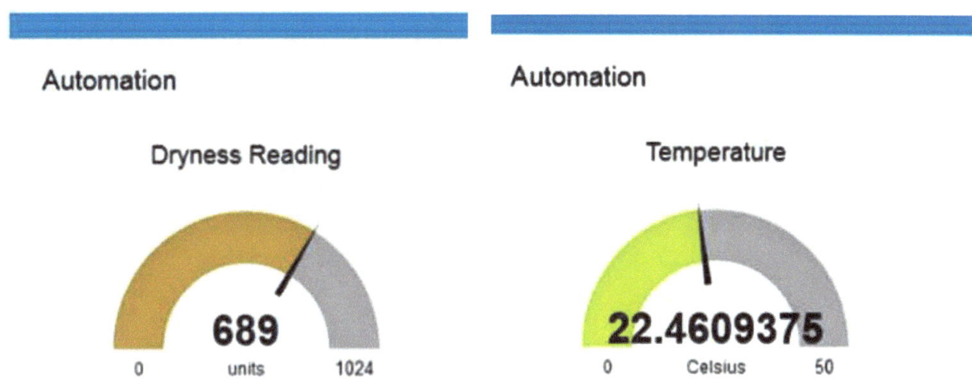

Fig. (9). The output of the sensor values.

For making this IoT-based system cost-effective, we used the ESP type microcontroller which has a very low price. Also, the power consumption of the smart system is less. Fig. **10** represents the comparison of recorded and estimated temperatures.

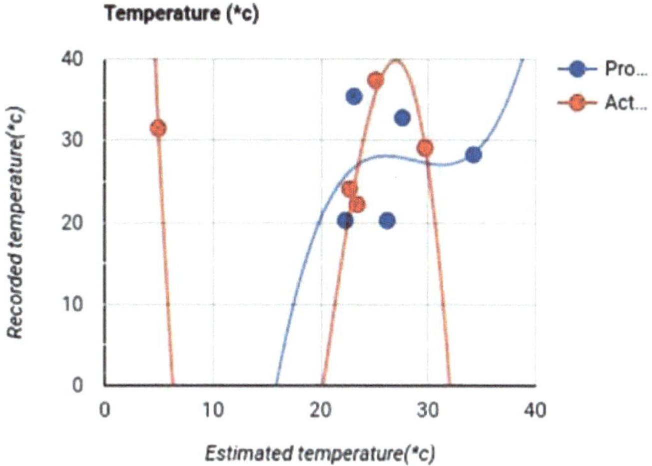

Fig. (10). Comparison of Recorded and Estimated temperature.

As the temperature increases in the atmosphere, it leads to a decrease in the soil moisture and humidity. Also, we have to maintain the SM value for maintaining irrigation at a sustainable water flow. Hence, on getting the actual temperature data, it will be compared with prediction temperature data for giving instructions to the irrigation system. This will allow the individual to get good yielding from the corresponding irrigation fields.

The humidity content in the atmosphere plays a vital impact in the prediction of rain. Both are proportional parameters. On getting the rainfall data from the corresponding sensor, it is proposed to check the moisture value to decide the pump status. Fig. **11** represents the actual and projected received rainfall. Upon getting the rainfall and humidity data, the smart irrigation system will make the decision itself.

Soil Moisture (SM) depends on humidity, and soil characteristics. It has control of the amount of water vapors and heat transfer to the atmosphere. If the SM drops, it will cause a decrease in the growth of cultivated crops. This results in poor yielding from the planted crops. Also, soil texture plays an important role in maintaining moisture. As the temperature is continuously recorded, then the prediction value reaches near the actual values. We have to check SM's actual and estimated data to maintain the moisture in the irrigation field. We also set a threshold value of 50% percent in the ON-OFF condition for the irrigation systems pump for maintaining the correct water level in the irrigation field. Figs. **12 & 13** represent the details of pressure recorded and the comparison of SM.

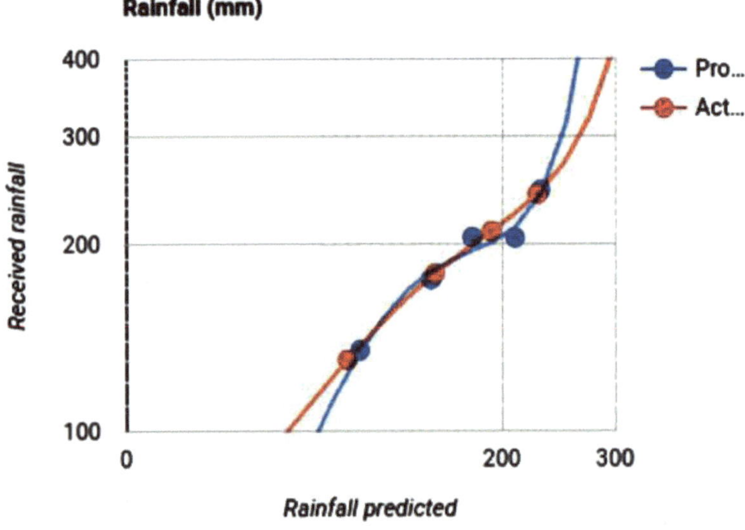

Fig. (11). Projected and actual received Rainfall.

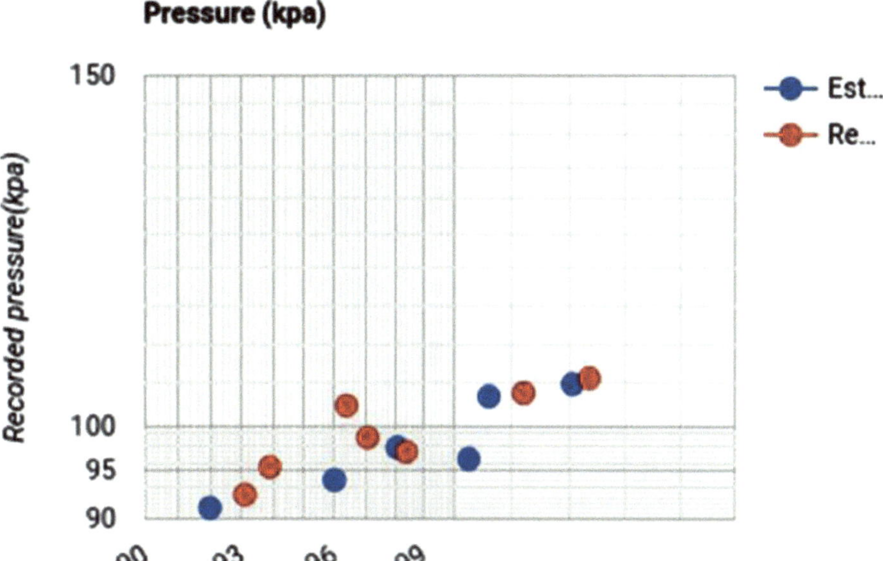

Fig. (12). Details of pressure recorded.

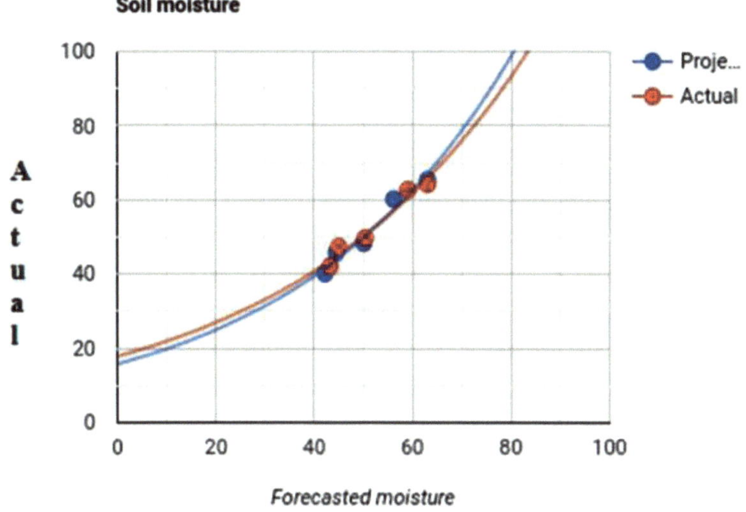

Fig. (13). Comparison of soil moisture.

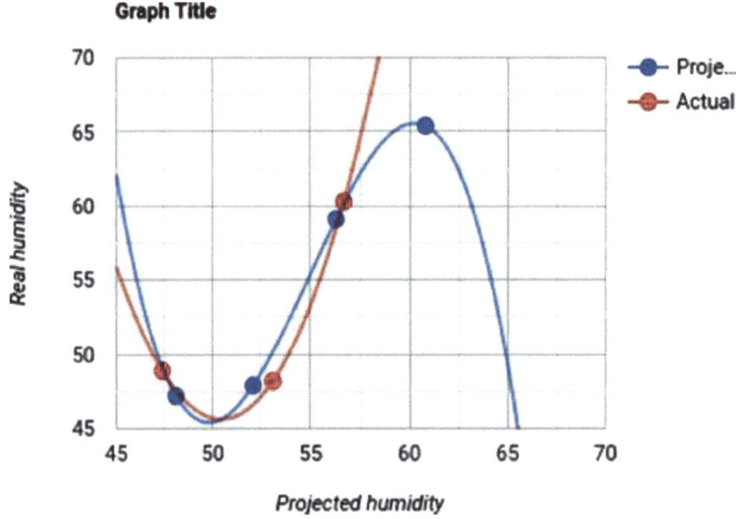

Fig. (14). Humidity values on an irrigation system.

It states the amount of water content in the air. If humidity increases, the probability of rain will increase as shown in Fig. **14**. So we have to put a note on the rainfall data simultaneously for checking the pump status to be either in ON or OFF condition. Hence humidity plays a vital role in this Smart weather system.

6. NOVELTY OF THIS RESEARCH WORK

For customer convenience, this system contains a high-tech watering system. Using ANN, the next day's weather appeared to have been forecast. Overall, the models' accuracy is sufficient to be used with existing works and methodologies. The suggested technique may measure actual meteorological factors including air humidity, soil moisture, and rainfall through the dashboard. This data will be blended with data from weather stations to enhance the forecast system. As a result, the suggested framework is less expensive than other methods.

CONCLUSION

In this study, an improved smart meteorological data system was developed and deployed. This system's installation process is meticulously planned and made user-friendly. The results of these studies indicate that these machine learning models can forecast weather features consistently enough to compete with conventional methods. In a specific area, using past data, the surrounding sites were also forecasted. Moreover, here it is shown that it is more effective than concentrating simply on the area where weather forecasting is done. The proposed strategy is capable of measuring actual weather parameters from the environment like the humidity in the air, moisture in the soil, and rainfall received through the dashboard. This prediction algorithm will improve even more as a result of this data, which will be combined with data from weather stations. As a result, the proposed framework is less costly than the conventional approaches.

REFERENCES

[1]   H. Dai, "Machine learning of weather forecasting rules from large meteorological data bases", *Adv. Atmos. Sci.,* vol. 13, no. 4, pp. 471-488, 1996.
        [http://dx.doi.org/10.1007/BF03342038]

[2]   K. Zhou, Y. Zheng, B. Li, W. Dong, and X. Zhang, "Forecasting different types of convective weather: A deep learning approach", *J. Meteorol. Res.,* vol. 33, no. 5, pp. 797-809, 2019.
        [http://dx.doi.org/10.1007/s13351-019-8162-6]

[3]   J. Xia, H. Li, Y. Kang, C. Yu, L. Ji, L. Wu, X. Lou, G. Zhu, Z. Wang, Z. Yan, L. Wang, J. Zhu, P. Zhang, M. Chen, Y. Zhang, L. Gao, and J. Han, "Machine learning-based weather support for the 2022 winter olympics", *Adv. Atmos. Sci.,* vol. 37, no. 9, pp. 927-932, 2020.
        [http://dx.doi.org/10.1007/s00376-020-0043-5]

[4]   K.U. Jaseena, and C. Binsu, "Deterministic weather forecasting models based on intelligent predictors: A survey", *J King Saud University - Comp.Inf. Sci.* 2020, vol 34. no.6, pp.3393-3412.
        [http://dx.doi.org/10.1016/j.jksuci.2020.09.009]

[5]   I.H. Sarker, "Machine learning: Algorithms, real-world applications and research directions", *SN Computer Science,* vol. 2, no. 3, p. 160, 2021.
        [http://dx.doi.org/10.1007/s42979-021-00592-x] [PMID: 33778771]

[6]   G. Gui, F. Liu, J. Sun, J. Yang, Z. Zhou, and D. Zhao, "Flight delay prediction based on aviation big data and machine learning", *IEEE Trans. Vehicular Technol.,* vol. 69, no. 1, pp. 140-150, 2020.
        [http://dx.doi.org/10.1109/TVT.2019.2954094]

[7]   H. Chen, V. Chandrasekar, R. Cifelli, and P. Xie, "A machine learning system for precipitation estimation using satellite and ground radar network observations", *IEEE Trans. Geosci. Remote Sens.,* vol. 58, no. 2, pp. 982-994, 2020.
        [http://dx.doi.org/10.1109/TGRS.2019.2942280]

[8]   D. Sun, J. Wu, H. Huang, R. Wang, F. Liang, and H. Xinhua, "Prediction of short-time rainfall based on deep learning", *Math. Probl. Eng.,* vol. 2021, pp. 1-8, 2021.
        [http://dx.doi.org/10.1155/2021/6664413]

[9]   S. Manandhar, S. Dev, Y.H. Lee, Y.S. Meng, and S. Winkler, "A data-driven approach for accurate rainfall prediction", *IEEE Trans. Geosci. Remote Sens.,* vol. 57, no. 11, pp. 9323-9331, 2019.
        [http://dx.doi.org/10.1109/TGRS.2019.2926110]

[10]   S. Madan, P. Kumar, S. Rawat, and T. Choudhury, "Analysis of weather prediction using machine learning & big data", *2018 International Conference on Advances in Computing and Communication Engineering (ICACCE),* 2018, pp. 259-264 Paris, France.
        [http://dx.doi.org/10.1109/ICACCE.2018.8441679]

[11]   A. Dolara, A. Gandelli, F. Grimaccia, S. Leva, and M. Mussetta, "Weather-based machine learning technique for Day-Ahead wind power forecasting", *2017 IEEE 6th International Conference on Renewable Energy Research and Applications (ICRERA),* 2017, San Diego, CA, USA.
        [http://dx.doi.org/10.1109/ICRERA.2017.8191267]

[12]   J. Booz, W. Yu, G. Xu, D. Griffith, and N. Golmie, "A deep learning-based weather forecast system for data volume and recency analysis", *International Conference on Computing, Networking and Communications (ICNC),* 2019, pp. 697-701 Honolulu, HI, USA.
[http://dx.doi.org/10.1109/ICCNC.2019.8685584]

[13]   S. Jamal, T.H. Bappy, R. Pervin, and A.S.A. Rabby, Weather status prediction of dhaka city using machine learning.*Computational Methods and Data Engineering. Advances in Intelligent Systems and Computing.,* V. Singh, V. Asari, S. Kumar, R. Patel, Eds., vol. 1227. Springer: Singapore, 2021.
[http://dx.doi.org/10.1007/978-981-15-6876-3_22]

[14]   T. Saba, A. Rehman, and J.S. AlGhamdi, "Weather forecasting based on hybrid neural model", *Appl. Water Sci.,* vol. 7, no. 7, pp. 3869-3874, 2017.
[http://dx.doi.org/10.1007/s13201-017-0538-0]

[15]   A.G. Salman, B. Kanigoro, and Y. Heryadi, "Weather forecasting using deep learning techniques", *2015 International Conference on Advanced Computer Science and Information Systems (ICACSIS),* 2015, pp. 281-285 Depok, Indonesia.
[http://dx.doi.org/10.1109/ICACSIS.2015.7415154]

[16]   A. Doroshenko, V. Shpyg, and R. Kushnirenko, "Machine learning to improve numerical weather forecasting", *2020 IEEE 2nd International Conference on Advanced Trends in Information Theory (ATIT),* 2020, pp. 353-356 Kyiv, Ukraine.
[http://dx.doi.org/10.1109/ATIT50783.2020.9349325]

[17]   G.P. Zhang, Neural networks for time-series forecasting.G. Rozenberg, T. Bäck, and J.N. Kok, *Handbook of Natural Computing.* Springer: Berlin, Heidelberg, 2020.
[http://dx.doi.org/10.1007/978-3-540-92910-9_14]

[18]   D. Fabbian, R. de Dear, and S. Lellyett, "Application of artificial neural network forecasts to predict fog at canberra international airport", *Weather and Forecasting.* vol. 22, no. 2, pp. 372-381.
[http://dx.doi.org/10.1175/WAF980.1]

[19]   X. Ren, X. Li, K. Ren, J. Song, Z. Xu, K. Deng, and X. Wang, "Deep learning-based weather prediction: A survey", *Big Data Research,* vol. 23, 2021.
[http://dx.doi.org/10.1016/j.bdr.2020.100178]

[20]   V. Ravindran, R. Ponraj, C. Krishnakumar, S. Ragunathan, V. Ramkumar, and K. Swaminathan, IoT-based smart transformer monitoring system with raspberry Pi.*2021 Innovations in Power and Advanced Computing Technologies (i-PACT),* 2021.Kuala Lumpur, Malaysia
[http://dx.doi.org/10.1109/i-PACT52855.2021.9696779]

[21]   V. Ravindran, and C. Vennila, "An energy-efficient clustering protocol for iot wireless sensor networks based on cluster supervisor management", *Comptes rendus de l'Académie bulgare des Sciences,* vol. 74, no. 12, 2021.
[http://dx.doi.org/10.7546/CRABS.2021.12.12]

[22]   V. Ravindran, and C. Vennila, "Energy consumption in cluster communication using mcsbch approach in WSN", *J. Intell. Fuzzy Syst: Application. Eng.Tech.* vol. 43, p. 1, 2022, 11.
[http://dx.doi.org/10.3233/JIFS-212632]

[23]   S.P. Yadav, D.P. Mahato, N.T. Linh, Ed., *Distributed Artificial Intelligence: A Modern Approach* CRC Press, 2020.
[http://dx.doi.org/10.1201/9781003038467]

[24]   S.P. Yadav, S. Zaidi, A. Mishra, and V. Yadav, "Survey on machine learning in speech emotion recognition and vision systems using a recurrent neural network (RNN)", *Arch. Comput. Methods Eng.,* vol. 29, no. 3, pp. 1753-1770, 2022.
[http://dx.doi.org/10.1007/s11831-021-09647-x]

CHAPTER 10

Hybrid Machine Learning Techniques for Secure IoT Applications

Udayabalan Balasingam[1,*], **S. B. Prathibha**[2], **K. R. Swetha**[3], **C. Muruganandam**[4] **and Urmila R. Pol**[5]

[1] *Department of Information Science and Engineering, East Point College of Engineering and Technology, Bengaluru, Karnataka, India*

[2] *Department of Computer Science and Engineering, Sri Siddartha Institute of Technology, Tumakuru, Karnataka, India*

[3] *Department of CSE, BGS Institute of Technology. Adichunchanagiri University, Mandya, Karnataka, India*

[4] *Department of Computer Science, AVVM Sri Pushpam College, Affiliated to Bharathidasan University, Poondi, Thanjavur, Tamil Nadu - 613503, India*

[5] *Department of Computer Science, Shivaji University, Kolhapur, Maharashtra-416003, India*

Abstract: Web sensing devices capture and transmit data from the physical environment to a central place using rapid advances in software, hardware, and IoT technologies. Depending on the source, the overall count of web-connected devices is estimated to be between 50 and 100 billion by 2025. The amount of data released will increase as the population expands and technology improves, which is already happening. The Internet of Things (IoT) technology connects and interacts with the physical and virtual worlds. A gadget linked to the Internet is called an IoT. Intellectual data handling and investigation are required to construct smart IoT requests. This article gives knowledge about the Machine learning (ML) algorithms available for dealing with IoT data challenges, using smart cities as the primary use case. This article looks at common IoT diagnostic applications. This research compares and evaluates the predicted precision and understandability of supervised and unattended ML models. These technologies are briefly addressed in desktop, mobile, and cloud computing settings.

Keywords: Cloud, Hybrid, Internet, Supervised, Security.

---

[*] **Corresponding author Udayabalan Balasingam:** Department of Information Science and Engineering, East Point College of Engineering and Technology, Bidrahalli, Bangalore, Karnataka -560049, India; E-mail: udayabalan@gmail.com

1. INTRODUCTION

With recent advancements in Internet protocols and computing systems, it is now possible to communicate from device to device more easily than ever before using IoT. Sensors and actuators and physical items that are interconnected to the web [1, 2] are all included in this category. Computing has always aimed to make human activities and experiences easier and more enjoyable. The IoT requires data to either enhance service consumers or improve the operation of the IoT framework. To extract information, computers must be capable of retrieving unprocessed data from many network resources. Given that the IoT will be a significant source of fresh data, it will be critical in making IoT applications smarter. Massive volumes of data may be mined for patterns and fresh insights using technologies like data mining. These strategies apply to a wide variety of algorithms. Data types, models, and efficient algorithms that are appropriate for the data attributes are all determined as part of the data analytics methodology deployment process. Following our examinations, we may conclude: First and foremost, because data comes from a variety of sources, it is necessary to adopt or build algorithms that are capable of dealing with the information. Second, the large number of resources that supply real-time data raises concerns about the scalability and velocity of data. Finally, determining the most appropriate data model is crucial for pattern recognition and the IoT process. As a result of these issues, various new development opportunities have arisen.

Massive volumes of data need the development of innovative information processing methods that improve understanding, decision-making, and the automation of business processes [3]. The developing sensors are continually moving. The development sensors detect the start of development. The controller analyzes the data and sends it to relevant destination. It depends on Raspberry Pi's devotion and lawful activity by then. We need to introduce intelligent data to the world to solve the vast data issues. Smart Data is now defined as "data that may be used to solve problems and improve decision-making processes." [4]. Some Smart Home apps leverage IoT. It is utilized in an IoT-based Monitoring System [5, 6]. Bluetooth and WiFi are used to connect mobile devices with cloud servers. Bluetooth, however, now has a 10M correspondence zone. IR cannot travel through dividers or other obstructions. The application's vulnerability is in IR. We are using IoT to solve this issue. With the IoT, we can improve our lives by connecting Smart Homes, Smart Buildings, and Intelligent Cars. We're working on an IoT project for a smart city. We employ a development finder sensor to measure the traits, then examine the data and decide. The Raspberry Pi is a tiny processor that can handle sensor data safely. Finally, smart data can represent IoT data.

2. ML ALGORITHM

ML predicts unknown structural linkages in a system with minimum information. ML is utilized for projects like, copying and pasting knowledge from another source, learning by example and experimentation, and discovery [7]. Inductive learning can estimate an unknown function. Induction is based on a training set of data (or a data set). The issue domain model requires a set of attributes or variables xi with values i=1 to n. Some of these traits are unnecessary and detract from the performance of most learning algorithms. Aspect/feature selection methods aim to reduce irrelevant properties [8]. Machine–learning-based classifications are vital in decision support and to classify new situations into problem categories.

A proper classification is used as an example of the unknown correlation in classification ML. The observed system's output is approximated from its inputs. Less common knowledge representations include mathematical or logical formulations, decision trees, and hypersurfaces. The composite classifier's components must all outperform each other. To do this, the main elements must be precise and distinct. Appropriate attribute divisions must be created for each classifier to increase ensemble element variation.

2.1. Supervised and Unsupervised Learning

In supervised learning, the input dataset contains labels that are either "true" or "correct." It then uses the ground truth to refine its estimations, and the process is repeated. Almost every ML algorithm seeks to minimize the cost or achieve a specific goal. According to standard practice, the cost function measures the difference between the algorithm and the ground truth. In case of unsupervised algorithms [9], it is not possible to link explicit labels to the training dataset because the training dataset does not contain any labels. To better understand the data, interpretations from the raw data are used to simulate the hidden or underlying structure and distribution [10].

3. INTRODUCTION TO IOT

The IoT is designed to help users all over the world save time, energy, and money by connecting their devices. This technique has the potential to reduce costs in a wide range of industries, including manufacturing.

As a result of large-scale investments and numerous studies that have been conducted, in recent times, the IoT has grown as a popular trend. Four components make up the IoT: sensors, processing networks, data analysis, and system monitoring, to name a few. IoT advancements in current days have included the increased use of RFID tags, the use of less expensive sensors, the use of web technologies, and the development of new communication protocols [11]. The IoT is a collection of technologies that, to function properly, must all be connected *via* the internet. Fig (**1**) shows the data characteristics of IoT. It is necessary to improve communication protocols as a result. When it comes to the IoT, communication protocols are made up of three fundamental components:

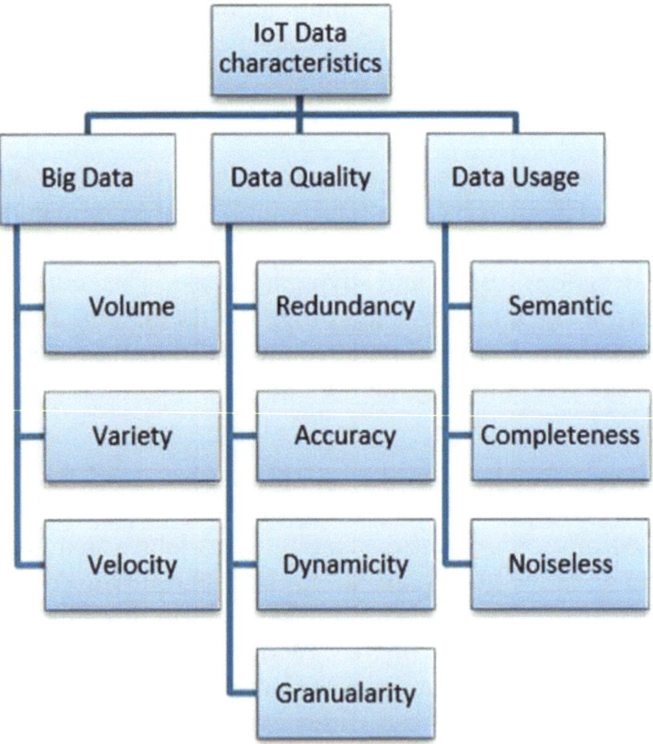

Fig. (1). IoT Data Characteristics.

1. Direct-to-Device (D2D) communication allows for communication between mobile phones that are nearby. This is the next generation of cellular networks and represents a significant advancement.
2. When using a Device to Server (D2S) connection, all data is sent to servers that may be located nearby or far away from the devices. When it comes to cloud computing environments, this type of communication is widely used.
3. Server-to-server (S2S) communication: When running in this mode, servers communicate with one another and share data. This is a term that is frequently heard in the context of cellular communication networks.

It takes a long time to prepare the data for these communications. This problem must be addressed by implementing data handling methods such as analytics at the edge, stream analysis, and IoT analysis at the database level. The selection of one of the processes listed above are dependent on the application and the requirements of the application [12]. To prepare data for further use, fog and cloud processing are two analytical procedures that can be used in conjunction with one another. In part, because the IoT is an innovative concept for the Internet and smart data, it is a difficult field of computer science to comprehend. Data preparation and processing are significant challenges for researchers working on the IoT. There are four different IoT data mining models [13]. IoT is classified into two sections: the primary division has layers for information gathering, organization, event handling, and data mining services; the second section contains layers for other services. The second strategy, which is similar to the first, proposes distributed data mining for data deposition across multiple sites, which is similar to the first. The use of grid computing for heterogeneous, large-scale, and high-performance applications has also been proposed as a data mining approach for these types of applications. An integrated multi-technology architecture, as well as a futuristic Internet infrastructure, are included in the final model, which is a data mining architecture.

RFID data warehousing was the focus which included learning how to handle my RFID stream data, among other things. A framework was established for assessing data mining skills and methodologies across a range of popular applications. This research looked at classification and grouping, association analysis, time series investigation, and framework discovery. In e-commerce, industry, healthcare, and municipal area, data mining generates data that is analogous to IoT data. The findings were then utilized to assign data mining functionality to applications, allowing for the selection of the best-suited data mining functionality for each application [14]. A study performed a poll to determine the difficulties associated with preparing and analyzing IoT data using data mining techniques. The study emphasized the importance of increased communication to give added-value services to both city management and citizens. The authors examine the technology, protocols, and architectures that are enabling smart cities. In the technical segment, the writers looked at data from the Padova Smart City.

4. METHODS OF ML FOR THE LEARNING

ML methods for the learning of classifications are described.

4.1. Improved Understanding Techniques

Easy-to-understand learning methods, the development of knowledge-based decision support systems and expert systems, among other applications, require mastering intelligible, human-readable knowledge. Decision trees (DT) and rule learning are two well-known AI approaches (RL), when the number of separate examples in a situation equals the number of independent instances.

4.2. Acquiring Implicit Data

This includes subjective, empirical, and inexplicable knowledge. For example, it can be represented using Bayes or neural networks. These include k-NN, Bayes networks, ANNs, and SVMs (SVM).Support Vector Machine (SVM) is a popular way of learning from examples. That is, it splits learning examples by a maximum distance. This hyperplane divides a few key boundary samples from each class. SVM discrimination boundaries use linear functions and a non-linear discriminant function is produced (kernel trick).

4.3. ML and Repetition

Unknown case prediction accuracy can be improved by training and combining redundant classifiers or ensembles. Elements are diverse in Random Forests [15]. An ensemble of symbolic classifiers successfully resample the learning data and the attributes set for induction. The sole basic ML method is CART [16]. To measure attribute relevance, Random Forests is also an option. Learnable hybrid models can be integrated in hybrid ensembles.

5. MODELS AND METHODS FOR HYBRID ML

Supervisory learning has as its purpose in the discovery of an approximation to an unknown function by employing a collection of previously tagged instances in a specific context. It is possible to study different hypotheses using various approaches, employ a range of search tactics, and apply different types of issues using various methodologies. The numbers [17] refer to the number of times a word is used. When it comes to decision trees, a strategy known as divide-an--conquer is used. Among other tree-based algorithms, this is the core notion of the well-known CART and C4.5 algorithms. Multivariate trees are ways of categorizing issues that allow for the study of a large number of different representations to be employed in the process. Multiple variable judgments are usually seen in internal nodes when dealing with categorization challenges.

Whenever there is a fear of regression, they appear in the leaf nodes. A decision tree and a linear threshold unit are combined in a Perceptron Tree, which is a type of decision tree. There exist trees of decisions and decision support systems. When a Naive Bayes classifier is built from examples that occur at a node in a standard univariate decision tree, the decision tree is referred to as a Naive Bayes hybrid. Multivariate and model trees are both expansions of functional trees in terms of structure. In the inner nodes and leaves of the decision tree, they make use of functions. Model trees are multivariate trees with linear or other functional models at the leaves that are used to make decisions. Combining several foundation learning methodologies to achieve stacked generalization [18] is a technique known as hybrid ensembles.

6. HYBRID ALGORITHMS IN IOT APPLICATIONS

Learning algorithms are commonly employed in real-world applications because of their unmatched capacity to handle problems that they encounter. These technologies are used to create machines that can learn on their own. In recent years, learning algorithms have become increasingly popular in practice. The current improvement of learning algorithms is being pushed by novel algorithms, large amounts of data, and methods with low computational costs [19 - 21].

6.1. Energy

Some utilize Arduino MEGA to save energy. This is a minimal IoT ML implementation. But we can certainly include other items like lighting and air conditioners in this IoT. For example: the coffee machine has two states: off and on. This is a difficult division that can be enhanced by supplying additional states to boost energy-saving performance. However, I believe this type of energy modeling works, but not for a single machine. The huge number theory will function better if we extend the scale to the entire power grid. ARIMA-based predictive models are used in this application.

6.2. Routing

Traffic routing is a promising topic to work on because of the mix of sensors and ML algorithms. The LarKC platform is being used by researchers in Milano to develop a system. Using data from traffic and weather, the entire system is capable of recommending several routes to the desired location.

6.3. In Living

In addition, IoT applications are appropriate for the household. Light, humidity, and temperature sensors, as well as pulse rate sensors, are all used in an apartment to monitor the environment. It's a sort of future vision of what life would be like in 20 years. The implementation utilizes the free source WEKA toolkit. To illustrate learning, a user's temperature preferences were tracked over time *via* a user interface. Dependent on this data, the MLP algorithm learns user preferences and predicts preferred temperature based on the time of day.

6.4. Industry

Many companies and governments employ IoT and ML algorithms. With billions of machine data, such applications are highly desired. Most of these applications require ML techniques to visualize data.

We want to save energy by forecasting demand and allocating it dynamically. We could accomplish this before, but we couldn't provide the consumer the specific facts and energy savings. But with smart meters for gas, electricity, and water, we can track equipment usage. We can also do load balancing and dynamic allocation. An IoT system with cameras and controllers can save many human resources in manufacturing. If the system detects an anomalous operation, it can alert and take action. It can also forecast when a field may fail, allowing you to take action before it happens. By forecasting the failure, factories can save a lot of resources. Tracking personal health data in healthcare is a problem. Doctors can analyze patients better if they have multiple wearable gadgets tracking data. And it's much cheaper than hiring a personal nurse. The insurance industry examines the financial paperwork. Now we may leverage data from mobile devices. We can give personal insurance by gathering and analyzing data. We want to know when our customer will be purchasing, what he wants to buy, and how much? The sensors can be installed in the store and data is collected online *via* shopping apps. It allows people to buy more of what they desire. In transportation, we can use both human and vehicle flow data. If the supply of vehicles meets the demand, it's an efficient allocation to buses and subways. We can reduce idling costs and improve service levels by dynamically allocating restricted resources. Since their inception, ML and Deep Learning (DL) have advanced to the point that they are now a practical technology with a wide range of applications.

The purpose of dividing the discussion of ML and DL into two sections is to provide readers with a comprehensive overview of each. DL in IoT applications is shown in Fig (2). In general, learning algorithms attempt to improve task performance through training and learning from previous experiences. For example, in intrusion detection, they help distinguish between normal and aberrant behaviors of the system. The events from which the algorithms learn are a collection of activities that are typical of a system. Supervised, unsupervised, and reinforcement learning are all types of learning (RL). Even though many current DL implementations require supervised learning methods to learn representations, recent research has enhanced DL systems that learn important input representations without the usage of pre-labeled training data. Unsupervised learning techniques are used to analyze data that has not been labeled. Unsupervised learning methods classify incoming data depending on how similar the data is to each other in the first place. RL is the third variant of ML. The data from the environment is used to train RL algorithms. To gain an understanding of an environment and to identify relevant approaches for an agent in a variety of settings, supervised and unsupervised learning data are used in the RL's training data. If an action is incorrect, the problem persists until the proper action is recognized.

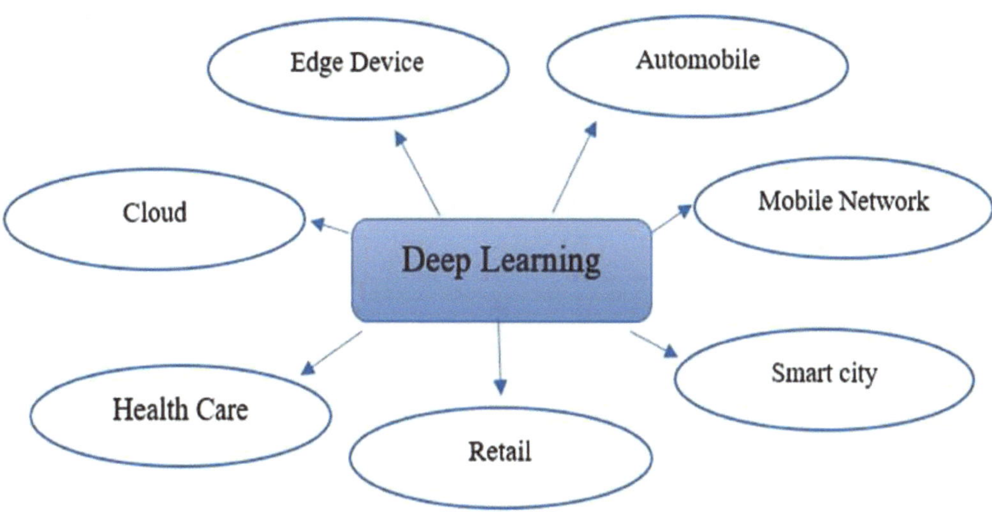

Fig. (2). DL in IoT.

RL is hence error-based learning. ML and DL methods for IoT security are highlighted here. First, we review traditional ML approaches, their benefits and drawbacks, and IoT security applications. Second, we examine DL algorithms, their benefits, and drawbacks in IoT security. The IoT is transforming our lives. ML transforms machine knowledge into human understanding. As a result of the ability to deal with large amounts of data, those applications are becoming increasingly important to our lives and are being pursued by venture capital firms. Those applications, on the other hand, can only make predictions based on past events; the future is still somewhat unpredictable, and this is where the magic lies.

7. ML TECHNIQUES IN IOT SECURITY

The use of most recent ML algorithms is critical for IoT security. Researchers are now studying GANs and Federated Learning. These new technologies and IoT security: Adversarial GANs have altered ML. In a zero-sum game, two neural networks compete with each other. It has a generator and a discriminator. A discriminator learns. Candidate data is generated by the generator network and classified by the discriminator (for instance mapping certain features to their respective labels). The discriminator is deceived, and desires to strengthen itself against the generator. The determination of the source occurs after the generator has convinced the discriminator of the sample's origin. In terms of IoT security, GANs have shown to be quite successful. Rather than centralized GANs, the authors used distributed GANs. Access to all IoT data should be centralized, and thereby risk privacy but not weights as in a GAN. Distributed GANs had 20% better detection accuracy, 25% better precision, and 60% fewer false positives than centralized GANs.

A GAN generator should provide samples close to training data and adversarial examples. However, it might be different for IoT. In short, ML can both improve accuracy and harm the learning process. It is critical to enhance positive aspects while minimizing unfavorable ones, namely, security and federated learning. It also protects user privacy. Modeling without user data is possible with FL. So, most ML models work. Encrypted updates are stored in a cloud server, where all FL devices will also update. This enhances the common model. It outperforms centralized computing. The cloud and central servers stay anonymous throughout model upgrades. FL can protect privacy and improve efficiency in mobile and distributed networks (*e.g.*, IoT). It's challenging to get widespread devices to contribute quickly. The convergence of FL models is hampered by the lack of Scheduling participants that is challenging. Also, device reliability is a concern. So real-time IoT networks have evolved. No device can participate until the FL model converges. Because FL models train iteratively, lack of a few devices can influence the learning quality.

8. DISCUSSION

With the IoT, the real and virtual worlds are linked and interacted with a network of interconnected devices. Smart IoT requests necessitate extensive data analysis and inquiry on part of the user. This article delivers knowledge about the ML algorithms available for dealing with IoT data issues, utilizing smart cities as the primary use case, and also looks at popular IoT diagnostic applications. This study analyzes and contrasts the anticipated accuracy and clarity of supervised and unsupervised methods. The usage of ML models in real-world applications and the difficulties presented are also clarified. New algorithms, massive amounts of data, and low-cost computation approaches are all being used to examine how to improve learning algorithms' accuracy.

CONCLUSION

In this review work, we discuss ML techniques in IoT networks, which are becoming increasingly popular. The IoT is a promising technology that connects both living and nonliving things globally. The IoT is gaining popularity, but cyber security is still a concern, leaving it open to various cyber-attacks. For a network to be effective, it must be entirely safe; otherwise, individuals may be unwilling to use it. To meet this urgent demand, a system for extracting useful information from large amounts of data, categorizing it into distinct categories, and forecasting end-user behavior or sentiment must be developed, including simple and condensed configuration of convolutions, as well as multiplication and addition of a single scalar value. In addition, this study addresses algorithms used for IoT cyber security.

REFERENCES

[1]   L. Atzori, A. Iera, and G. Morabito, "The internet of things: A survey", *Comput. Netw.,* vol. 54, no. 15, pp. 2787-2805, 2010.
[http://dx.doi.org/10.1016/j.comnet.2010.05.010]

[2]   C. Cecchinel, M. Jimenez, S. Mosser, and M. Riveill, "An architecture to support the collection of big data in the IoT", *2014 IEEE World Congress on Services,* 2014, pp. 442-449 Anchorage, AK, USA.
[http://dx.doi.org/10.1109/SERVICES.2014.83]

[3]   J. Manyika, M. Chui, B. Brown, J. Bughin, R. Dobbs, C. Roxburgh, and A.H. Byers, *Big Data: The Next Frontier for Innovation, Competition, and Productivity.* McKinsey Global Institute, 2011, p. 156.

[4]   A. Sheth, "Transforming big data into smart data: Deriving value via harnessing volume, variety and velocity using semantics techniques and technologies", *IEEE 30th International Conference on Data Engineering,* 2014, Chicago, IL, USA.
[http://dx.doi.org/10.1109/ICDE.2014.6816634]

[5]   N.C. Park, "IoT routing architecture with autonomous systems of things", *IEEE World Forum on Internet of Things (WF-IoT),* 2014, pp. 442-445.
[http://dx.doi.org/10.1109/WF-IoT.2014.6803207]

[6]   J. Fox, A. Donnellan, and L. Doumen, "The deployment of an IoT network infrastructure, as a localised regional service", *IEEE 5th World Forum on Internet of Things (WF-IoT),* 2019, Limerick, Ireland.
[http://dx.doi.org/10.1109/WF-IoT.2019.8767188]

[7]   J.G. Shanahan, "ML. soft computing for knowledge discovery", In: *The Springer International Series in Engineering and Computer Science.* vol. 570. Springer: Boston, MA, 2000.
[http://dx.doi.org/10.1007/978-1-4615-4335-0_7]

[8]   I.H. Witten, E. Frank, and M.A. Hall, *Data Mining.: Practical ML tools and techniques* 3rd. Elsevier Inc, 2011.

[9]   M. Khanum, T. Mahboob, W. Imtiaz, H. Abdul Ghafoor, and R. Sehar, "A survey on Unsupervised ML Algorithms for automation, classification and maintenance", *Int. J. Comput. Appl.,* vol. 119, no. 13, pp. 34-39, 2015.
[http://dx.doi.org/10.5120/21131-4058]

[10]   B. A. Pathak, "A survey on k-means clustering and web-text mining", *Int. J. Sci. Res.,* vol. 5, no. 4, pp. 1049-1052, 2016.
[http://dx.doi.org/10.21275/v5i4.NOV162776]

[11]   C. Sundar, "Sundar: An analysis on the performance of k-means clustering algorithm for Cardiotocogram clustering", *Int J Comput Sci & Applic.,* vol. 2, no. 5, pp. 11-20, 2012.
[http://dx.doi.org/10.5121/ijcsa.2012.2502]

[12]   M.E. Celebi, K. Aydin, Ed., *Unsupervised learning algorithms.* 1st. Springer International Publishing: Switzerland, 2016.
[http://dx.doi.org/10.1007/978-3-319-24211-8]

[13]   V. Cherkassky, and F.M. Mulier, *Learning from Data: Concepts, Theory, and Methods* 2nd. John Wiley - IEEE Press, 2007.
[http://dx.doi.org/10.1002/9780470140529]

[14]   S. Amari, "Backpropagation and stochastic gradient descent method", *Neurocomputing,* vol. 5, no. 4-5, pp. 185-196, 1993.
[http://dx.doi.org/10.1016/0925-2312(93)90006-O]

[15]   V.J. Mathews, and Z. Xie, "A stochastic gradient adaptive filter with gradient adaptive step size", *Trans. Signal Process.,* vol. 41, no. 6, pp. 2075-2087, 1993.
[http://dx.doi.org/10.1109/78.218137]

[16]   J.A. Flanagan, and T. Novosad, "Maximizing WCDMA network packet traffic performance: Multi-parameter optimization by gradient descent minimization of a cost function", *PIMRC,* vol. 1, 2003, pp. 311-315 Beijing, China.
[http://dx.doi.org/10.1109/PIMRC.2003.1264284]

[17]   F.F. Lubis, "Gradient descent and normal equations on cost function minimization for online predictive using linear regression with multiple variables", *2014 International Conference on ICT For Smart Society (ICISS),* 2014, pp. 202-205 Bandung, Indonesia.
[http://dx.doi.org/10.1109/ICTSS.2014.7013173]

[18]   S. Bin, L. Yuan, and W. Xiaoyi, "Research on data mining models for the IoT", *International Conference on Image Analysis and Signal Processing,* 2010, pp. 127-132 Zhejiang.
[http://dx.doi.org/10.1109/IASP.2010.5476146]

[19]   K. Greff, R.K. Srivastava, J. Koutník, B.R. Steunebrink, and J. Schmidhuber, "LSTM: A Search space odyssey", *IEEE Trans. Neural Netw. Learn. Syst.,* vol. 28, no. 10, pp. 2222-2232, 2017.
[http://dx.doi.org/10.1109/TNNLS.2016.2582924] [PMID: 27411231]

[20]   A. Abeshu, and N. Chilamkurti, "Deep Learning: The frontier for distributed attack detection in fog-to-things computing", *IEEE Commun. Mag.,* vol. 56, no. 2, pp. 169-175, 2018.
[http://dx.doi.org/10.1109/MCOM.2018.1700332]

[21]   S. Yadav, F. Al-Turjman, V. Yadav, M. Kumar, and T. Stephan, *Transforming Management with AI, Big-Data, and IoT* Springer, 2021.

SUBJECT INDEX

A

AI 1, 20
   assisted diagnostics 20
   based smart grids 1
AirNet dataset 96, 98
Air pollution 77, 102
Air quality 64, 77, 96, 98
  automated indoor 98
  sensors 77
Algorithms 92, 93, 99, 100, 102, 146, 147,
    170, 171, 181, 182, 183, 186, 187, 188,
    191
  data mining 102
  deep-learning 99
Analysis, sensitivity 163
ANN 143, 168
  methodology 168
  technique 143
Artificial 1, 3, 4, 8, 19, 54, 68, 73, 79, 87, 91,
    141, 142, 143, 144, 145, 146, 147, 161,
    162, 167, 168, 169, 172
  intelligence 1, 3, 4, 8, 19, 54, 68, 73, 79,
    87, 91
  neural networks (ANN) 141, 142, 143, 144,
    145, 146, 147, 161, 162, 167, 168, 169,
    172
Automation 18, 77, 95, 108, 112, 113, 114,
    123, 182
  industrial 112
  systems 77
Automobile 18, 52
  innovative 18

B

Bins 19, 55, 125, 130, 133, 135, 137, 138
  overflowing 133
  rubbish 137
  sensible garbage 125
Bio-degradable wastes 130
Biological contaminants 128
Blockchain technology 16, 55, 101

Breast arterial calcification (BAC) 97

C

CCTV cameras 74
Chennai municipal waste management system
    132
Circuit 151, 166, 173
  embedded-based 166
  sensing 173
Circumstances, crucial decision-making 24
Cisco hardware 113
Cloud 22, 64
  amenities 22
  based IoT 64
Cloud computing 20, 41, 42, 79, 87, 96, 122,
    184
  environments 184
Computational infrastructures for IoT 90
Computation technique 42
Computing 42, 185
  architecture 42
  grid 185
Congestion 18, 24
  reducing road 18
Conglomeration 26
Convolutional neural network (CNN) 92, 93,
    96, 97
Cyber security abuses 69

D

Database 72, 94, 137, 138
  hyperconnected cities ranking 72
Data 18, 110, 170, 185
  mining techniques 185
  procurement 170
  storage 110
  transmission 18
Decentralized decision-making methods 24
Decision trees 183, 186, 187
Deep learning 87, 88, 94, 99, 100, 102, 131
  algorithms 99, 131

9 789815 136197